The Wind Band and Wind Ensemble Before 1500

Books by David Whitwell

Philosophic Foundations of Education
Foundations of Music Education
Music Education of the Future
The Sousa Oral History Project
The Art of Musical Conducting
The Longy Club: 1900–1917
A Concise History of the Wind Band

The History and Literature of the Wind Band and Wind Ensemble Series

Volume 1 The Wind Band and Wind Ensemble Before 1500
Volume 2 The Renaissance Wind Band and Wind Ensemble
Volume 3 The Baroque Wind Band and Wind Ensemble
Volume 4 The Classic Period Wind Band and Wind Ensemble
Volume 5 The Nineteenth-Century Wind Band and Wind Ensemble
Volume 6 A Catalog of Multi-Part Repertoire for Wind Instruments or for Undesignated Instrumentation before 1600
Volume 7 Baroque Wind Band and Wind Ensemble Repertoire
Volume 8 Classic Period Wind Band and Wind Ensemble Repertoire
Volume 9 Nineteenth-Century Wind Band and Wind Ensemble Repertoire
Volume 10 A Supplementary Catalog of Wind Band and Wind Ensemble Repertoire
Volume 11 A Catalog of Wind Repertoire before the Twentieth Century for One to Five Players
Volume 12 A Second Supplementary Catalog of Early Wind Band and Wind Ensemble Repertoire
Volume 13 Name Index, Volumes 1–12, The History and Literature of the Wind Band and Wind Ensemble

www.whitwellbooks.com

David Whitwell

The Wind Band and Wind Ensemble Before 1500

THE HISTORY AND LITERATURE OF THE WIND BAND AND WIND ENSEMBLE, VOLUME 1

EDITED BY CRAIG DABELSTEIN

WHITWELL BOOKS • AUSTIN, TEXAS, USA

The Wind Band and Wind Ensemble Before 1500
Second Edition
Dr. David Whitwell
Edited by Craig Dabelstein
www.whitwellbooks.com

Whitwell Books
P.O. Box 342673
Austin, Texas, USA

Copyright © David Whitwell 2011
All rights reserved

All images used in this book are in the public domain except where otherwise noted.

Composed in Bembo Book
Published in the United States of America

Cover image: *Music and dance*, illumination from *Tacuina sanitatis* (Tables of Health), fourteenth century

The Wind Band and Wind Ensemble Before 1500 (paperback) isbn 978-1-936512-17-1

Foreword

THIS VOLUME IS THE FIRST OF SEVERAL which together attempt a general History and Literature of the Wind Band and Wind Ensemble. At the time these volumes were first written there was no comprehensive history of the wind band. In addition these volumes together provide library identification and shelf-marks for more than 30,000 wind band manuscripts and early prints before 1900 found in more than 450 libraries. Over several decades it was my practice when conducting in Europe to add some weeks to my trip to visit libraries and examine early works for wind band and many of these scores I worked into the repertoire of my own concerts.

Whereas general music history begins the Renaissance with the fourteenth century, because of developments in Church music, in terms of musical style for wind bands it is really the beginning of the sixteenth century when things really change. This was due to rather sudden advances in the art of the crafts of the wood workers and the metal workers which resulted in an almost complete change in the construction of wind instruments themselves during the sixteenth century. In particular, these changes made possible the first true bass wind instruments which, together with the consort principle, led to much more mature and satisfying music. For these reasons, in terms of the history of wind bands it is only the sixteenth century which is truly the Renaissance. And for this reason this volume considers medieval wind bands as continuing until the year 1500.

The real purpose in writing these volumes has been an attempt to demonstrate to band directors everywhere that they represent a medium that has performed at the highest levels of society over a very great span of time and that while all musicians take their turn at functional music, wind bands also performed music to be listened to. It is a very great mistake for any band director to assume that his role is limited to only entertaining the public.

David Whitwell
Austin, Texas

Contents

WIND MUSIC BEFORE THE CHRISTIAN ERA ... 1

1. *The Ancient East and Near East* ... 9
2. *Wind Music in Ancient Egypt* ... 15
3. *Hebrew Wind Music in the Old Testament* ... 19
4. *Wind Music in Ancient Greece* ... 29
5. *Wind Music of the Etruscans* ... 49
6. *Wind Music in the Roman Empire* ... 55

THE AGE OF THE MINSTREL ... 67

7. *The Early Medieval Jongleur* ... 71
8. *Late Medieval Minstrels* ... 77
9. *The Decline of Minstrelsy* ... 83

WIND ENSEMBLES IN THE MEDIEVAL CHURCH ... 89

10. *The Intolerance of the Church* ... 91
11. *Toward Acceptance of Instrumental Music* ... 95
12. *Wind Instruments in the Medieval Church Drama* ... 107

THE CIVIC WIND BAND ... 113

13. *Civic Wind Bands in Italy* ... 121
14. *Civic Wind Bands in England* ... 131
15. *Civic Wind Bands in the Low Countries* ... 137
16. *Civic Wind Bands in France* ... 143
17. *Civic Wind Bands in the German-Speaking Countries* ... 149

THE MEDIEVAL COURT WIND BAND ... 157

18. *The Wind Band in Medieval Courtly Life* ... 165
19. *The Wind Band and the Medieval Dance* ... 173
20. *The 'Lost' Repertoire of the Medieval Wind Band* ... 177
21. *Court Wind Bands in England* ... 181

22 *Court Wind Bands in France* ... 207
23 *Court Wind Bands in Spain* ... 219
24 *Court Wind Bands in Italy* ... 227
25 *Court Wind Bands in Burgundy* ... 243
26 *Court Wind Bands in the German-Speaking Countries* ... 261

NOTES ON THE INSTRUMENTS ... 279

BIBLIOGRAPHY ... 291

INDEX ... 307

ABOUT THE AUTHOR ... 313

Acknowledgments

This new edition would not have been possible without the encouragement and help of Craig Dabelstein of Brisbane, Australia. His experience as a musician and educator himself has contributed greatly to his expertise as editor of this volume.

> David Whitwell
> Austin, 2011

PART I

Wind Music Before The Christian Era

Wind Music Before The Christian Era

PERFORMANCE ON WIND INSTRUMENTS must be a very ancient joy, perhaps older than speech as we understand it. Those first wind players must have found their instruments in natural objects, such as shells and cane.

While some scholars date primitive wind instrument specimens from more than 80,000 BC, most of the oldest specimens are from the Upper Paleolithic Period (30,000–10,000 BC) and include already the various forms of flutes known ever since. The most simple are mere whistles, made from perforated reindeer phalanges, such as those found in France (La Madeleine and Solutré) and in Moravia (Pekárna). But more complex flutes existed: a fipple flute, found in Moravia; an instrument made of a bird bone, with three finger holes, found at Isturitz, Basses-Pyrénées; a flute found in Hungary, made from a bear femur, which may be a transverse flute; and panpipes, which have been found in several locations. Cave paintings suggest music was not yet appreciated as a separate art, but existed for ritual and funeral use. But it is difficult to believe these early flute players did not also play for their own enjoyment.

Replica of a paleolithic bone flute from Geißenklösterle, Germany.
Photo by José-Manuel Benito Álvarez / CC-BY-SA

From the Neolithic Period (10,000–2,500 BC) we begin to find evidence of drums, in the form of surviving specimens made of pottery. Surviving ocarinas found in Austria and Hungary already have finger holes cut for diatonic music![1]

It was in the Bronze Age (ca. 2,500–650 BC) that the trumpet and reed pipes were born. Now instruments were widely dispersed, as evidenced by two long curved trumpets discovered in Norway.

[1] Grove, 6:313. (Hereafter, references to 'Grove' refer to *The New Grove Dictionary*, ed. Stanley Sadie, 1980)

How we wish we knew more about the performance practices of these very ancient wind instruments, but most of them were used in performances before the invention of writing. Nevertheless, is it possible to deduce something about how these instruments were used in society?

One common characteristic of most of the oldest civilizations is that music was always associated with the gods.[2] It is clear that the earliest peoples did not associate music with the other arts, such a painting and sculpture, as we do today. Perhaps it was simply that music is the only art you can not see. It is easy to understand how painting, for example, could be thought of as a craft, for in looking at a painting you can immediately see the craft. But music is different. While neither the craft, nor music itself, can not be seen, it is immediately understood on an experiential level even by people with no training in music. No doubt it was this mysterious aspect, something which you could experience but not see, which they associated with the gods.

[2] Alfred Sendrey, *Music in the Social and Religious Life of Antiquity* (Rutherford: Fairleigh Dickinson University Press, 1975), 31.

The area of the Near East which we call Mesopotamia consisted first of isolated city-states, among the oldest of which were Ur, Susa and Kish. The area known as Babylonia consisted of Sumeria to the south and Akkad to the north. During the third millennium BC these peoples were united by the Semitic king, Sargon I.

Based on the surviving evidence, Sumeria, ca. 3,000 BC, is the oldest civilization we know which developed a sophisticated tradition of music. Since they believed music was of divine origin, they created temples for a number of gods, all of whom they believed had to be entertained, to keep them in good spirits, by singing and playing of instruments. Among these gods was one called *Enlil*, the father of humanity, who governed with a musical instrument called *al*.

Soon after the beginning of the second millennium the Amorites invaded Sumeria, ending the Sumerian Empire. From the Sumerian capital, Babylon, we take the name of the people of the next period. The Babylonians (2,000–562 BC) were extraordinary people, excelling in mathematics, astronomy, geography and medicine. They founded schools in which they taught cuneiform writing and they first introduced the 354-day calendar with twelve-hour days.

With respect to culture, the Babylonians seemed to have little of their own and we can therefore understand that they absorbed completely that of the Sumerians, including their musical traditions. We find a new god, however, *Ea*, who was god of the mysteries and arts, especially associated with the flutist-psalmist.

The Assyrians (750–606 BC), who took their name from the god *Ashur*, were a fierce and warlike collection of tribes who conquered Babylonia. They built the great capital city of Nineveh and began to develop unusual skills in the art of sculpture.[3] But, if it were not for the great stone-reliefs now in the British Museum, this empire would probably never be mentioned today, for after their defeat in 612 BC they disappeared from history.

Aside from the stone-reliefs, we can see these feared warriors had also some appreciation for music in the fact that whenever they put a city to the sword, they spared the musicians who, with the rest of the valuable booty, were sent back to Nineveh.[4]

In Egypt (2,686–52 BC), as in other ancient civilizations, the spiritual nature of music caused it to be linked in myth with the gods. We find this especially interesting with respect to the limited hieroglyphic language of Egypt. For example, the symbol which represents the god who created earth is also used to represent the god *Hesu*, who created music.[5] Another dual god, *Hathor*, was both the goddess of love and the goddess of music. A hymn to Hathor found in the temple of Dandera, seems to refer to the 'music of the spheres,' a familiar notion among the ancient philosophers, most notably Pythagoras.

> To thee, the heaven and its stars make music,
> Sun and moon sing praises to thee,
> The whole earth is making music for thee.[6]

Another goddess, *Merit*, was considered to be the personification of music. The strange dwarf god, *Bes*, was usually associated with childbirth but is usually pictured playing a variety of musical instruments.

The Greek myths and mythical gods are perhaps also an important chapter in our civilization's history. These myths, while only colorful stories to us, were for the early Greeks not

[3] Carl Engel, *The Music of The Most Ancient Nations* (London: Reeves, 1909), 24ff.

[4] Henry G. Farmer, 'The Music of Ancient Mesopotamia,' in *The New Oxford History of Music* (London: Oxford University Press, 1966), 237.

[5] Sendrey, *Music in the Social and Religious Life of Antiquity*, 37.

[6] Quoted in Lise Manniche, *Music and Musicians in Ancient Egypt* (London: British Museum Press, 1991), 12.

fables, but at the very least an important handed down oral tradition from a period before the arrival of Greek writing. While we can't think of them as genuine oral history, perhaps there may yet be embedded in these stories small nuggets of historical possibilities. Consider, for example, the myth of the sea god, Triton, and his 'invention' of the trumpet. He, we are told, in the war against the giants, blew into a sea conch producing sounds so new and frightening that the giants, thinking they had encountered a terrible and ferocious monster, took flight. Well, if we leave out the part about the giants, it certainly is easy to imagine this as a possible scenario for the discovery of the trumpet-type instrument. That is to say, some distant man walking along the shore, picking up a large conch and blowing through it to remove the water and sand, may have produced a frightening sound.

1   *The Ancient East and Near East*

THE MODERN READER WILL FIND MOST INTERESTING the accounts of wind ensembles in the Hebrew, Greek, and Roman societies, but as accounts of civilization begin in the East and move West, I must begin with a few brief notes on the wind and percussion music of the ancient Near and Far East.

The earliest references to the Far East are almost exclusively of percussion instruments. The Emperor Chao-hao of China (2,598 BC) prescribed the use of small drums to play for the changing of the watchmen.[1] Kastner tells a nice story from China in the second century BC. It seems an emperor named Lieu-Pang became irritated by the resistance he encountered in sieging a city and decided to reduce it to ashes. One night, as he made a tour of the walls to find an ideal place to attack, he heard a concert of voices and instruments from within the city. He was surprised and, after listening for a while, said to his officers, 'It must be that these people are very well ruled, since they love music. I consider their resistance as a mark of their attachment to their duty; thus I will revoke my order and give them life and liberty.'[2]

Similarly, the Indians, even in battle, used only percussion instruments, in particular timpani and whips which gave a 'deafening and frightening noise.'[3] We are told they played on the skin, but also on the sides of the instrument for signal purposes.[4]

One early writer, Arrian, a second century AD historian of the campaigns of Alexander the Great, reported that the Indians were noted for singing 'barbaric songs.' He adds, quoting Nearchus,

> For the Indians, be it said, are an extremely musical race and have loved dancing ever since the days when Dionysus came with his wild revelers to their country.[5]

According to several early sources, it was this Indian tradition of using percussion in battle which spread into Parthia, a kingdom in the eastern part of Alexander the Great's empire.[6]

[1] Amyot (trans.), *Dix préceptes adressés aux gens de guerre*, quoted in Georges Kastner, *Manuel Général de Musique Militaire* (Paris, 1848), 41.

[2] Kastner, *Manuel Général*, 23.

[3] Suidas, quoted in Kastner, *Manuel Général*, 40.

[4] Ibid.

[5] Arrian, *The Campaigns of Alexander* (New York: Penguin, 1978), 530, quoting Nearchus, *Indica* 7.8–9. Livy, in his *History of Rome* 5.39, also describes the troops of the Gauls attacking with 'barbaric songs' and 'cries like the howling of wolves.'

[6] Justin, Appian, and Plutarch, cited in Kastner, *Manuel Général*, 40, fn. 3–6.

The Parthians had instruments made of hollowed out wood and covered with skin and brass bells which made a 'deafening noise resembling the cries of ferocious beasts mixed with thunder.'[7] According to Plutarch, the very sound of these instruments contributed to the Roman's defeat in one of their many battles with the Parthians.

[7] Kastner, *Manuel Général*, 40.

> During this time, the enemy arrived, made more terrible by their cries and their victory chants; they put themselves to simultaneously hitting a multitude of timpani, at the great surprise of the Romans, who were waiting for a completely different kind of attack.[8]

[8] Plutarch, *Vitarum comparatarum* 2. Also, Grove, 14:254.

Parthian iconography shows a broader range of instruments in non-military life. A second century BC frieze pictures the double-pipe reed instrument, together with a panpipe, playing for a ritual Dionysian celebration. These instruments appear also in bronze and terracotta statuettes from the same period.[9]

[9] Grove, 14:254.

The origin of these instruments in this area is difficult to trace, but it is obvious that their roots go back very far in the general Mesopotamian cultures. A seal cylinder of the Sumerian King, Gudea of Sumeria (2,600 BC), reads, 'Enlulim, the shepherd of the lulim-kids, for the Lord Ningirsu, was given a share in his cult to cultivate diligently flute [playing] to fill the forecourt of Eninnu with joy.'[10] Even the more complex flute with a recorder mouthpiece seems to have been known in this area at a very early age, judging from the Babylonian clay example which formerly belonged to the Royal Asiatic Society in London.[11] Sachs believed that the reed instrument must have originated from this Near Eastern region, judging from the fact that the earliest names for it seem to be Semitic in origin.[12]

[10] Curt Sachs, *The History of Musical Instruments* (New York: Norton, 1940), 71.

[11] Ibid., 72.

[12] Ibid. For example, *halhallatu*, in Semitic, developed into *hālîl* in Hebrew.

Primitive horns were also known in this area at a very early date. A Carchemish relief in the British Museum shows a short, thick horn from ca. 1,250 BC.[13] Even earlier, ca. 1,400 BC, King Tushratta made a gift to King Amenophis IV of Egypt which included some forty horns, each covered with gold and precious stones.[14]

[13] Ibid., 73.

[14] Ibid.

Continuing west, the armies of the Persian Empire began to march with a trumpet signal from the tent of the king and began combat by holding up these instruments and performing a 'war hymn.'[15] Herodotus, the fifth century BC historian,

[15] Kastner, *Manuel Général*, 23, 30.

made the interesting observation that when the Persians, under Xerxes, attacked the Greeks at Artemisium, they marched not in rows but in the shape of a great crescent.[16]

A letter from the Macedonian General, Parmenio (400–330 BC), to Alexander the Great, regarding the capture of the palace of the Persian King, Darius III, reports 'concubines of the king who played musical instruments, to the number of 329.'[17] One wonders how many of them played the single-body double reed instrument like similar young women in ancient Greece.

Later Persian iconography is also interesting. A rock relief in a cave at Taq-i Bustan, near Kermanshah, shows a military band consisting of timpani, cylindrical drum, reed pipe and two trumpets from before 590–628 AD.[18]

In Syria, at the eastern end of the Mediterranean Sea, one finds a rare early reference to the small transverse flute. Poseidonius (ca. 135–145 BC) in his *Histories of Apameia*, wrote,

> They grasped daggers and small lances covered with rust and dirt; they put on hats with visors, which afforded shade, but did not prevent breathing at the throat; they carried with them drinking-horns full of wine and food of every variety, and beside these lay small (cross) flutes and single (body) pipes, implements of revel, not of battle.[19]

The double-bodied reed pipe was also known in ancient Syria. The performer on this instrument in the court of King Antiochus (280–261 BC), Sostratus, was so esteemed that his sons were made part of the king's bodyguard.[20]

The rhetorician and biographer, Flavius Philostratus (early third century AD) gives an extraordinary account of a visit on the Isle of Rhodes with the most famous double-pipe player of that age, Canus of Rhodes. In response to a question by the traveler, Apollonius, Canus indicated a broad range of music in use at that time.

> (The purpose of my music is) that the mourner may have his sorrow lulled to sleep by the pipe, and that they that rejoice may have their cheerfulness enhanced, and the lover may wax warmer in his passion, and that the lover of sacrifice may become more inspired and full of sacred song.

[16] Herodotus, *The Histories* (New York: Penguin, 1977), 8.15ff.

[17] Quoted in Athenaeus, *The Deipnosophists* 13.607.

[18] Grove, 14:550.

[19] *On the War Between the Apameans and Larisaeans*, bk.3, quoted in Athenaeus, *The Deipnosophists* 4.176.

[20] Athenaeus, *The Deipnosophists* 1.19.

Upon further questioning, Canus admits it is the music itself which accomplishes these ends, not the double-pipe 'constructed of gold or brass and the shin of a stag, or perhaps the shin of a donkey.' Next this early player gives a rare glimpse into the basic technique of playing the instrument:

> namely reserves of breath ... and facility with the lips consisting in their taking in the reed of the pipe and playing without blowing out the cheeks; and manual skill I consider very important, for the wrist must not weary from being bent, nor must the fingers be slow in fluttering over the notes.[21]

[21] Philostratus, *The Life of Apollonius of Tyana*, bk. 5, ch. 21.

The wide range of music available to the early double-pipe player, as given by Canus above, reminds one of an account by Claudius Aelianus (second century AD) which amusingly suggests even broader applications.

> But the mares of Libya are equally captivated by the sound of the pipe. They become gentle and tame and cease to prance and be skittish, and follow the herdsman where ever the music leads them; and if he stands still, so do they. But if he plays his pipe with greater vigor, tears of pleasure stream from their eyes. Now the herdsmen of the mares hollow a stick of rose-laurel, fashion it into a pipe, and blow into it, and thereby charm the aforesaid animals. And Euripides speaks of some 'marriage songs of shepherds' (Alc. 577); this is the pipe-music which throws mares into an amorous frenzy and makes horses mad with desire to couple. This in fact is how the mating of horses is brought about.[22]

[22] Aelianus, *On the Characteristics of Animals*, 12.44.

Finally, a few comments need to be made regarding the nomadic people of the Near East and lower Central Europe who crossed this area from approximately 1,000 BC to 1,000 AD.

One of these early cultures was the Assyrians. These people become recognizable about 1,800 BC and by 1,200 BC began to dominate much of Mesopotamia. These people used the trumpet as can be seen in a relief now in the British Museum (Nr. 124820), showing trumpets being used to synchronize the efforts of men heaving an enormous stone monument. Also housed in the British Museum is a far more primitive 'trumpet,' an end-blown shell of Assyrian origin.

The first of the standard Chinese histories reported that the Huns used trumpets and timpani when they fought the Chinese Han Empire in the third and second centuries BC.[23]

[23] *Shih-chi*, 110–111.

A Chinese traveler of the second century BC, Chang Ch´ien, returned from captivity among the Huns and is said to have introduced the transverse flute in his homeland.[24]

[24] Grove, 13:265.

A description of the trumpets of the Huns, in the battle of Catalaunian Fields (451 AD), says they 'sounded like the roaring of lions.'[25]

[25] Jordanes, *Getica* 16.212.

Although accounts, especially in the field of music, are extremely rare regarding these nomadic peoples, one must assume that since they covered great distances by horse, they must have acquired all the basic wind and percussion instruments known in the more stable civilizations. For example, a double-pipe found near Jánoshida, in Hungary, was probably carried there by the Avar tribes.[26]

[26] Grove, 13:265.

2 Wind Music in Ancient Egypt

THE USE OF WIND INSTRUMENTS IN ANCIENT EGYPT must be deduced from iconography, due to a lack of sufficient extant literature. During the period known as the Old Kingdom (ca. 2,686–2,181 BC), the earliest in which a clear pattern of musical practice can be observed, two wind instruments seem to have clearly been established. The most frequently pictured is a long flute, played in the transverse manner, but end-blown. The other is a single or double-pipe, fashioned with a reed.[1] Percussion instruments are limited to various hand-clappers. Music making seems to have been prevalent at this time, although with the exception of the harp the instruments all seem to have been played only by males.

The Middle Kingdom (ca. 2,133–1,786 BC) iconography continues the traditions of the earlier period.[2] It is in the following period, known as the New Kingdom (ca. 1,567–1,085 BC), that we have iconography for a new instrument—the trumpet.[3] Two extraordinary tomb paintings from this period not only show the trumpet, but clearly show it in its military environment. A painting from Tomb 90 of the Theban necropolis (ca. 1,425–1,405 BC) shows a male figure, in helmet, playing a trumpet about two and one half feet in length, held parallel to the ground. A painting in Tomb 74, from the same time and place, shows two trumpeters, marching with the instruments carried over their shoulders. Four additional soldiers seem to be carrying a small horn-like object.

In the New Kingdom iconography we also frequently see another wind instrument, the aulos, or double-pipe. This was an instrument with two bodies, frequently pictured in Greek and Roman iconography as well, and was probably played with a double reed. Sometimes the instrument is pictured being played with hands crossed over and sometimes with the hands playing the nearest pipe. It is here pictured being

[1] A painting from the Fifth Dynasty tomb of Necheftka and a relief from the tomb of Nekauhor, of the same period, each shows the two instruments playing in an ensemble with singers. The flute is held to the left in one case and to the right in the other; the reed pipe is played parallel to the ground and appears about twelve inches long in one scene and nearly two feet long in the other.

[2] An example of a Middle Kingdom flutist, again with a singer and harpist, can be found in the tomb of Tkhhotep at Meir, ca. 1,991–1,786 BC.

[3] Grove, 6:71, says that a tomb of Kagemni, Dynasty 5–6, of the Old Kingdom, may show the earliest known representation of a trumpet (participating in a ritual). Sachs, in *The History of Musical Instruments* (New York, 1940), 100, says the trumpet was used in the worship of Osiris, as well as in the military.

performed by women, usually in entertainment scenes. In sections of a wall painting from the eighteenth dynasty (ca. 1,425–1,375 BC) we see a richly costumed player accompanying two almost naked dancers and another player playing for a banquet.[4]

4 British Museum, Nr. 37948. The University Museum, Philadelphia, has obtained such an instrument, taken from the royal cemetery at Ur, ca. 2,800 BC (Sachs, *History of Musical Instruments*, 72).

Dancers and a double-pipe (aulos) player from the tomb of Nebamun at Thebes, ca. 1424–1375 BC.

These instruments do not seem to change in development in the following thousand years. In the so-called 'Greek' period of Egyptian history, beginning in the fourth century BC, another new wind instrument appears, the short transverse flute. Not only does this instrument appear in iconography of this period, but a passage from Athenaeus attributes the invention of the instrument to the God, Osiris, and calls it the *photinx*.[5]

5 Athenaeus, *The Deipnosophists* (quoting Juba's *History of the Stage*, bk. 4), 4.175ff.

The double-pipe is also mentioned in the early literature. Herodotus describes the Egyptian festival held in the town of Bubastis, in honor of the cat-headed Goddess, Pasht.

When the people are on their way to Bubastis they go by river, men and women together, a great number of each in every boat. Some of the women make a noise with rattles, others play double-pipes all the way, while the rest of the women, and the men, sing and clap their hands … When they have reached Bubastis, they make a festival with great sacrifices, and more wine is drunk at this feast than in the whole year beside. Men and women (but not children) are wont to assemble there, to the number of seven hundred thousand, as the people of the place say.[6]

[6] Herodotus, *The Histories* 2.59–60.

In another place, Herodotus writes of the Egyptians,

their heralds and double-pipe players, and cooks inherit the craft from their fathers … no others usurp their places … they ply their craft by right of birth.[7]

[7] Ibid., 6.60.

The earliest writer on the worship of Isis, Apuleius, second century AD, mentions two instruments rarely encountered in early Egyptian literature or iconography: the panpipes and the single bodied-pipe, which is presumed to have been a double reed instrument.[8]

Finally, one might mention the Alexandrian inventor, Ctesibius, third century BC, who was famous for elaborate toys powered by water or air. For Ptolemy's queen, Arsinoe, he constructed a water-powered clock, with sounding trumpets![9]

[8] Apuleius, *Metamorphoses*, 11.9.273; ed. Rudolf Helm (Berlin: Teubner, 1931) 11.8–16.

[9] Grove, 5:84.

3 Hebrew Wind Music of the Old Testament

THE OLD TESTAMENT contains numerous descriptions of the use of wind instruments, sometimes in large numbers. These references are more valuable to us today if taken as representative of general practice, and not as specific historical accounts. While the principals of the Old Testament may be presumed to be actual people, who in some cases can be accurately dated (i.e., David, ca. 1.000 BC, or Solomon, ca. 950 BC, etc.), the accounts which we call the books of the Old Testament were written generations, and sometimes many centuries, after the actual people and events they describe. With regard to music, these accounts were subject to error and exaggeration through generations of oral retelling before they were placed in written form and, in addition, tremendous linguistic problems sometimes prevent a literal translation into a modern language.

Nothing illustrates the problem in attempting a literal reading in a modern translation of the Old Testament better than the famous passage in Daniel 3:5 and 3:15, which describe the court musical ensemble of Nebuchadnezzar. First, this passage was written four centuries after Nebuchadnezzar. Second, the surviving text was first translated from Hebrew to Greek, and then into Aramaic. The resulting problems in translation are so difficult that transcribers tend to simply replace the original instruments with names of instruments familiar to the contemporary reader. Thus the Revised Standard Version (RSV, 1952) describes the ensemble as consisting of, 'the sound of the horn, pipe, lyre, trigon(?), harp, and bagpipe.' The King James Version (or Authorized Version, AV), written for the early seventeenth-century reader, lists a typical Renaissance band: cornett, flute, harp, sackbut, psaltery, and dulcimer! Obviously, neither literally represents the actual instruments used: *karnâ, mašrôkitâ, kaytroś, sabběkâ, pěsant-těrîn, sîpōneyâ,* and *sûmpônya*.

The first of these instruments seems obviously related to the Hebrew *keren*, a horn, usually appearing in the Old Testament as *keren hayyôvel*, rams-horn, meaning perhaps the shofar. A chief problem in the Old Testament is a not infrequent lack of distinction between the shofar and the trumpet, *hăsōserāh*.[1] The second of the instruments given in Daniel appears nowhere else in the Bible. The root means 'to whistle' and it may be the only reference to the panpipe instrument. The following three are probably string instruments. The following two words have no agreed upon modern meaning.[2]

In general, the instrument often translated as 'pipe' was *hālîl*, assumed to be a double body, double reed instrument like the aulos. The percussion identification is made difficult by the fact that the word for cymbal and bells is the same in both Greek and Latin.

The problem of exaggeration in the accounts of music practiced by the ancient Hebrew people can be seen in Josephus's account of Solomon's dedication of the first Temple. He assures us the ceremony included a performance by 200,000 trumpets—a figure which might exceed all the trumpets of antiquity![3]

This brief discussion should suffice to make the point that one can not take what one reads in the Old Testament as historically accurate with respect to wind and percussion instruments. However, in examining the *function* of these instruments in the Old Testament, one can form a picture of the general way winds were used by these ancient peoples. The use of these instruments falls easily into three broad fields: their use in religious ritual, in the military, and in civic functions.

With regard to the use of the trumpet in religious rituals, one immediately thinks of the extensive description given in Numbers 10:1–10.

[1] David Wulstan, 'The Sounding of the Shofar,' *The Galpin Society Journal* 26 (May 1973): 31, gives an excellent discussion of the linguistic problems.

[2] Sachs, *History of Musical Instruments*, 83ff., has a unique hypothesis regarding both the final word and the meaning of this passage, based on his reading of the Greek text.

[3] Josephus, *Jewish Antiquities* 8.95.

> The Lord said to Moses, 'Make two silver trumpets; of hammered work you shall make them; and you shall use them for summonsing the congregation, and for breaking camp. And when both are blown, all the congregation shall gather themselves to you at the entrance of the tent of meeting. But if they blow only one, then the leaders, the heads of the tribes of Israel, shall gather themselves to you. When you blow an alarm, the camps that are on the east side shall set out. And when you blow an alarm the second time, the camps that are on the south

side shall set out. An alarm is to be blown whenever they are to set out. But when the assembly is to be gathered together, you shall blow, but you shall not sound an alarm. And the sons of Aaron, the priests, shall blow the trumpets. The trumpets shall be to you for a perpetual statute throughout your generations. And when you go to war in your land against the adversary who oppresses you, then you shall sound an alarm with the trumpets, that you may be remembered before the Lord your God, and you shall be saved from your enemies.

On the day of your gladness also, and at your appointed feasts, and at the beginnings of your months, you shall blow the trumpets over your burnt offerings and over the sacrifices of your peace offerings.[4]

4 All Old Testament quotations here are taken from the Revised Standard Version, New York, 1952. This version is frequently in error with respect to the correct identification of wind and percussion instruments.

Aside from the extraordinary list of specific trumpet functions one finds here, this passage reveals much additional information. First, as the opening sentence demonstrates, this passage refers to real trumpets, not the ram's horn shofar. In fact, one can say that all of the Old Testament books which fall into this early period of approximately 1,250–1,210 BC (Numbers, Exodus, and Judges) are speaking of the trumpet. The later books, written in the fifth and sixth centuries BC (I & II Chronicles, I & II Kings, Isaiah, Ezekiel, I & II Samuel, and Joshua), begin to show the replacement of the trumpet with the ram's horn instrument.[5] The early Hebrews, who were probably originally Bedouins living in the desert, became

5 This evolution was probably due to the scarcity of metals in the desert, and perhaps a desire to rid themselves of Egyptian associations.

A coin from the Jewish Bar Kokhba revolution showing two silver trumpets

acquainted with the real trumpet in Egypt, through that portion of the Hebrew people who went to that country and then brought it back. There seems little doubt that at the same time they also brought with them from Egypt the double-pipe, and perhaps some of the percussion instruments.

The reservation of the trumpets for the priests, a statement which can be found in other places in the Old Testament as well, was probably a practical necessity, similar to restrictions in medieval Europe, where only the official civic musicians were allowed to perform after dark. This must have been a means of preventing confusion at a time when such basic communication depended on the trumpet signals. The reference to the 'alarm' proves that a recognizable repertoire of signals existed. Even more interesting is the distinction between one and two trumpets playing, for clearly this means two-part music. People at a distance could obviously not determine if one or two were playing, if they were playing in unison (with ram's horns they would have been able to make such a distinction, as each is a natural overtone series unique unto itself).

This early Egyptian–Hebrew trumpet, assuming it had similar characteristics to the Greek and Roman instruments, must have been capable of a rather loud sound. In Exodus 19, in a reference from the same general time frame as Numbers, Moses asks for a 'long blast' on the trumpet to call the people to the mountain. Two days later, competing with thunder and lightning, there was 'a *very* loud blast, so that all the people who were in the camp trembled.' Then, 'as the sound of the trumpet grew *louder and louder*,' God himself answered in thunder!

Exodus contains some interesting percussion references as well. The only small bells mentioned anywhere in the Old Testament are found here, on the robe of the high priest.[6] The small drum, similar in appearance to the modern tambourine, without the 'jingles,' is called *tof* in Hebrew (*duff* in Arabic). In Exodus 15:20, one reads that the sister of Moses was a performer on this instrument, an instrument usually associated with merrymaking.[7]

[6] Exodus 28:34ff and 39:25ff.

[7] See II Samuel 6:5, and Psalms 81:2.

In I Chronicles there is a description of David holding a ceremony around the ark of the covenant with shouting, 'to the sounds of the horn, trumpets, and cymbals, and made loud music on harps and lyres.'[8] Here we are given the actual names of three of the players of the 'bronze cymbals' and of seven trumpet players.[9] Two of these same trumpet players appear later and were 'to blow continually before the ark.'[10]

During a ceremony organized by King Solomon, one reads of the performance by no fewer than one hundred and twenty trumpets by the altar, in addition to cymbals, harps and lyres.[11] Additional examples of the use of winds in various aspects of religious ritual are the horns and trumpets accompanying the taking of the oath to the Lord[12] and the only appearance of the double-pipe in a religious context, leading a group of prophets.[13]

In the military sphere the trumpet is frequently found, as in almost every society. There are the usual references to the trumpet being used for signals in battle,[14] but more interesting are the two great battles in which trumpets played a primary role.

The earliest of these stories is the famous surprise attack by Gideon when, at night, he surrounded the enemy and gave them the impression that a much greater army was accompanying him.

> So Gideon and the hundred men who were with him came to the outskirts of the camp at the beginning of the middle watch, when they had just set the watch; and they blew the trumpets and smashed the jars that were in their hands. And the three companies blew the trumpets and broke the jars, holding in their left hands the torches, and in their right hands the trumpets to blow; and they cried, 'A sword for the Lord and for Gideon!' They stood every man in his place around about the camp, and all the army ran; they cried out and fled. When they blew the three hundred trumpets, the Lord set every man's sword against his fellow and against all the army; and the army fled.[15]

[8] I Chronicles 15:28.

[9] I Chronicles 15:19, 15:24. Another musician named in the Old Testament is Jubal, the 'father' of all musicians! (Genesis 4:21)

[10] I Chronicles 6:6.

[11] II Chronicles 5:2ff.

[12] II Chronicles 15:14.

[13] I Samuel 10:5. The Revised Standard Version is incorrect in two of the four instruments here: 'flute' should read double-pipe (*hālîl*) and 'tambourine' should read small drum, or *tympanon* after the Greek.

[14] II Chronicles 13:12; II Samuel 18:16 and 20:22; and Numbers 10:9.

[15] Judges 7:19–22.

The more famous passage tells the story of the use of trumpets to blow down the walls of Jericho.

> And seven priests shall bear seven trumpets of ram's horns before the ark; and on the seventh day you shall march around the city seven times, the priests blowing the trumpets. And when they make a long blast with the ram's horn, as soon as you hear the sound of the trumpet, then all the people shall shout with a great shout; and the wall of the city will fall down flat.[16]

[16] Joshua 6:4–5.

And so, we are told, it did!

The Battle of Jericho, by Julius Schnorr von Carolsfeld (1794–1872)

The descriptions of wind instruments in civic functions have parallels not only with the ancient civilizations to the west, but with medieval usage in Western Europe. These include the use of double-pipes to play for processions[17] and for banquets.[18] The trumpet appears as the civic watchman[19] and to celebrate the coronation of a new king.

[17] I Kings 1:40.

[18] Isaiah 5:12. This is incorrectly given as flute in the Revised Standard Version.

[19] Ezekiel 33:1.

> And the captains and the trumpeters beside the king, and all the people of the land rejoicing and blowing trumpets.[20]

[20] II Kings 11:13. See also I Kings 1:34, 1:39, and II Chronicles 23:13.

We should also mention that the *Dead Sea Scrolls*, in the material called 'The War of the Sons of Light and the Sons of Darkness,' there is detail about the use of trumpets in battle which goes far beyond similar passages in the Old Testament. An early date for this material is suggested in the fact that both the older silver trumpets seems to be present as well as the later ram's horn instrument.

Before the battle the trumpets are consecrated (III, 1-11) in a long passage which begins,

> On the trumpets of assembly for the entire community, they shall write: *The Enlisted of God*.
> On the trumpets of assembly for officers, they shall write: *The Princes of God*.
> On the trumpets of enrollment they shall write: *The Rank of God*.

After the battle lines are drawn up to face the enemy (VII, 8 – IX, 9) the trumpets give a series of specific calls, to arms, for the charge, for recall, etc., followed by even more detail:

> The trumpets shall keep sounding for the slingers until they have hurled a full seven times. Then the priests shall blow the recall for them, and they shall return to the first line to take their stand in their assigned position. Thereupon the priests shall sound a blast on the trumpets of assembly ...
> Then the priests are to sound blasts on the six trumpets used for rousing to the slaughter—a sharp insistent note for directing the battle. And the Levites and all the people with ram's horns are to sound a single blast—a great war-like trump to melt the heart of the enemy. At the sound of that blast, the war-darts are to issue forth to fell the slain. Then they are to accelerate the notes of the ram's horns, and the

priests are to blow upon the trumpets a sharp, insistent sound to direct the wings of the battle ... Thereupon the priests are to sound upon the trumpets the signal of recall—a low, quavering subdued note ...

And all the people shall silence their war-cries, while the priests keep blowing the trumpets for carnage.

There are also passages here which describe the troops going into battle not in rows but in geometric formations, one of which the Romans called *forfex* or the 'scissors-formation.'

4 *Wind Music in Ancient Greece*

How can one account for the remarkable accomplishments of ancient Greece? Out of its quasi-federation of city-states, each too unique in terrain and ethnic stock to ever permit a 'nation' in our understanding of the word, came some of the most extraordinary people ever born. Could one speak of philosophy today without reference to Socrates, Plato and Aristotle, or of literature without mention of Homer, Sophocles, or Aristophanes? Is there a musician alive who has not heard of Pythagoras?

The political institutions centered on two city-states in particular: Sparta, in Lacedaemonia, on the Peloponnesus Peninsula, enriched by the Dorian invaders of the eleventh century BC, and Athens, further north in Attica, settled by the Ionians in the fifteenth century BC. Many other cities, although of relatively less influence, are nevertheless familiar names today, such as Corinth, Thebes, and Syracuse.

Music exercised an almost unique power on the Greek mind, beginning with the Pythagoreans of the sixth century BC, who it is believed discovered the mathematical relationships among the tones of the natural scale. This, together with the obvious mathematical character of rhythm, led to the acceptance of music as an 'exact' science, to be included alongside geometry, arithmetic and astronomy. It followed, they believed, that the contemplation of music might reveal insights into the other 'exact' sciences. The study of music, for example, might reveal insights into astronomy—relative to the 'music of the spheres' or the relationship of the planets, which some believed were ordered in ratios consistent with the structure of the overtones over a fundamental pitch. According to Athenaeus, it was this belief that 'the universe was bound together by musical principles' that convinced Pythagoras himself to 'take up music as no mere hobby.'[1]

Pythagoras and his school were wrong, as it turned out. The contemplation of music does not reveal conceptual insights, but rather (equally important) non-conceptual, experiential insights. Therefore, it was only a matter of time before doubts

[1] Athenaeus, *The Deipnosophists* 14.632.

began to arise about music's favored status as an 'exact' science. In the fourth century BC, we can see Aristotle (in *Politica*) struggling to answer questions which had been raised. These questions are very familiar to us today; for example, 'Does music have a fundamental value or is it only an entertainment?' When Aristotle discusses, 'Is it necessary for school children to learn to actually play an instrument or is it enough to only be educated to appreciate music as listeners?,' we think of those today who would eliminate school bands and teach only 'General Music.'

The commonly known instruments, at the time of Aristotle, were a trumpet, two kinds of reed instruments, a flute, the small harp prototypes (kithara and lyra), and a type of lute. Lacking sufficient extant music, our insights into the nature and function of the wind instruments must come primarily from literature.[2]

The trumpet, called *salpinx*, was a straight cylindrical tube, perhaps in several sections.[3] The earliest reference to the trumpet in Greek literature is from the eighth century BC, in *The Iliad*.[4] Here Homer mentions the civic trumpeter who sounds the alarm when the foe approaches the gates of the city, very much like the medieval trumpeter of Western Europe twenty-five centuries later. Oddly enough, Homer did not mention the use of trumpets in his account of the battle of Troy, although Vergil, in his account of the same battle, did and even gave the name of one player.

> Misenus lay extended on the shore—
> Son of the god of winds;—none so renown'd
> The warrior trumpet in the field of sound,
> With breathing brass to kindle fierce alarms,
> And rouse to dare their fate in honorable arms.
> He serv'd great Hector, and was ever near,
> Not with his trumpet only, but his spear.[5]

It is in the realm of military music that we have the most surviving information about the trumpet. Xenophon wrote, in the early fifth century BC, that the Spartans used it for giving signals in their navy.[6] After the defeat of Cyrus in 401 BC, by his younger brother, Artaxerxes II, the Greek troops began one of the great adventures in human history, their escape into

[2] Direct *aesthetic* hierarchy is rarely mentioned in Greek literature. Ovid, *Metamorphoses*, bk. 11, relates a mythical musical contest between Pan with his panpipes and Apollo with his kithara, which Apollo won. On the other hand, Aristotle, *Problemata* 19.43, says the double-pipe was more pleasant than the lyra.

[3] One actual instrument survives and is in the Museum of Fine Arts, Boston (Acc. No. 37.301). The most striking icon is a sixth century BC vessel in the Vatican Museum, Rome (Nr. 498).

[4] Homer, *Iliad*, bk. 18, line 243.

[5] Vergil, *Aeneis* 6.242–248, here in the translation by John Dryden (London, 1803).

[6] Xenophon, *Hellenica*, bk. 4.

Warrior playing the salpinx. Attic black-figure lekythos, late sixth – early fifth century BC

© Marie-Lan Nguyen / CC-BY

Babylonia known as the 'Retreat of the Ten Thousand.' Xenophon was there in person and in his account he gives more precise information on the use of trumpet signals.

> When the trumpet gives the signal to rest, get ready your baggage; at the second signal, lead the beasts of burden; at the third, follow your general.[7]

A mention of trumpet signals in the armies of Alexander the Great can be found in Plutarch.[8]

[7] Xenophon, *Anabasis*, bk. 2. Xenophon also mentions here a rustic form of the instrument, 'After this there entered persons who played tunes on the horns used for signaling, and who sounded off measures, and as it were double-pipe notes, on trumpets made of raw ox-hides.' Quoted in Athenaeus, *Deipnosophists* 4.151.

[8] Plutarch, *Lives*, 'Alexander,' 25.

Although such references are not frequent in the extant literature, we can assume that the use of trumpet signals in the army was a sufficiently established tradition that, on occasion, the use of false signals to fool the enemy could be employed as a tactic. There are two such examples from the fifth century BC.

> Pericles, general of the Athenians, laid siege on a city which defended itself vigorously. By sounding the trumpets at night and creating great cries on the side of the city which faced the sea, the enemy, fearing a surprise attack from this side, ran through another gate freeing the entrance for Pericles.

Alcibiades used an analogous ruse.

> Approaching Cyzicus in the night, he sounded the trumpets from a side where he was not, and the enemy ran there in mass, while he entered without trouble from the abandoned location.[9]

9 Frontin, quoted in Kastner, *Manuel Général*, 32.

Among the most interesting accounts of Greek trumpet music are those found relative to the trumpet contests of the early olympics.[10] These began with the 96th Olympiad, in 396 BC, and were apparently not musical contests as such, but rather physical in nature—even as the modern olympic motto, *citius, altius, fortius* ('faster, higher, stronger'). Some of these trumpet players were famous: Timaios of Elis, Dionysios of Ephesos, and Heradorus of Megara. We are told the latter consumed, in a typical meal, six pints of wheat bread, twenty pounds of meat and six quarts of wine! A famous lady trumpeter, Aglais of Megacles, was known to have a comparable appetite.

10 See Edgar Turrentine, 'Notes on the Ancient Olympic,' *Instrumentalist* (April 1969).

There is one more reference to trumpet playing which I mention only because the use of wind music to accompany the auto-de-fe occurs from time to time. During Alexander the Great's campaign in India he encountered a man named Calanus, one of a group of Indian ascetics who had developed a fatal case of pneumonia. This man, to save time and trouble, decided to immolate himself. Alexander had his trumpets sound a salute as the fire began its work.[11]

11 Arrian, *The Campaigns of Alexander* (New York: Penguin, 1978), 352.

The instrument which appears most frequently in Greek iconography is the aulos, the twin-body instrument which looks like a 'V' on its side. Long incorrectly translated as 'flute,' this instrument was actually a reed instrument, which here will be referred to as a 'double-pipe.'[12] No one knows if a single or a double reed accompanied this instrument, but contemporary descriptions that it was an 'exciting' tone perhaps suggest it was a double reed. Aristotle, for one, says the instrument was *too* exciting to be used in educational music—the proper time to use it being for the relief of the passions. 'The ancients,' says Aristotle, 'were therefore right in forbidding the double-pipe to youths and freemen, although they had once allowed it.'[13] While we can not definitely establish the *kind* of reed, an almost inadvertent comment by Strabo reveals the source of the cane.

> Haliartus is no longer in existence, having been razed to the ground in the war against Perseus; and the country is held by the Athenians, a gift from the Romans. It was situated in a narrow place, between the mountain situated above it and Lake Copais, near the Permessus and Olmeius Rivers and the marsh that produces the double-pipe reed.[14]

Finally, the double-pipe existed in many different sizes and often was played with a leather band around the head to aid cheek pressure.[15]

We first read of the double-pipe in Homer's account of the fall of Troy (1,184 BC). Here, Agamemnon, during a lull while soldiers are resting, looks around the plain of Troy. He marvels at the many bonfires before Ilium and listens to the playing of double-pipes and flutes.[16]

I have remarked above that no trumpets were mentioned by Homer in his account of this famous battle. On the other hand, the appearance of the double-pipe is not unexpected, for this instrument was the favored instrument with the Greek armies. Why, asks Agesilaus (444–361 BC), King of Sparta, do the Spartans go into combat to the sound of the double-pipe? Because, he says,

> One can observe, as they advance thus, measure for measure, which are the cowards and which are the brave; because the rhythm of the anapests gives arder to courageous men, the same as it betrays the fainthearted; thus when the foot hesitates to follow the cadence of the double-pipe, the coward finds himself exposed in front of all eyes.[17]

[12] I distinguish the aulos from another instrument, also a reed instrument, but with one body, which I call a single-pipe. Neither term refers to a single or double *reed*.

[13] Aristotle, *Politica*.

[14] Strabo, *Geographica* (first century BC), 9.30.

[15] See Athenaeus, *The Deipnosophists* 14.176–185. Here one finds a discussion of at least nine different sizes of double-pipes, the largest of which had a primitive bell tied on the end, made from a 'piece of horn.'

[16] Homer, *Iliad*, bk. 10, line 15.

[17] Plutarch, quoted in Kastner, *Manuel Général*, 27.

Youth playing the aulos, detail of a banquet scene, ca. 460 BC–450 BC, by Euaion Painter

The double-pipe probably was nearly equal in volume to the trumpet, but there is a more compelling reason why the Greek armies preferred the double-pipe to the trumpet: it could play the entire scale and thus melodies, rather than mere signals. In fact, the double-pipe could play two pitches at once, due to its unique construction. Aristotle tells us that when accompanying a singer, for example, the double-pipe player would play one part in unison with the singer and at the same time a second part as an apparent independent accompaniment.[18]

[18] Aristotle, *Problemata*, 19.16.

The ability of the Greeks to march to music had strategic implications noticed by Machiavelli, at about the time Western Europe began to rediscover this concept:

for whiche cause the antiquitie had Shalmes, Flutes, and soundes perfectly tymed: For as moche as like as he that daunseth, proceadeth with the tyme of the Musick, and goyng with the same doeth not erre, even so an armie obeiyng, in movyng it self to the same sounde, doeth not disorder: and therefore, thei varied the sounde, accordyng as thei would varie the mocion, and accordyng as thei would inflame, or quiete, or staie the mindes of men.[19]

The analogy Machiavelli makes between using music to control armies and music to control dancers is very appropriate, for the Greeks, especially the Spartans, used dance as part of the education of young boys to help prepare them to be soldiers.[20]

It was in this context that Socrates stated that the best dancer is also the best warrior.[21] The most important of these dances was the *pyrrhiche*, which was danced to the double-pipe. In four parts, it consisted of all the necessary movements for attack and defense. First, the *podisme* consisted of very fast feet movement, preparing one to catch the enemy as he fled, or to escape its pursuit. The second part, the *xiphisme*, was a kind of simulated combat. The third part consisted of very high leaps, frequently repeated, which prepared the soldier for clearing walls and ditches. The final part, the *tetracome*, was tranquil and majestic.[22]

Xenophon described three additional dances of this nature. One, the *karpaia*, began as

> one performer lays aside his arms and begins to sow and plow, often turning around as if in fear; a robber approaches, and when the first dancer sees him he snatches up his arms and fights in front of his oxen, keeping time with the double-pipe music; finally the robber binds the man and drives off the team.[23]

Another dance, 'The Persian,' involves clashing of wicker shields and alternately squatting and standing up, to the accompaniment of the double-pipe. Still another, was danced by the Arcadians,

> who rose up in full armour and marched in step to the warlike measures of the double-pipe, neatly adapting themselves to the rhythm while they danced.[24]

---

[19] Machiavelli, *The Art of War*, trans. Peter Whitehorne (London: Niclas Inglande, 1560; reprint New York: AMS Press, 1967), 93.

[20] In the severe physical regimen which the Spartans called education, gymnastics was divided into two branches: dance and wrestling.

[21] Curt Sachs, *World History of the Dance* (New York: Norton, 1937), 239.

[22] See Kastner, *Manuel Général*, 9ff. There were other military dances, such as the *bryaliktai*, *byllichai*, and *dactyle*, all of which Kastner believed to be of very old origin, all related to a kind of sword dance said to have been invented by the Goddess, Minerva.

[23] Quoted in Athenaeus, *The Deipnosophists* 1.15.

[24] Ibid., 15–16.

The origin of these dances with the double-pipe must be very ancient, for the corresponding practice of troops marching in co-ordination with the music of the double-pipe is mentioned so far back in Greek literature that myth can no longer be separated from history. For example, there was a battle supposedly fought sometime in the twelfth century BC when the Heracleidae ('children of Heracles') defeated Eurystheus of Argos, claiming the Peloponnesus Island. It was from this battle that the Spartans dated their civilization. Tradition has it that although Eurystheus hurled his troops upon the Heracleidae, the latter did not panic but rather had their double-pipes march in front playing a 'rhythmic chant.' The double-pipes, we are told, enabled the troops to faithfully keep their ranks and defeat the enemy.[25]

Plutarch tells a similar story of a later Spartan General, Lycurgus.

> When the army was drawn up in battle array and the enemy near, the king sacrificed a she-goat, commanded the soldiers all to put garlands on their heads, and the double-pipers to play the hymn to Castor, and then he himself began the paean of advance. It was a magnificent and terrible sight to see them marching to the tune of the double-pipes, with no gap in their lines and no terror in their souls, but calmly and gaily led by music into the perilous fight. Such men were not likely to be either panic-stricken or over-reckless, but steady and assured, as if the gods were with them.[26]

Other Greek armies besides the Spartans used the double-pipe, including the Thebes and the Lydians.[27] The latter, under Alyattes (617–560 BC) used treble and bass double-pipes with panpipes in front of their army.[28]

No less than an oracle of the Gods predicted victory for the Spartans so long as they marched to the sound of the double-pipes. In a very famous battle, that of Leuctra, in 371 BC, against the Thebans, they failed to use the double-pipes (for they had traditionally recruited these players from Thebes itself) and lost. Modern historians speak only of the greater military tactics of the Thebans, but for the ancient historians the failure to use double-pipes was sufficient reason for the defeat.[29]

[25] Kastner, *Manuel Général*, 26.

[26] Plutarch, *Lives*, 'Lycurgus,' 22.

[27] Kastner, *Manuel Général*, 26ff.

[28] Herodotus, *The Histories* 1.17.

[29] Kastner, *Manuel Général*, 26ff.

This association of armies and double-pipes enables us to appreciate an old anecdote about the painter, Theon. He had painted the picture of a warrior in attack upon the enemy. But before unveiling it he first hired a double-pipe player to stand behind the canvas and perform. Having thus placed the viewers in the proper mood, he unveiled the painting to enthusiastic applause.[30]

Before leaving the subject of the Greek wars, it should be mentioned that the early writers on military tactics did not fail to observe the effects of wind instruments on the horses and other animals which participated. Some of the most extraordinary stories in early Greek literature center on battles lost when the horses responded to the wrong double-pipe melodies. In one such mishap in 510 BC, the Sybarites were defeated so soundly that in a single day they passed out of history altogether.[31] Charon of Lampsacus tells a similar story of a battle between the people of Cardia and the Bisaltians, the leader of whom was named Naris.

[30] Ibid., 28, fn. 2.

[31] Athenaeus, *The Deipnosophists* 12.520.

> He, when a child, had been sold in Cardia, and after serving as a slave to a Cardian had become a barber. Now the Cardians had an oracle that the Bisaltians would come against them, and they would often talk about it as they sat in the barber-shop. So Naris, escaping from Cardia to his native land, put the Bisaltians in readiness to attack the Cardians, and was appointed leader by the Bisaltians. All the Cardians had schooled their horses to dance at their drinking-parties to the accompaniment of the double-pipes, and rising on their hind legs and, as it were, gesticulating with their front feet, they would dance, being thoroughly accustomed to double-pipe melodies. Knowing these facts, Naris purchased a pipe-girl from Cardia, and on her arrival in Bisaltia she taught many double-pipers; accordingly he set out with them to attack Cardia. And when the battle was on, he gave orders to play all the pipe-melodies which the Cardian horses knew. And when the horses heard the piping, they stood on their hind legs and began to dance; but since the whole strength of the Cardians lay in their cavalry, they were beaten in this way.[32]

[32] Ibid.

Vergil believed that the very sound of the trumpet inspired the horse for battle.

> The fiery courser, when he hears from afar
> The sprightly trumpets, and the shouts of war,
> Pricks up his ears; and, trembling with delight,
> Shifts place, and paws, and hopes the promis'd fight.

On his right shoulder his thick mane reclin'd,
Ruffles at speed, and dances in the wind.
His horny hoofs are jetty black and round;
His chine is double; starting with a bound
He turns the turf, and shakes the solid ground.
Fire from his eyes, clouds from his nostrils, flow:
He bears his rider headlong on the foe.[33]

Elephants, on the other hand, which were more used to percussion sounds in India, were often startled by the sound of the trumpet. For example in one battle, Hannibal's elephants, frightened by the Roman trumpets and horns, stopped and began backing up upon their own soldiers, causing great disorder.[34]

One also finds the double-pipe was played in all the celebrations of Greek daily life: weddings, social gatherings, entertainments, and funerals.[35] There were also celebrations on the order of state holidays. The Spartans, for example, celebrated the 'Feast of Hycinthia' for a period of three days. The official events included boys singing to double-pipe accompaniment and,

> full choirs of young men singing some of their national songs, and dancers mingling among them go through the figures in the ancient style, accompanied by the double-pipe and the voice of the singers.[36]

Apparently the great tradition of choral odes accompanied by the double-pipe had evolved by the third century BC, into a form with more emphasis on the double-pipe. One, Pratinas of Philius, in any case complains that instead of the double-pipe accompanying the chorus in the traditional fashion, 'the choruses now sing a mere accompaniment to the double-pipe players.'[37] In the case of the *Hyporcheme*, a form including singing, double-pipes, and dance, Pratinas grew quite angry when the double-pipe ursurped the attention of the audience.

> What uproar is this? What dances are these? What outrage hath assailed the alter of Dionysus with its loud clatter? ... 'Tis the song that is queen ... the double-pipe must be content to be leader in the revel only, in the fist-fight of tipsy youngsters raging at the front door. Beat back him who has the breath of a mottled toad, burn up in flames that spit-wasting, babbling raucous reed, spoiling melody and rhythm in its march.[38]

[33] Vergil, *Georgics* 3.130–140 (trans., John Dryden, London, 1803). This passage reminds us of a similar one in the Old Testament (Job 39):

> Do you give the horse his might?
> ...
> He paws in the valley, and exults
>   in his strength;
> He goes out to meet
>   the weapons.
> He laughs at fear, and is
>   not dismayed;
> He does not turn back from
>   the sword.
> Upon him rattle the quiver,
> The flashing spear and
>   the javelin.
> With fierceness and rage he
>   swallows the ground:
> He cannot stand still at the sound
>   of the trumpet.
> When the trumpet sounds, he
>   says, 'Aha!'
> He smells the battle from afar,
> The thunder of the captains; and
>   the shouting.

[34] Livy, *History of Rome* 30.33; Polybius, *The Histories* 4.491.

[35] Homer, *Iliad*, bk. 18; Aristotle, *Problemata* 19.1, and *Politica* 8.5.

[36] Athenaeus, *The Deipnosophists* 4.139.

[37] Ibid., 14.617.

[38] Ibid.

Many of the choral odes had preludes, which may on occasion have been examples of purely instrumental music. In addition there seems to have been some pure instrumental performance on these festive programs. Semus of Delos writes,

> Since the term 'concerted music' is unknown to many persons, I must tell its meaning. It was a kind of contest in harmony, double-pipe music and dance rhythm exactly corresponding, with no singer adding words to the performance.[39]

We may assume that cult performances included the double-pipe as well. One reads of this instrument being used for the sacrifices at Delos, during the worship of Artemis Chitonea by the Syracusans, by boys dancing on Mount Helicon, and in the cult of Dionysus:[40]

> and bent its Bacchic revelry with the high-pitched, sweet-sounding breath of Phrygian double-pipes.[41]

There were also contests for double-pipe players. Plutarch tells us that Alexander the Great organized many such contests, for he, himself, did not have much interest in the usual boxing and wrestling contests.[42] Here again, apparently, the contests over a period of time had developed from artistic events into popular ones. Athenaeus (second century BC) notes,

> Today, however, people take up music in a haphazard and irrational manner. In early times popularity with the masses was a sign of bad art; hence, when a certain double-pipe player once received loud applause, Asopodorus of Phlius, who was waiting in the wings, said, 'What's this? Something awful must have happened!' … And yet the musicians of our day set as the goal of their art success with their audiences.[43]

For this reason, Aristotle took a dim view of these contests. Thinking of the literature, he noted, 'The vulgarity of the spectator tends to lower the character of the music.' Students, he felt, 'should stop short of the arts which are practiced in professional contests, and not seek to acquire those fantastic marvels of execution which are now the fashion in such contests.'[44]

[39] Semus, *History of Delos*, bk. 5, quoted in Athenaeus, *The Deipnosophists*.

[40] Athenaeus, *The Deipnosophists* 14.629 and Harvard University Press edition, 6:329, fn. 'c.'

[41] Strabo, *Geographica* 10.3.13.

[42] Plutarch, *Lives*, 'Alexander,' 4.

[43] Athenaeus, *The Deipnosophists* 14.631.

[44] Aristotle, *Politica*.

One repertoire work from these double-pipe contests has been described for us by Strabo. This work, performed at the games at Delphi, consists of five formal parts, somewhat like movements, telling of a battle between Apollo and a dragon. It consisted of a prelude; commencement of the battle; the battle proper; the victory; and finally the death of the dragon, 'the double-pipe players imitating the dragon as breathing its last in hissings.'[45]

There must have been among these players many who were well-known and even legendary in their own day. No doubt one among them was Pythochares, who is said to have repelled an attack of wolves by playing a loud and noble strain on his double-pipe![46]

As one might suppose, any society which had double-pipe contests also had a thriving profession of double-pipe teachers. This was necessary for, in spite of the frequent appearances of the instrument in Greek literature and art, it was apparently not an easy instrument to play well. This is reflected in several versions of a Greek myth about the Goddess Minerva having invented the double-pipe, but throwing it away when she discovered the exertion in playing it deformed her face.[47] Plutarch, in his famous book, *Lives*, mentions a negative view of the aulos. Pericles (495–429 BC), the famous statesman and general of Athens, objected to the time and effort required to master this instrument, such effort he believed to be unworthy of a noble person. To illustrate this he mentioned a story about Antisthenes who, when someone remarked that one Ismenias was an excellent aulos player, said 'It may be so, but he must be a wretched human being otherwise he would not have been an excellent aulos player.' Aristotle also noted that he considered the instrument too difficult to be used in the education of children.[48]

Even after twenty-five centuries, it is possible today to indentify some of the teachers and a large number of the treatises on double-pipe performance. Athenaeus mentioned such treatises by Euphranor, Archytas, Pyrrander, Phillis of Delos, and two each by Aristoxenus and Archestratus.[49]

Unfortunately all of these double-pipe treatises are lost and surviving Greek literature gives us only an occasional glimpse of the double-pipe teacher at work. Plutarch tells of two different double-pipe teachers, Ismenias the Theband and Antigeni-

[45] Strabo, *Geographica* 9.3.10.

[46] Aelianus, *On the Characteristics of Animals* (second century AD), 11.28.

[47] Charles Gayley, *The Classic Myths* (Boston, 1893), 112; and Kastner, *Manuel Général*, 11, fn. 3.

[48] *Politica* 8.6.

[49] Athenaeus, *The Deipnosophists* 4.184, 14.634. There were double-pipe schools at Olypiodorus and at Orthagoras.

das, who regularly paraded before their students examples of both good and poor double-pipe players, as an illustration of how to play and how not to play.[50] I like the comment by the double-pipe teacher, Caphisias, who worked in the court of Alexander the Great. When one of his pupils constantly practiced with a very loud sound, Caphisias whacked him and said, 'Good playing consists not in bigness, but bigness depends on good playing.'[51]

We have seen the use of the double-pipe in many facets of Greek life. Its acceptance seems to have been so common that the historian Polybius (second century BC) makes special mention of the people of Cynaetha as the only people of Arcadia who did not use the instrument. He implies that the disorganization of their society was somehow connected with this.

> One must not believe that the ancient Cretans and Lacedaemonians (Spartans) introduced the double-pipe and a marching rhythm into battle, instead of the trumpet, without good reason; nor was it by chance that the earliest Arcadians carried the art of music into their entire social organization, so that they made it obligatory and habitual not only for boys but also for young men up to thirty years of age, although in all other respects they were most austere in their habits of life ... it is no disgrace (for them) to confess that one knows nothing, but it *is* deemed a disgrace among them to decline (to be unable) to sing. What is more, they practice marching songs with double-pipe accompaniment in regular order, and further, they drill themselves in dances and display them annually in the theatres with elaborate care and at public expense ... But the people of Cynaetha came at the end to neglect these customs (and therefore) they plunged right into friction and rivalry with one another and finally became so brutalized that among them alone occurred the gravest acts of sacrilege.[52]

There was another reed instrument known to Greek society, one played exclusively by girl entertainers who were either prostitutes or at least associated with them. This instrument was described as a single-pipe, probably a kind of aulos with one body instead of two. As such, it would have been easier to play and more practical for entertainment purposes. These girls with their single-pipes seem to have been a common feature of important, but private, banquets. They must have been attractive young ladies as there are many references to their aristocratic hosts falling in love with them, showering them with gifts, and even having acknowledged children by them.[53]

[50] Plutarch, *Lives*, 'Demetrius,' 1.

[51] Athenaeus, *The Deipnosophists* 14.629.

[52] Quoted in Athenaeus, *The Deipnosophists* 14.626ff. See also Polybius, *The Histories* 4.

[53] Athenaeus, *The Deipnosophists* 13.577–608.

By this association some of the single-pipe girls achieved considerable status and wealth; Polybius observes that some of the finest houses were named for them.[54]

The girls seem to have been introduced after the meal, as a form of entertainment while the hosts drank. One such banquet, documented at length by Hippolochus, was given by Caranus, of Macedonia, for twenty of his friends to celebrate his marriage. We are told that as the guests entered they received as gifts gold tiaras and silver cups. The first course included duck, ringdove, chicken, and a goose; the second course featured rabbit, more geese, young goats, pigeons, turtle-doves, partridge, and other fowl. The custom was for the guests to sample this and then pass the rest back to their servants. More gifts followed, and then drinks.

Now the single-pipe girls entered, together with other entertainers. 'To me,' writes Hippolochus, 'these girls looked quite naked, but some said that they had on tunics. After a prelude they withdrew.' Another round of gifts: jars of gold and silver, perfume, and a great silver platter with a roast pig, filled with a variety of small fowl. Again gifts were distributed: more perfume, more gold and silver, and breadbaskets made of ivory.

Next more entertainers appeared, including naked female jugglers who performed tumbling acts among swords and blew fire from their mouths. This was followed by more gifts: a large gold cup for each guest, a large silver platter filled with baked fish, a double jar of perfume and gold tiaras twice the size of the first ones. The sounding of a trumpet announced the end of the banquet and the enriched guests, according to Hippolochus, all went out to look for real estate agents!

The single-pipe girls who appeared at great banquets did not apparently come inexpensively. Menander, complaining about the high cost of sacrifices, estimated the costs of 'single-pipe girls and perfume, harp-girls, Mendean and Thasian wine, eels, cheese, and honey' at one talent (approximately $40,000 in 1982 US Dollars).[55] Plato complained that those who could not carry on a decent conversation were the ones responsible for 'driving high the market price of single-pipe girls.'[56]

[54] Letter to Lynceus, quoted in Athenaeus, *The Deipnosophists* 4.1ff.

[55] Menander, *The Carouse*, quoted in Athenaeus, *The Deipnosophists* 4.146.

[56] Plato, *Protagoras*, quoted in Athenaeus, *The Deipnosophists* 3.96ff. The more practical Aristotle suggested the city commissioners 'see that female reed-players … are not hired at more than two drachmas.' (*Atheniensium Respublica*, 49)

Sometimes these girls were auctioned off at the banquet, but only after sufficient drinks had loosened both the purse and appetite of the guests. Persaeus describes a banquet he attended in the third century BC:

> There was a philosopher drinking with us, and when a single-pipe girl entered and desired to sit beside him, although there was plenty of room for the girl at his side, he refused to permit it, and assumed an attitude of insensibility. But later, when the single-pipe girl was put up for the highest bidder, as is the custom in drinking-bouts, he became very vehement during the bargaining, and when the auctioneer too quickly assigned the girl to someone else, he expostulated with him, denying that he had completed the sale, and finally that insensible philosopher came to blows, although at the beginning he would not permit the single-pipe girl even to sit beside him.[57]

The popularity of these single-pipe girls may be measured in the fact that Phylarchus maintained that only in the vicinity of Ceos could one not find them.[58]

The flute which was known to ancient Greece was the pan-pipe instrument, although as in almost every culture it appears only as a rural instrument. It therefore is rarely mentioned in Greek literature, usually in an association with some of the mythical characters. One of these examples deals with the creation of the instrument.

> Then, of unequall wax-joyn'd Reeds he fram'd,
> This seven-fold pipe: of her 'twas *Syrinx* nam'd.[59]

The transverse flute is the missing instrument of Greek antiquity. We can find it nearby to the east, in Syria, and there is a stunning Etruscan stone carving of a man playing this instrument, in Perguis, to the west, but it appears in no Greek iconography nor in literature which discusses the Greek cities. It seems it should be there, but it is not.

Percussion instruments are rarely mentioned in Greek literature and they do not seem to have progressed beyond noise-making devices. For example, Euripides mentioned that sometimes soldiers put small bells on their horses and on their own belts for the purpose of terrorizing the enemy.[60]

[57] Persaeus of Citium, *Convivial Notes*, quoted in Athenaeus, *The Deipnosophists* 13.607.

[58] Phylarchus of Athens or Naucratis (historian, third century BC), *History* 23, quoted in Athenaeus, *The Deipnosophists* 13.610.

Pan with pan pipes, ceramic, painted, Greece, fifth to third century BC

[59] Ovid, *Metamorphosis*, trans. George Sandys, (Lincoln: University of Nebraska Press, 1970), 1.

[60] Kastner, *Manuel Général*, 48.

I have tried to limit this discussion to historical events, but one should not overlook entirely the myths which are so much a part of Greek literature. Many of the gods and goddesses have associations with wind and percussion instruments (Pan, Apollo, Mercury, Curetes, Dionysis, etc.), which must be taken as yet another reflection of the importance of wind music in the life of the Greeks. Although these myths are only stories, and not history, it is reasonable to assume that many of them have very ancient roots in actual events. For example, consider the Sea-God, Triton, who, in the war against the giants, blew into a sea conch producing sounds so new and frightening that the giants, thinking they had encountered a terrible and ferocious monster, took flight. In the process the trumpet was born, according to the myth. It makes a nice story and perhaps, from some time in the remote past of man, it might even contain a basic truth. It certainly seems reasonable that some distant man picked up a sea conch and blew into it at an earlier date than the man who first fashioned a primitive instrument from an animal horn.

Considering how influential music was in the life of the Greeks, it is very unfortunate that so little actual music has survived; the handful of fragments extant do not permit a general study. If, however, one examines the comments of the early writers carefully, through deduction one can gain some insight into what this early wind music must have been like.

The first element of Greek music was its modal system. Music students today are often given the impression that modes such as Dorian and Phrygian are tonalities, distinguished by their varying steps and half-steps within their scales. But to the Greeks they were not systems of steps and half-steps so much as the music of indigenous populations.. They used these terms as we today might say 'German' music as opposed to 'French' music. The Dorians, Ionians, Phrygians, Aeolians, and Lydians were actual people to the Greeks; when these terms were used in a musical sense, it meant music *in the style* of these peoples. When we read, for example, that the Spartans preferred Dorian music, we must remember that it was the Dorians who settled Lacedemonia and were the stock for the future Spartans. The Greeks themselves recognized a broad distinction among these styles. Aristotle, for example, defines Dorian as 'music of a moderate and settled temper ...

grave and manly'; Mixolydian 'makes men sad and grave ... woeful and quiet'; Hypodorian is 'magnificent and steadfast'; whereas Phrygian is 'exciting and orgiastic ... inspires enthusiasm.'[61]

Aristotle says, 'even in mere melodies there is an imitation of character, for the musical modes differ essentially from one another, and those who hear them are differently affected by each (mode).'[62] So, Alexander the Great, in an often retold story, upon hearing a double-pipe player from Thebes perform in the Phrygian mode was 'suddenly inflamed by a supernatural furor,' alarming his guests as he 'took to his arms as if he were preparing for battle.'[63]

According to Aristides Quintilianus (writing much later, in the second or third century AD), the Greek melodies were also cast in one of three forms.

> The diatonic is the most natural, the chromatic is artificial and by this reserved for the connoisseur; and the enharmonic is the most difficult of all and only accessible to the consumate musicians.[64]

This seems to be confirmed by Thucydides (471?–400 BC) who wrote that in Sparta, where they preferred the diatonic, a player named Timothy of Milesia, was banished by the magistrates for having introduced into the city the use of an 'artificial and chromatic genre.'[65] Such stories suggest that perhaps Spartan melodies were of a rather simple tonal nature.

Regarding harmony in Greek music, comments by Aristotle seem to suggest nothing was unusual about two-part writing and in some passages he seems to imply even more complex harmonies were heard:

> we delight in concord because it is the mingling of contraries which stand in proportion to one another ... (Speaking of accompaniment) ... though they do not play the same other notes as the singer.[66]

Aristotle also suggests that Greek music contained some variety in rhythmic values:

> some (rhythms) have a character of rest, others of motion, and of these latter again, some have a more vulgar, others a nobler movement.[67]

---

[61] Aristotle, *Problemata* 19.48; *Politica* 8.5, 8.7. Theophrastus of Eresus (372–287 BC, a disciple of Aristotle) wrote in his *On Inspiration* that a person suffering from sciatica would always be free from attacks if one played the double-pipe in the Phrygian mode over the part of the body affected. (Quoted in Athenaeus, *The Deipnosophists* 14.624)

[62] *Politica* 8.5.

[63] Kastner, *Manuel Général*, 19. Machiavelli, retelling this story in the early sixteenth century ('Alexander beyng at the Table, and one soundyng the sounde Frigio, it kendled so moche his minde, that he laied hande on his weapons.') regretted that in his day military music had so lost its power that, far from inspiring great actions, it only inspired 'rumor.' (Machiavelli, *The Art of War*, 93)

[64] Aristides Quintilianus, *On Music*, 1. 'Ex his naturalius est diatonum, quippe omnibus etiam indoctis omnino cani potest. Artificiossissimum, chroma. Soli enim docti illud modulantur. Accuratissimum est enharmonium, quod peritissimis musicis est receptum; multis autem est impossibile.'

[65] Quoted in Kastner, *Manuel Général*, 19, fn. L.

[66] Aristotle, *Problemata* 19.38, 19.39. See also Plato, *Laws*, 2.655A, 669D–670C, 7.802D.

[67] *Politica* 8.5.

The wide use of music by the Greeks for dance and for the control of military men and animals raises the interesting possibility that meter was also present as part of their rhythmic organization. One passage in Plutarch also seems to suggest such a definite concept of pulse. He speaks of the fleet carrying the ashes of Demetrius (337–283 BC) as part of his funeral obsequies.

> The most famous double-pipe player of the time, Xenophantus, was sitting close to it playing a solemn melody, to which the rowers kept time in rhythm. The beat of their oars, like funeral mourning, answered the strains of the double-pipe.[68]

[68] Plutarch, *Lives*, 'Demetrius,' 53.

Finally, one comment by Aristotle clearly suggests that Greek music, or at least some Greek music, was not the product of simple improvisation, but that regular 'repertoire' works existed which were known and recognized by the public.

> Why do men take greater pleasure in listening to those who are singing such music as they *already know*?[69]

[69] Aristotle, *Problemata* 19.5.

The knowledge and appreciation of music implied in this statement, and in all that we have mentioned above, is a hallmark of the ancient Greek civilization.

One ancient Greek myth is, in its unique way, a testimonial to the value of good music for the citizen. Philetaerus, writing in the fourth century BC, exclaims, 'Zeus, it is indeed a fine thing to die to the music of double-pipes!'[70] Being able to arrange such an event, he believed, demonstrated conclusively to the gods that one appreciated music. For such persons, should one go to 'Hades' one is permitted 'to revel in love affairs,' whereas 'those whose manners are sordid, having no knowledge of music,' are condemned to spend eternity carrying water in a fruitless effort to fill 'the leaky jar.'

[70] Philetaerus, *The Double-pipe Lover*, quoted in Athenaeus, *The Deipnosophists* 14.633.

The reader may be astonished to find reference to this same myth seven hundred years later in the New Testament. In Matthew 9:23 we have the story of Jesus raising a girl from the dead. He enters the house where she lies and he sees the double-pipe players [mistranslated in modern editions as 'flutes'] standing around her bed and he cries out 'Get those flute players out of here, the girl is not dead but only sleeping!' Then he took her hand and raised her up.

5 *Wind Music of the Etruscans*

The Etruscans (Latin: *tusci*) inhabited the western region of Italy, known today as Tuscany. These peoples, of East Mediterranean origin, migrated in the eighth and ninth centuries BC, and formed a strong cultural entity until their absorption into the Roman Empire in 27 BC.

Because they traded with the Greeks, they form an important link between the city states of Greek antiquity and the Roman Empire. This is quite evident, for example, in the ancient history of the trumpet, which several writers claim was an invention of the Etruscans.

> Athenaeus: 'Horns and trumpets are an invention of the Etruscans.'[1]
> Diodorus of Sicily: 'It remains for us now to speak of the Tyrrhenians (Etruscans) ... they were the inventors of the *salpinx*, as it is called, a discovery of the greatest usefulness for war and named after them the "Tyrrhenian" trumpet.'[2]
> Aeschylus: 'Herald, give the signal and restrain the crowd; and let the piercing Tyrrene trumpet, filled with human breath, send forth its shrill blare to the folk!'[3]
> Sophocles: 'I hear thy call and seize it in my soul, as when a Tyrrhenian bell speaks from mouth of bronze!'[4]
> Euripides: 'Then the Tyrrhenian trumpet blast burst forth, ritfe fire, as the signal for the fight.'[5]

[1] Athenaeus, *The Deipnosophists* 4.184. (late second century BC)

[2] Diodorus, *The Library of History* 5.40. (first century BC)

[3] Aeschylus, *Eumenides* 567. (fifth century BC)

[4] Sophocles, *Ajax* 16–17. (sixth century BC)

[5] Euripides, *The Phoenician Women* 1377–1378. (fifth century BC)

This has been puzzling to scholars, because the salpinx trumpet can be found in both Greece and Egypt before the migration into this part of Italy. What then, are these early writers referring to? It seems possible, on the basis of iconography, to suppose that it was the Etruscans who developed the two new 'trumpets' familiar in Roman music, but not found in earlier Greek traditions. The *cornu*, a great hoop-shaped instrument of bronze or iron, with transverse grip (looking somewhat like a capital 'G'), is seen pictured in virtually every Roman military icon. The second, and a bit less frequently seen, is the *lituus*, with a bell bent backwards (looking like a horizontal letter 'J'). Both of these instruments appear in the iconography of Etruria considerably earlier than that of Rome.[6]

[6] Both of these instruments seem to have developed from the trumpet, rather than from the animal horn as is the case of the primitive *buccina*. An excellent early (fourth century BC) example of both the cornu and the lituus in Etruria can be seen in a fresco of the tomb of Castel Rubello, Orvieto. Roman examples can be seen frequently in iconography of the early second and first centuries BC. Two actual early lituus instruments survive, one Etruscan (National Etruscan Museum, Villa Giulia, Rome, Nr. 51216) and one Roman (Rome, Museo Gregoriano Etrusco, Room 3).

The Etruscans also seem to have experimented with the double-pipe of Greece, adding to it a kind of bell.[7] This new looking instrument may have had a new name at this time. The Roman, Varro, wrote (first century BC) that *Subulo* was a word given by the Etruscans to their 'reed-pipe' players.[8]

[7] A fifth century BC fresco in the tomb of Leopardi, near Tarquinia, shows a bell on each body similar to that of the modern oboe. Later Roman examples show larger bells, bent back.

[8] Varro, *On the Latin Language* 7.35.

Fresco, tomb of Leopardi, fifth century BC, showing the bell on each body of the double-pipe

The Etruscans seem to have particularly cultivated wind instruments and one sees them in many icons of public processions.[9] A late fifth century BC funeral urn (Chiusi, Museo Civivo, Nr. 2260) shows a double-pipe player leading a wedding procession. Cornu and lituus players can be seen in funeral processions in the tombs of Bruschi and Tifone, near Tarquinia. Professional double-pipe players also performed during the lying-in-state, sacrificial rites and magic lamentations for the dead.[10]

No doubt winds were used in all cult and quasi-religious ceremonies. Vergil mentions the cornu as being, together with wine and forecasting from animal entrails, a basic tool of the priest.

[9] Grove, 6:288.

[10] Ibid., 289. An excellent example of a double-pipe player performing for the lying-in-state can be seen in the fragment of a tomb stone from Chiusi, now in Museo Barracco, Rome.

> That gentle ground to gen'rous grapes allow.
> Strong stocks of vines it will in time produce,
> And overflow the vats with friendly juice,
> Such as our priests in golden goblets pour
> To gods, the givers of the cheerful hour,
> Then when the bloated Tuscan blows his horn,
> And reeking entrails are in chargers borne.[11]

[11] Vergil, *Georgics* 2.263–269, here in the John Dryden translation, 1803.

As in Greece, these wind instruments are also part of life on a more day-to-day basis. Alcimus wrote that the Etruscans, 'knead bread, practice boxing, and flog their slaves to the accompaniment of the double-pipe.'[12] Another writer, Eratosthenes, confirms that boxing matches were accompanied by the double-pipe.[13]

As we might expect, accounts exist regarding the use of wind instruments in hunting in Etruria. Such an account by Claudius Aelianus (second century AD) must be regarded as either exaggerated or of a school of the most charismatic double reed players who ever lived!

[12] Quoted in Athenaeus, *The Deipnosophists* 12.518. The British Museum has had on display a beautiful pot (B 64) from the sixth century BC, Etruria, which shows two boxing figures and a man playing the double-pipe (see images below). In a wall painting on the tomb of Golini I, Orvieto (fourth century BC) one can see a double-pipe player playing in the kitchen while servants work. In a similar tomb painting (in Scudi, Tarquinia, third century BC), one can see a double-pipe player (in a toga) playing for a banquet.

Black-figured amphora, Etruscan, ca. 510-500 BC, found at Vulci, Italy
© Trustees of the British Museum

There is an Etruscan story current which says that the wild boars and the stags in that country are caught by using nets and hounds, as is the usual manner of hunting, but that music plays a part, and even the larger part, in the struggle. And how this happens I will now relate. They set the nets and other hunting gear that ensnare the animals in a circle, and a man proficient on the double-pipes stands there and tries his utmost to play a rather soft tune, avoiding any shriller note, but playing the sweetest melodies possible. The quiet and stillness easily carry (the sound) abroad; and the music streams up to the heights and into ravines and thickets—in a word into every lair and resting place of these animals. Now at first when the sound penetrates to their ears it strikes them with terror and fills them with dread, and then an unalloyed and irresistible delight in the music takes hold of them, and they are so beguiled as to forget about their offspring and their homes. And yet wild beasts do not care to wander away from their native haunts. But little by little these creatures in Etruria are attracted as though by some persuasive spell, and beneath the wizardry of the music they come and fall into the snares, overpowered by the melody.[14]

[13] Eratosthenes, *Olympic Victors*, 1, quoted in ibid., 4.153.

[14] Aelianus, *Of the Characteristics of Animals* 12.46.

Indoor entertainment, especially the dance, also depended on this instrument. Livy wrote that Etruscan dancers were popular in Rome.

> The *ludiones* summoned from Etruria, dancing to the melodies of the reed-pipe (*tibia*) player without any singing ... performed movements which were in no way unseemly, in the Etruscan manner.[15]

[15] Livy, *History of Rome* 7.2.

6   *Wind Music in the Roman Empire*

Discussion of Roman music must begin with its military, for this music carried across Europe by those legions influenced many peoples.[1] The most important instrument in the Roman army was the trumpet (*tuba*; the player, *tubicine*). Developed from Greek and Etruscan prototypes, the Roman trumpet appears in iconography to be a straight tube, something close to four feet in length, but with a very small bore. Literature abounds with references to the tone of this trumpet as a 'brazen' roar, 'clangor,' or 'strifeful.'[2] These descriptions, together with the extremely puffed cheeks of the players in surviving iconography, suggest that the instrument was difficult to blow.

Also present in most military references, and in iconography as well, was the *cornu*, an instrument probably developed by the Etruscans, as we have discussed previously. These two instruments are mentioned with the armies very early in the Roman era, beginning with the period of Servius Tullius, ca. 578 BC.[3] A system seems to have been worked out whereby the cornu gave the signals to the standard bearers of smaller units of the army, while the trumpets gave signals to the army as a whole. Polybius (second century BC) gives examples of the latter.

> In the time of war it is the noise of the trumpets which wakes the morning. At the dinner hour, they sound equally close to the general's tent, because it is at this time that the guard changes.[4]

[1] For example, the civic museum in Worms, Germany, contains a trumpet mouthpiece left behind by the Romans in the first century BC.

[2] Plutarch, *Lives*, 'Numa Pompilius,' 20; Vergil, *Aeneis*, 5, 7; Ovid, *Metamorphosis* 1.

[3] Grove, 16:148; Kastner, *Manuel Général*, 20. An extensive discussion of Roman military music may be found in Günther Wille, *Musica Romana* (Amsterdam: Schippers, 1967), 75–100.

[4] Quoted in ibid., 33. Josephus, *The Jewish Wars* 3.89ff., writes that in camp the Roman trumpets gave a wake signal, a second to prepare to march, and a third for departure.

Relief on Trajan's Column, Rome, showing players of the trumpet and cornu
Photograph by Wknight94 / CC-BY-SA

This system seems to have been well enough established, and the signals and their style of performance familiar enough to the ordinary Roman soldier, that on one occasion when Hannibal attempted to gain an advantage by having his trumpeters try to confuse the Romans with false signals, he found he was unable to fool them.[5] On the other hand, we know of one occasion when the chain of signals began prematurely. Hirtius, in his *History of the War of Africa*, reported that he heard the trumpets give the order for attack, and then the signal passed on to the legions by the cornus, while Julius Caesar was still making up his mind to attack or not.[6]

There is not sufficient extant information to know how many of these trumpet and cornu players were used with an army of a particular size. There is an extant listing of players in the third Augustan Legion in Lambaesis (Numidia) which gives a surprisingly large contingent of thirty-nine trumpet players and thirty-six cornu players.[7] Plutarch, speaking of the sounds of the trumpets, 'coming from every direction,' seems to confirm such large numbers of players.

> Moving stealthily over the ground between, they charged the camp about midnight, and with loud shouts and blasts of trumpets from every direction, by their din threw the Gauls … into complete confusion.[8]

[5] Kastner, *Manuel Général*, 35.

[6] Quoted in ibid., 34.

[7] G. Wilmanns, ed., Inscriptiones Africae latinae, *Corpus inscriptionum latinarum* (Berlin, 1881), 8, Nr. 2557, 295.

[8] Plutarch, *Lives*, 'Camillus,' 23.

Roman soldiers carrying the cornu, from a relief on Trajan's Column, Rome.

Polybius, too, in his account of a battle between the Romans and the Celts, speaks of 'the dreadful din, for there were innumerable cornu blowers and trumpeters.'[9] In another place Polybius speaks of trumpets playing the signal for retreat,[10] the signal for attack[11] and even on occasion for the purpose of fooling the enemy.[12] Another historian, Arrian, mentions the trumpets playing their call of alarm and for the departure of ships.[13]

The great historian, Livy, also frequently refers to trumpet signals, including to attack,[14] a call for silence,[15] for retreat,[16] to assemble the troops,[17] to begin the battle[18] and playing to frighten the elephants of Hannibal.[19] Livy also tells of an occasion when the Carthaginian and Gallic armies attempted to sound a specific Roman trumpet signal for some military purpose, but the trumpeter, a Greek, did not know the signals well and the ruse failed.[20]

Suetonius mentions some interesting non-military examples of Roman trumpet playing including for the entry into Rome[21] and as a call to begin construction work.[22] There are two rather extraordinary tales involving the trumpet recalled by Suetonius. The first involved a ghost trumpeter!

> As Caesar stood, in two minds, an apparition of superhuman size and beauty was seen sitting on the river bank playing a reed pipe. A party of shepherds gathered around to listen and, when some of Caesar's men, including some of the trumpeters, broke ranks to do the same, the apparition snatched a trumpet from one of them, ran down to the river, blew a thunderous blast, and crossed over. Caesar exclaimed: "Let us accept this as a sign from the Gods, and follow where they beckon."[23]

The other curious story is a testimonial to the dangers in being a trumpeter for the emperor, in this case Tiberius.

> While sacrificing, the emperor took an erotic fancy to the acolyte who carried the incense casket, and could hardly wait for the ceremony to end before hurrying him and his brother, the sacred trumpeter, out of the temple and indecently assaulting them both. When they jointly protested at this disgusting behavior he had their legs broken.[24]

---

[9] Polybius, *Histories* 2.29, lines 6–7.

[10] Polybius, *The Rise of the Roman Empire* (New York: Penguin, 1981), 91. See also Tacitus, *Annals* 15.30 to dismiss guests after dinner.

[11] Ibid., 412, 414. See also Tacitus, *Annals* 4.24, 25.

[12] Ibid., 381.

[13] Arrian, *The Campaigns of Alexander* (New York: Penguin, 1978), 289, 304. See also Livy, *The War with Hannibal* (New York: Penguin, 1980), 602. On ibid., 601, Livy quotes the prayer which was given as part of this departure ceremony.

[14] Livy, *The Early History of Rome* (New York: Penguin, 1979), 60. On page 81 of this work Livy provides a list of the six classes of Romans with respect to battle. Trumpeters were ranked in the next to lowest class.

[15] Ibid., 158.

[16] Ibid., 382.

[17] Livy, *The War with Hannibal* (New York: Penguin, 1980), 248.

[18] Ibid., 328.

[19] Ibid., 661.

[20] Ibid., 306

[21] Suetonius, *The Twelve Caesars* (New York: Penguin, 1989), 272.

[22] Ibid., 222.

[23] Ibid., 28.

[24] Ibid., 136.

Less frequently mentioned is the *lituus*, which was apparently assigned to the cavalry, and the *buccina*. This last instrument, made from an animal horn, was used for giving signals during the night, when the louder trumpet might prevent sleep entirely.[25]

[25] Kastner, *Manuel Général*, 33.

Reference to percussion instruments in the Roman army is quite rare. Tacitus relates a battle fought in the first century BC, during which a lunar eclipse occurred. The frightened soldiers took it as an omen of the gods and immediately began a cult ceremony directed at the god in question.

> Accordingly, the silence was broken by a boom of brazen gongs and the blended notes of trumpet and cornu.[26]

[26] Tacitus, *Annals* 1.26.

After their military usage, perhaps the most important appearance of wind instruments in Roman life was in the ceremonies of two important cult celebrations. One of these was the annual commemoration of the temple of the Goddess, Cybele, celebrated each April 4. A description of this celebration is given in a poem of Catullus (84–54 BC), where we see the large size double-pipe (*tibia*), cymbals, and small drum (*tympanum*, looking like a tambourine) together with a crowd of celebrants with their shrill cries.

> To the Phrygian forests, to the fame of Cybele,
> Where the cymbals sing loud and the smitten drums
> Resound and on rounded reed and the double-pipe
> Breathe out a booming bass, where the maenads,
> Ivy-wreathed and wanded and wagging their heads,
> Shriek shrilly and shake the emblems;
> Take the way of the wandering worshipers-thither
> Devotion directs us to dance and adore.[27]

[27] Catullus, 'Poem 63.'
Phrygiam ad domum Cybebes,
  Phrygia ad nemora deae,
ubi cymbalum sonat uox, ubi
  tympana reboant,
tibicen ubi canit Phryx curuo
  graue calamo,
ubi capita Maenades ui
  iaciunt hederigerae,
ubi sacra sancta acutis
  ululatibus agitant,
ubi sueuit illa diuae uolitare
  uaga cohors,
quo nos decet citatis
  celerare tripudiis.

This festival was born of an ancient myth of the God, Saturn. An oracle having told that he would be deposed by his son, Saturn sought to prevent this by eating all of his offspring. Finally his wife, Rhea, tricked him after giving birth by concealing a stone in infant garments, which Saturn swallowed. To keep the baby secret, Rhea's servants beat on empty helmets and shields to create noise to cover its cries. It is in imitation of this that we find so many percussion instruments participating.

An account by Ovid provides additional information about this celebration: it lasted three days, it included games, the law courts closed in observance, and it featured a procession.

> Let the sky revolve thrice on its never-resting axis; let Titan thrice yoke and thrice unyoke his steeds, straightway the Berecyntian pipe will blow a blast on its bent horn, and the festival of the Idaean Mother will have come. Eunuchs will march and thump their hollow drums, and cymbals clashed on cymbals will give out their tinkling notes: seated on the unmanly necks of her attendants, the goddess herself will be borne with howls through the streets in the city's midst. The stage is clattering, the games are calling. To your places, Quirites! and in the empty law-courts let the war of suitors cease![28]

The other cult celebration at which wind and percussion instruments were present was the festival of Dionysus. This celebration was less public, as it emphasized drinking and sexual depravity. Again we quote first the poetry of Catullus.

> And, all around, the maenads pranced in a frenzy,
> Crying the ritual cry, 'Euhoe! Euhoe!,'
> Tossing their heads; some of them brandishing
> The sacred vine-wreathed rod, some bandying
> Gobbets of mangled bullock, others twining
> Their waists with belts of writhing snakes, and others
> Reverently bearing, deep in caskets,
> Arcane things which the uninitiated
> Long, but in vain, to see, while others stretched
> Fingertips to play the drum,
> Struck a shrill clang from the semicircular cymbals,
> With raucous playing on the horn or made
> The double-pipe scream.[29]

The historian Livy (59 BC–17 AD) gives a much more detailed description of this cult ceremony. These were, he writes, secret, occult rites performed at night.

> There were initiatory rites which at first were imparted to a few, then began to be generally known among men and women. To the religious element in them were added the delights of wine and feasts, that the minds of a larger number might be attracted. When wine had inflamed their minds, and night and the mingling of males with females, youth with age, had destroyed every sentiment of modesty, all varieties of corruption first began to be practiced, since each one had at hand

[28] Ovid, *Fasti* 4.179–188.
Ter sine perpetuo caelum versetur in axe,
    ter iungat Titan terque resolvat equos,
protinus inflexo Berecyntia tibia cornu
    flabit, et Idaeae festa parentis erunt.
ibunt semimares et inania tympana tundent,
    aeraque tinnitus aere repulsa dabunt:
ipsa sedens molli comitum cervice feretur
    urbis per medias exululata vias.
scaena sonat, ludique vocant. spectate, Quirites,
    et fora Marte suo litigiosa vacent.

[29] Catullus, 'Poem 64.'
quae tum alacres passim lymphata mente furebant euhoe bacchantes, euhoe capita inflectentes. harum pars tecta quatiebant cuspide thyrsos, pars e diuolso iactabant membra iuuenco, pars sese tortis serpentibus incingebant, pars obscura cauis celebrabant orgia cistis, orgia quae frustsra cupiunt audire profani; plagaebant aliae proceris tympana palmis, aut tereti tenuis tinnitus aere ciebant; multis raucisonos efflabant cornua bombos barbaraque horribili stridebat tibia cantu.

the pleasure answering to that to which his nature was more inclined. There was not one form of vice alone, the promiscuous matings of free men and women, but perjured witnesses, forged seals and wills and evidence, all issued from this same workshop: likewise poisonings and secret murders, so that at times not even the bodies were found for burial. Much was ventured by craft, more by violence. This violence was concealed because amid the howlings and the crash of drums and cymbals no cry of the sufferers could be heard as the debauchery and murders proceeded.[30]

As in the cult of Cybele, the instruments were used for noise making, rather than musical purposes. In this case, as Livy pointed out, for the more macabre reason of covering up the cries of the victims! Pliny (first century AD) mentions that during sacrifices wind music was used for the same reason—to help assure that the agony of the animals would not distract the celebrants from hearing their prayers.[31]

There was also a festival of Juno, who was the mythical daughter to Saturn and wife to Jupiter. Ovid describes some of the music used.

> Here, to the sound of auloi and solemn chanting,
> The long procession passes every year
> Through streets bedecked, with white Falerian heifers
> From their own fields, while all the people cheer.[32]

Before leaving the discussion of cults, we must mention that two of the instruments enjoyed their own 'holy days.' Although the trumpets were not used as extensively as the double-pipes in religious and cult ceremonies, they nevertheless enjoyed certain status because of their association with the leaders of the state and its armies.[33] Accordingly, each 23 March and 23 May a festival day called the *Tubulustrium* occurred. This ceremony was a blessing of the instruments, or as Ovid wrote, 'to purify the melodious trumpets.'[34] Varro indicated that he believed that this ceremony took place in the Shoemaker's Hall.[35]

[30] Livy, *History of Rome* 39.8.5–14.
… occultorum et nocturnorum antistes sacrorum. Initia erant quae primo paucis tradita sunt deinde vulgari coepta sunt per viros mulieresque. Additae voluptates religioni vini et epularum, quo plurium animi illicerentur. Cum vinum animos incendisset, et nox et mixti feminis mares, aetatis tenerae maioribus, discrimen omne pludoris exstinxissent, corruptelae primum omnis generis fieri coeptae, com ad id quisque, quo natura pronioris libidinis esset, paratam voluptatem haberet. Nec unum genus noxae, stupra promiscua ingenuorum feminarumque erant, sed falsi testes, falsa signa testamentaque et indicia ex eadem officina exibant: venena indidem intestinaeque caedes, ita ut ne corpora quidem interdum ad sepulturam exstarent. Multa dolo, pleraque per vim audebantur. Occulebat vim quod prae ululatibus tympanorumque et cymbalorum stsrepitu nulla vox quiritantim inter stupra et caedes exaudiri poterat.

[31] Pliny, *Natural History* 28.2.18–19. ('tibicinem canere, ne quid aliud exaudiatur … ')

[32] Ovid, *Amores* 3.13.

[33] An excellent example of three trumpets participating in an offering procession can be seen in the first-century alterpiece in the Pio-Clementine Museum, Belvedere Pavilion, Museo del Vaticano, Rome.

[34] Ovid, *Fasti* 3.849–850.

[35] Varro (116–26 BC), *On the Latin Language* 6.14.

The double-pipe players, present at everyone else's cult celebration, themselves enjoyed a special double-pipe holiday, held each 13 June, called 'lesser *Quinquatrus*.'[36] This festival commemorates an occasion when the double-pipe players of Rome went on strike, enraged at some ordinance of the government which reduced their wages. On this occasion (third century BC) all the double-pipe players left Rome and retired to Tibur. They were missed.

> The hollow double-pipe was missed in the theatre, missed at the altersi; no dirge accompanied the bier on the last march.[37]

Apparently negotiation did not result in their return to Rome so the government devised a plan to trick them into returning. A wealthy citizen in Tibur threw a great party in their honor and when they were 'reeling with heady wine' their host arranged for wagons to return them to their lodging. But instead the wagons took the sleeping double-pipe players to Rome and in order to help them save face upon their unexpected arrival they were given masks and long gowns. Hence the double-pipe festival in Rome was always celebrated with the double-pipe players parading through the streets wearing masks and long gowns.

As Ovid mentioned above, the double-pipes were frequently used in the funeral rites. Apparently this had become something of a status symbol, for in the same place Ovid mentions that a government regulation was drawn up to limit the number of double-pipe players in funeral processions to no more than ten.[38] The principal funeral song was the *Nenia*, which praised the dead person with double-pipe accompaniment. Sometimes trumpets and cornu players appeared in purely instrumental music.[39]

The double-pipe was also found in many kinds of entertainment activities available to Romans. They seem to have been frequently found at banquets, as they were in Greece. Martial (first century AD) wrote a poem listing all that he could offer if a friend would attend a banquet. After listing a wide variety of food, he promises,

> It's a poor sort of dinner; yet, if you deign to grace it,
> You'll neither say nor hear

[36] Ibid., 6.17. Horace (65–8 BC) makes an interesting comparison with the ancient double-pipe and the instrument known to Imperial Rome. 'The double-pipe—not, as now, bound with brass and a rival of the trumpet (Tibia non, ut nunc, orichalco vincta tubaeque aemula), but slight and simple, with a few stops—was once of use to lead and aid the chorus and to fill with its breath benches not yet too crowded, where ... folk gathered—sober folk, too, and chaste and modest.' (*The Art of Poetry*, 202–208). An excellent example of a double-pipe being played during a Roman sacrifice (the axe is poised over the cow) can be seen in the sarcophagus carving (second century AD) in the Museo del Palazzo Ducale, Mantua. Some icons from this period show a single-pipe, which is not mentioned in literature. Examples are the carvings in the household alterpiece and the offering relief, both in the Palazzo dei Conservatori, Rome.

[37] Ovid, *Fasti* 6.666ff.

[38] Ibid., 6.663–664.

[39] Grove, 13:103. A grave stone from the second century BC shows a funeral procession led by a double-pipe player (London, British Museum). An outstanding example from the first century BC (a relief in the Museo Civico, Aquila), shows a funeral procession with a genuine ensemble: four double-pipe players, two cornu and one lituus players! A relief from the first century AD (Museo Lateranense, Rome), shows a seated double-pipe player performing during the lying-in-state.

One word that's not sincere,
You can lounge at ease in your place,
Wearing your own face,
You won't have to listen while your host reads aloud from some thick book
Or be forced to look
At girls from that sink, Cadiz, prancing
Through the interminable writhings of professional belly-dancing.
Instead, Condylus, my little slave,
Will pipe to us—something not too rustic, nor yet too grave.[40]

At some banquets, perhaps on more formal occasions, the double-pipe was put to more serious purpose. According to the historian Valerius Maximus (first century AD), during banquets the elders would compose, to the accompaniment of the double-pipe, their ancestors' outstanding deeds in song, so that by this they might make the younger men more eager to imitate them.[41]

A form of entertainment which one associates in particular with the Roman Empire is the games of the arena.[42] Here too, wind ensembles performed interludes and accompanied the cries of the contestants.[43] There is one extraordinary passage by Polybius (second century BC) which describes a special performance organized by the Roman General, Lucius Anicius, to celebrate his defeat and capture of King Genthius of the Illyrians.

> Having summoned the most distinguished artists of Greece and constructed a very large stage in the Circus (arena), he first brought on the double-pipe players; these were Theodorus of Boeotia, Theopompus, Hermippus, Lysimachus, all of them the most distinguished. Posting them, then, at the front of the stage with the chorus, he directed them to play all together. As they started to perform their music to accompany the dance motions which corresponded to it, he sent word to them that they were not playing in the right way, and ordered them to whoop up the contest against one another. Since they were puzzled at this, one of the officials indicated that they should turn and advance upon one another and act as if they were fighting. Quickly the players caught the idea, and taking on motions in keeping with their own licentious characters they caused great confusion. For the double-pipe players by a concerted movement turned the middle choruses against those at the ends, while they blew on their double-pipes unintelligible notes, and all differing, and then they drew away in turn upon each other; and at the same time the members of the choruses clashed noisily against the players as they shook their gear at them and rushed

[40] Valerius Martial, *Epigrams*, Nr. 78.

[41] Valeri Maximi, *Factorvm et Dictorvm Memorabilivm*, 2.1.10ff. Maiores natu in conuiuiis ad tibias egregia superiorum opera carmine conprehensa pangebant (peragebant?) quo ad ea imitanda iuuentutem alacriorem redderent.

[42] A mosaic in the amphitheater at Zliten (ca. first century AD) shows a trumpet and two cornu players performing while two gladiators engage in combat (see image opposite page).

[43] Will Durant, *Caesar and Christ* (New York: Simon and Schuster, 1944), 384.

The mosaic from the amphitheatre at Zliten. The top panel shows a trumpet and two cornu players performing while the gladiators engage in combat.

upon their antagonists, to turn again and retreat. And so in one case a member of the chorus girded himself, and stepping out of the ranks he turned and raised his fists as if to box against the double-pipe player who plunged against him; and then, if not before, the applause and shouts that arose from the spectators knew no bounds. Furthermore, while these were contending in a pitched battle, two dancers entered with castanets, and four boxers mounted upon the stage accompanied by trumpeters and horn players. All these contests went on together, and the result was indescribable.[44]

44 Polybius, *Histories* 30.

The more conventional theater also used the double-pipe. The prologue to *Stichus*, a play by Plautus, mentions that a slave musician, named Marcipor, composed and performed the accompaniment throughout on a double-pipe. Sometimes, according to Seneca (ca. 4 BC–65 AD), fairly large numbers of instruments must have been used in the theater.

> Do you not see how many voices there are in a chorus? Yet out of the many only one voice results. In that chorus one voice takes the tenor, another the bass, another the baritone. There are women, too, as well as men, and the double-pipe is mingled with them. In that chorus the voices of the individual singers are hidden; what we hear is the voices of all together. To be sure, I am referring to the chorus which the old-time philosophers knew; in our present day exhibitions we have a larger number of singers than there used to be spectators in the theaters of old. All the aisles are filled with rows of singers; brass instruments surround the auditorium; the stage resounds with double-pipes and instruments of every description; and yet from the discordant sounds a harmony is produced.[45]

45 Seneca, *Ad Lucilium Epistulae Morales* 84.9–10. Examples of iconography which show the double-pipe being played in the theater are the vase from the fourth century BC, in the Hermitage, Moscow, and the second century BC relief (INV. NR. 6687) in the Museo Nazionale, Naples

To accomplish all this wind instrument performance, players early in the Roman Empire began organizing themselves into associations very much like the guilds of medieval Europe. There were separate guilds (called *collegia*) for trumpet, horn, double-pipe, and bagpipe players.[46] According to Plutarch, these began in the seventh century BC, and in any case we know the double-pipe guild was one of the oldest professional organizations in Rome.[47]

These guilds were modeled on the Italian municipality, having a hierarchy of magistrates. They also had their own deities, festivals and sought patrons.[48]

46 Durant, *Caesar and Christ*, 335. See also, *Corpus Inscriptionum Latinarum* 1/2, 998, 989; 6.240; 1054; 33449; and J. Quasten, *Musik und Gesang* (Münster: Aschendorff, 1930), 21ff.; G. Wille, *Musica Romana: Musik im Leben der Römer*, 33ff.

47 Grove, 16:147.

48 Durant, *Caesar and Christ*, 335.

Funerary inscription for members of the guild of the *tibicens* (*collegium tibicinum*), ca. first century BC.
© Marie-Lan Nguyen / CC-BY

Two final notes: first, the panpipe flute is found here as it was in Greece, a rural instrument, outside the wind practice of government or aristocratic circles. In a passage by Vergil, one notes that the players complained that playing the panpipe (*fistula*) 'chafed their lips.'[49]

Some members of aristocratic families played wind instruments themselves for pleasure, including at least two of the Emperors. Early writers maintain that Elagabalus (third century AD) played the double-pipe and cornu, while the famous Nero was a performer on the bagpipes.[50] Can it be, therefore, that Nero did not 'fiddle while Rome burned,' but rather blew?

[49] Vergil, *Eclogues* 2.34.

[50] Curt Sachs, *The History of Musical Instruments* (New York, 1940), 141; also, Durant, *Caesar and Christ*, 624.

PART II

The Age of the Minstrel

The Age of the Minstrel

AFTER THE WIND MUSIC OF THE ROMAN EMPIRE and before the numerous wind ensembles which can be documented in the later Middle Ages, the traditions and techniques of wind performance were kept alive by that musician known as the minstrel.

In the larger story of wind music he takes on a significance greater than his own moment on the stage due to the role he unwittingly played in the development of instrumental music in the early Christian Church.

Objection to the 'character' of the minstrel was one of the reasons the early Church denounced all instrumental music; even to the present day some Christian churches do not permit instrumental music. Because the early Christian, or Roman, Church was so much a part of medieval life and thought, this exclusion unquestionably delayed the birth of true wind ensemble music in Western Europe. It seems the best explanation why multi-part instrumental music follows by so long multi-part vocal music. In addition, the Christian clergy were often Western Europe's early historians and librarians. Thus it may be said that only after the wind music begins to appear in the Roman Church do we begin to have many surviving accounts of wind ensembles in the cities and courts as well.

Therefore, because of this role the minstrel played in the development of church music, and because when he formed wind ensembles they were the first in Western Europe, the story of the modern wind ensemble must begin with him.

7 *The Early Medieval Jongleur*

DURING THE LATTER PART OF THE FOURTH CENTURY AD, as the effective protection of the Roman Empire was evaporating and the 'barbarians,' the German tribes, the Huns, and the Goths, began to flood into Central and Southern Europe, the first period of mass migration on the continent began. As the peoples of Europe began to pass from region to region, they were accompanied by a broad range of entertainers and fellow travelers: jugglers, story-tellers, actors, musicians, and performers of magic.

Our understanding of the specific functions of these early entertainers is weakened by the lack of precision by the early scribes; the names they gave them varied considerably. The earliest general term in medieval Latin is *Ioculator*, which one might translate simply as 'one who makes merry.' From this is derived *jouglere* and *jougleur* in French, *joglar* in Provençal, and *jugelour*, *jugelere*, and *jogeler* in English. The term *jongleurs*, although used by many writers today as a synonym for minstrel, was used by the early scribes to sometimes identify the highest class of entertainer, the scops; sometimes the musician; and sometimes the lowly buffoon or conjuror.

In Germany, by about the eighth century, one finds a new term, *Spielmann*, which is also used first in a generic sense. Among the Nordic nations there were *scaldes*, an order restricted to nobles and the aristocracy much as the *Scops* of Germany. The Nordic *gliman* (*gleeman* in English) was more specifically an actor, mime, or story-teller. In general, however, the best term until the later middle ages is *jongleur*, which here will mean the general entertainer, including the musician, for the first thousand years of the Christian era.

Another factor which complicates our perception of the early jongleur is that for centuries he must have been an entertainer with many abilities, not the specialist one finds later. In this regard, a catalog of skills claimed by one of them no doubt speaks for all.

> I can play the lute, vielle, pipe, bagpipe, panpipes, harp, fiddle, guittern, symphony, psaltery, organistrum, organ, tabor and the rote. I can sing a song well, and make tales to please young ladies, and can play the gallant for them if necessary. I can throw knives into the air and catch them without cutting my fingers. I can jump rope most extraordinary and amusing. I can balance chairs, and make tables dance. I can somersault, and walk doing a handstand.[1]

A twelfth-century educational treatise, called *Enseignamens*, for the would be jongleur offers a similar broad list of skills. It warns him to be prepared to, 'learn the arts of imitating birds, throwing knives, leaping through hoops, showing off performing asses and dogs, and dangling marionettes.'[2] Even those who thought of themselves as being primarily musicians probably had to include extramusical attractions to satisfy the audience. Joinville, in the thirteenth century, relates a performance by three trumpet players:

> When they began to play their trumpets you would have thought it was the voice of swans coming from the water, and they produced the sweetest and most gracious melodies, a marvel to hear. And these same minstrels did wonderful acrobatic feats. A towel was put under their feet and, holding themselves rigid, they turned a complete somersault, their feet returning to the towel. Two of them turned their heads to face behind them, and the eldest also, and when he turned it round again he crossed himself, for he was afraid of breaking his neck in the act of turning.[3]

These jongleurs wandered from village to village and from castle to castle, the better ones, or perhaps the luckier ones, receiving temporary employment by a noble. Aristocratic marriages, baptisms, knighthood ceremonies, and tournaments must have all required music from an early date. These were the fortunate few, so fortunate in some cases that they could request that their donations be only in the most valuable currency of the day.

> Come back tomorrow after dinner
> And I beg of you, each bring me
> A farthing tied up in your shirts;
> For in these Poitevin coins is little value:
> Greedy and parsimonious were they who had them struck,
> Never give them to a gentle minstrel.[4]

---

[1] Anonymous, quoted in Howard D. McKinney and W. R. Anderson, *Music in History: The Evolution of an Art* (Boston: American Book Company, 1940), 170.

[2] E.K. Chambers, *The Mediaeval Stage* (Oxford: Clarendon, 1903), 1:53.

[3] Frantz Funck-Brentano, *The Middle Ages*, trans. Elizabeth O'Neill (New York: Putnam, 1923), 184–185.

[4] *Huon de Bordeaux*, quoted in ibid., 190.

THE EARLY MEDIEVAL JONGLEUR 73

A caricature of a minstrel by
Nicholas de Larmessin, late
seventeenth century

Those jongleurs who played for the aristocracy also received valuable gifts of clothing, which must have been worth more than money during the cold winter. An early poet observed,

> We have seen princes who after having spent twenty or thirty marks on splendid garments wonderfully embroidered have given them a week later to minstrels.[5]

But for the great majority of jongleurs there was little hope of service in an important court. For them life must have been a very difficult road from village to village. They, perhaps, had no coat at all.

> But quite often in his shirt
> Was exposed to wind and blast.[6]

Even the clothes he wore might have to be left in payment for a meal, for lack of money.

> When he has got together sous three, four, five,
> Into the tavern he soon goes
> And feasts with it while it lasts.
> And when he has tasted the good wine,
> And the landlord sees he has spent all:
> 'Brother,' says he, 'seek another inn,
> Give me pledge of what you owe.'
> And he leaves with him his hose and shoes.[7]

Who is not filled with the deepest sympathy upon reading the early poet Rutebeuf's heartbreaking description of the poor jongleur?

> I cough with cold and with hunger gape,
> Through them I die and am finished with.
> I am without coverlet or bed;
> Lord, I know not where to go.
> My sides feel the straw,—
> A bed of straw is no bed,
> And in my bed there is nothing, but straw …
> Lord, I would have you know
> I have not wherewith to buy bread.[8]

[5] Ibid, 186.

[6] *De Saint Pierre de du jongleor*, quoted in ibid., 190.

[7] *Le Moniage Guillaume*, quoted in ibid.

[8] Quoted in ibid., 188.

Chambers paints a similar picture in his summary of the life of this early minstrel or jongleur.

> To tramp long miles in wind and rain, to stand wet to the skin and hungry and footsore, making the slow bourgeois laugh while the heart was bitter within; such must have been the daily fate of many amongst the humbler minstrels at least. And at the end to die like a dog in a ditch, under the ban of the Church and with the prospect of eternal damnation before the soul.[9]

[9] Chambers, *The Mediaeval Stage*, 1:48.

Although we know so little of this early minstrel, whom we call jongleur, one can see his contribution and it is a very great one. As he traveled during centuries of migration with the homeless, with merchants and students, with pilgrims and knights, he wove an evermore unified cultural language that laid the way for a truly European music. It is through him that so many European countries have a common popular foundation to their music and legends, and that the same instruments appear in all countries. He was indeed the tiller of the soil and the sower of seed.

8 Late Medieval Minstrels

A STREET IN PARIS in the thirteenth century, *rue de Jugleeurs*, was renamed in the fourteenth century, *rue des Ménétriers*.[1] This reflects a new name for the jongleur which had come into usage along with a gradual narrowing of the definition of his specialties. From the ninth century Latin *ministerialis*, meaning office-holder or functionary,[2] one finds by the fourteenth century *ménéstrel* and *ménstrier* in French and *menestrel* and *mynstral* in English firmly established as an entertainer who is primarily an instrumental musician. In this period also one finds the Trouveres, Troubadours, and Minnesingers, singers of the *chansons de geste*, and creators of a style almost more literary than musical in importance.

By the twelfth and thirteenth centuries those minstrels who mainly sang probably accompanied themselves with the small harp or viol. But for the most part, in the later middle ages the term 'minstrel' means an instrumentalist who is increasingly identified as primarily a player of wind instruments, specializing on members of the trumpet, flute, shawm, and bagpipe families. Indeed, one can see the proof that 'minstrel' usually meant wind instruments in the qualifying names of this period, such as *ménétriers de bouche* (mouth minstrels, or singers!) and *ménétriers de cordes* (string minstrels).[3] For the period 1450–1550 extensive evidence, both in iconography and in literature, associates 'minstrel' with the wind instrument performer. An English scribe, for example, observes,

> For the most parte all maner mynstrelsy
> By wynde they delyver thyr sound chefly.[4]

By the late middle ages the more capable of these minstrels were beginning to find a more stable existence, playing for aristocratic courts and as civic musicians, as the remainder of this volume will document. He must have been a welcome change in the otherwise monotonous routine of castle life in the middle ages. Gaston Phébus, a fourteenth century nobleman who resided in a castle high in the Pyrenees, gives as the typical day in his life:

[1] Chambers, *The Mediaeval Stage*, 2:231ff.

[2] Grove, 12:347.

[3] Walter Salmen, *Der Fahrende Musiker im Europäischen Mittelalter* (Kassel: Hinnenthal, 1960), 31. See also, Edmund Bowles, *Musikleben im 15. Jahrhundert* (Leipzig: Deutscher Verlag für Musik, 1977), 26. ('From iconography we know the role of music—which was above all wind music')

[4] Quoted in John Stevens, *Music & Poetry in the Early Tudor Court* (London: Methuen, 1961), 302.

Hunting; after the hunt, Mass; after Mass, the womenfolk and the minstrels.[5]

In the towns, which were just beginning to establish real independent identities, one finds the minstrels performing for weddings of the middle class merchants, celebrations such as the harvest, civic bonfires,[6] and even at public spas (Paris had twenty-six in 1292).

Iconography of the late middle ages usually pictures the minstrels dressed in short coats or capes with hoods. A city's or a nobleman's livery was an important form of protection for the minstrels when they traveled, aided in their hope for gifts from out-of-town hosts, and above all, set them apart from the vagabond minstrels. This dress seems to have been universal enough that frequently those who were not minstrels would attempt, by dressing as one, to gain a free meal at a monastery or priory. On occasion, even a knight might have need for such a disguise, as one can see in an early fourteenth-century poem.

> Now thei beth disgysed,
> So diverselych i-digt,
> That no man may knowe
> A mynstrel from a knygt
> Wel ny.[7]

The minstrels, too, must have needed disguise at times, for among the many church bans leveled against them was one forbidding them to wear ecclesiastical dress.[8]

What do we know of the music of these minstrels? Scholars have assumed that they did not play from the page, but rather improvised or played repertoire learned by hearing other minstrels. There were important opportunities to learn new literature this way through the astonishing minstrel 'schools,' called *scolae ministrallorum*. These schools were held regularly during the week before Laetare Sunday in Lent, when minstrel performances were not allowed, and on a more informal basis whenever large numbers of minstrels gathered in the same town for a large fair or Church council.

[5] Quoted in Romain Goldron, *Minstrels and Masters* (New York: Stuttman, 1968), 25.

[6] The bonfire was a regular feature of civic celebrations during the middle ages. The word comes from 'bones fire,' which reminds us of its ancient origin during an age when the more complete specimen was the guest of honor!

Miniature from *Jongleurs*; Ms. latin 1118, f. 112. Bibliothéque National de Paris.

[7] Chambers, *The Mediaeval Stage*, 45.

[8] Ibid., 82.

The most important schools were sponsored by individual cities. An extant civic document from Ieper, dated 1429, authorizes money for the school (23 livres tournois) as well as eight 'canettes' of wine for entertainment purposes.⁹ We know today of many of these cities which held minstrel schools: Bruges, in 1318; Ieper, from 1313 to 1432; Brussels, in 1370; Ghent, in 1378; Beauvais, from 1398 to 1436; Mons, from 1406 to 1422; Cambrai, from 1366 to 1440; and in parts of Germany between 1364 and 1389.¹⁰ The peak of this activity seems to have been in the late fourteenth and early fifteenth centuries, but this may only reflect incomplete extant documentation. Indeed, these schools may have begun much earlier than scholars have generally assumed, or at least so a document from 1192 suggests. Here one reads that the Hungarian king, Béla III, sent a minstrel named Elvinus to Paris to attend such a school.

> ... de van zencolen
> zo Parys helden scholen ...¹¹

These schools were attended by minstrels who were employed by both cities and courts. Knowledge of the schools seems to have been general enough that minstrels traveled great distances to attend them, as numerous extant documents attest. An entry in the wardrobe accounts of Edward III of England (1327–1377), for example, authorizes money to send two minstrels to the *scolas ministrallis in partibus trans mare*.¹²

The purpose of these schools was not to learn to play, for these were schools for professionals. They came to buy or trade instruments and especially to learn new literature. In 1413 the minstrels of Lille went to the school in Beauvais to learn new 'canchons.' Again in 1436 the 'ménestrelz' of the same city went to Cambrai with the specific goal 'pour apprendre des nouvelles chansons.'¹³ It is especially interesting that already in the fourteenth century there was recognition of national styles. A letter of Juan I, of Spain, dated 1377, speaks of 'manera d'Alemanya' and 'manera de Flandres.'¹⁴

There is every evidence that large numbers of minstrels attended these schools. One held in 1330 in Tournai had present, in addition to the ordinary minstrels, no less than thirty-one 'kings.'¹⁵ A 'king' was the leader of a minstrel guild. The possibility of large numbers of minstrels at these schools is sup-

---

9 Edmond Vander Straeten, *La Musique aux Pays Bas avant le XIXe Siècle* (1867–1888, reprinted, New York: Dover, 1969), 4:132.

10 Robert Wangermée, *Flemish Music and Society in the Fifteenth and Sixteenth Centuries*, trans. Robert Erich Wolf (New York: Praeger, 1968), 182; François Lesure, *Musique et Musiciens Français du XVI Siècle* (Geneve: Minkoff Reprint, 1976), 114; Grove, 3:181.

11 Alfred Bourgeois, *Les Métiers de Blois* (Blois, 1892), 1:96ff.

12 Chambers, *The Mediaeval Stage*, 1:53.

13 Salmen, *Der Fahrende Musiker*, 181–182.

14 H. Anglès, 'El músic Jacomi al servei de Joan I i Marti I durant als anys 1372–1404,' in *Homenatge a Antoni Rubió i Lluch* (Barcelona, 1936), 1:613–625.

15 Grove, 7:811.

ported by the known occasions when similar large gatherings were documented. One Italian town is said to have entertained 1,500 minstrels in 1324 and in 1340 there were 400 of them at the court in Mantua.[16] In England, in 1290, 426 minstrels arrived to help celebrate the marriage of Margaret of England and John of Brabant.[17] For the celebration of the Prince of Wales undergoing the ordeal of knighthood in 1306, in London, there is extant a roll of payments listing nearly 200 minstrels by name.[18] On this occasion there was a great feast during which two swans, covered with nets of gold, were brought into the hall by the minstrels.[19]

[16] Goldron, *Minstrels and Masters*, 38.

[17] Chambers, *The Mediaeval Stage*, 1:44, fn, 4.

[18] Ibid., 1: Appendix C.

[19] Edmonstoune Duncan, *The Story of Minstrelsy* (Detroit: Singing Tree, 1968), 73.

The great numbers of minstrels which must have attended many of the *scolae ministrallorum* offers, perhaps, a clue to one of the poems of Chaucer which has long puzzled scholars. In *House of the Dead*, Chaucer mentions bands of vast proportions. How else could he have imagined such large numbers of wind players, but perhaps having seen one of these schools?

First Chaucer describes a category of musicians who played 'sondry gleës.' They were more numerous than the stars in the sky ('mo than sterres in hevene'). He does not describe their instruments, in order to save us time!

> For tyme y-lost, this knowen ye,
> By no way may recovered be.

Next he discusses in more detail three large groups of harps, trumpets, and woodwinds, even giving names of some of the flute players. Some, he says, were Dutchmen.

> Then saugh I famous; olde and yonge,
> Pypers of the Duche tonge,
> To lerne love-daunces, springes,
> Reyes and these straunge thinges.

Then came the woodwind instruments, and while not as numerous as the musicians in the first group above, they nevertheless numbered in the tens of thousands!

> Tho saugh I standen hem behinde,
> Afar fro hem, al by themselve,
> Many thousand tymes twelve,
> That maden laude minstralcyes
> In corne muse and shalmyes,
> And many other maner pipe
> That craftely begunne to pipe,
> Both in doucet and in rede,
> That ben at feastes with the brede
> And many floute and lilting-horne,
> And pypes made of greene corne,
> As have thise litel herdegromes
> That kepen bestes in the bromes.[20]

One can not mention Chaucer without reference to his classic, *Canterbury Tales*. It was the absence of regular minstrels that caused this famous group of pilgrims to begin their telling of stories to one another. There was the miller, 'a Baggepype wel koude he blowe,' but in particular it is the flute playing squire who attracts our attention. Both in dress and in his numerous skills, he seems to be a surrogate for the otherwise missing minstrel.

> Singinge he was a floytinge al the day;
> He was as fresh as is the month of May.
> Short was his goune with sleves long and wide,
> Wel coude he sit on hors, and fayre ryde.
> He coude songes make, and wel endyte,
> Juste and eeke daunce, and well purtreye and wryte.

Chaucer says he could ride a horse well, draw well, dance, compose and notate his music. How many flute players today are so broadly educated?[21]

[20] 'loude minstralcyes' is a synonym for 'wind instrument band,' as we shall see later.

[21] It is interesting that this 'surrogate minstrel' could *notate* his own music. Perhaps we are not giving the medieval minstrel enough credit when we make the assumption that he only improvised and learned his music by ear.

9 The Decline of Minstrelsy

As the wandering jongleur of the early Middle Ages slowly developed from an entertainer of broad skills into the minstrel of the later Middle Ages, who was more and more a specialist, a natural classification among them occurred. This can be seen already in the thirteenth century in a supplication by the troubadour, Guiraut de Riquier, of Provence, dated 1273, addressed to Alphonso X of Castile. The subject was the state of minstrelsy and Guiraut de Riquier speaks of his concern for the confusion caused by the indiscriminate grouping of poets, singers, and entertainers of all kinds under the title jongleur. Alphonso's reply defines a hierarchy of three classes of jongleur. First are the composers (*doctors de trobar* and *trobaires*), followed by the jongleur proper, whom he saw as instrumentalists and reciters of, 'delightful' stories. The lowest category was the *bufos*, entertainers of common folk, who really had no claim to be called jongleurs at all.[1]

Even within the second category he gives, the instrumentalists themselves made a further classification for they clearly considered themselves as of a higher status than the teller of stories.

> A minstrel who wishes to act rightly
> Should not imitate the mountebank,
> But on his lips should ever have
> Gentle words and fine language.[2]

It was, however, the opportunities for regular employment which introduced an important new classification among the instrumental musicians. Now the minstrel who represented the city or court called himself a 'minstrel of honor' in an attempt to disassociate himself with the wandering musician. Setting himself thus apart from his itinerant brother was an important step towards gaining the rights of the citizen.

This term begins to appear in the fourteenth century as one can see in an English royal proclamation of 1316.

[1] Chambers, *The Mediaeval Stage*, 1:63.

[2] Quoted in Funck-Brentano, *The Middle Ages*, 192.

Edward by the grace of God, … to Sheriffes … greeting. Forasmuch as many idle persons, under colour of Minstrelsie, and going in messages and other feigned business, have been and yet be received in other men's houses to meat and drink, and be not therewith contented if they be not largely considered with gifts of the lords of the houses … We willing to restrain such outrageous enterprises and idleness, have ordained that to the houses of prelates, earls, and barons, none resort to meat and drink, unless he be a minstrel; and of these minstrels that there come none, except it be three or four minstrels of honour, at the most in one day, unless he be desired by the lord of the house. And to the houses of meaner men that none come—unless he be desired; and that such as shall so come, hold themselves contented with meat and drink, and with such courtesy as the master of the house will show unto them of his own goodwill, without their asking of anything. And if anyone do against this Ordinance, at the first time he is to lose his Minstrelsy, and at the second time to forswear his craft, and never to be received for a minstrel in any house.[3]

This desire of the minstrel to obtain the rights of the ordinary citizen can be understood clearly in the domain of civil rights. The earlier wandering minstrel had no legal rights and was deprived of most legal protection. The earliest comprehensive German law book, the *Sachsenspiegel*, tells us that even if the minstrel won a case in court and demanded justice, he was permitted only to 'beat the shadow' of his adversary.[4]

In some places, the minstrels could not transmit their possessions to their heirs[5] nor even, in one case, could they claim the rights to their own compositions.[6] Because the minstrels did not have access to normal courts, there seems to have been a period when special courts were established to have jurisdiction over the legal problems of these players. There are extant records from many of these special courts, called 'Curia Vigiliae' or 'Curia de Gayte.'[7]

The minstrel's inaccessibility to normal civic rights, and the accompanying lack of civic status in general, also contributed to their lack of welcome by the church. Even as late as 1461, one finds a plea by the minstrels of Elsass that they should be given the holy sacrament and treated as other Christians in spite of their being instrumentalists.[8]

In order to help overcome these prejudices, the minstrels residing in cities took a positive step forward by forming minstrel guilds.[9] These early guilds were not modeled on the wind instrument guilds of ancient Rome, of which these Western

3 Quoted in Duncan, *The Story of Minstrelsy*, 78–79.

4 Quoted in Wilhelm Ehmann, *Tibilustrium* (Kassel: Bärenreiter-Verlag, 1950), 6. See also *Specul. Saxon*, L.I, art. 38, and L.III, art. 45, ed. 1592, fol. 26 verso and 131 verso (Histriones, joculatores et omnes illegitimi … si in his coram judicio convicti fuerint notantur infamia et juris sunt alieni … Histrionbus, joculatoribus et his qui in servitutem se dedrunt emendatur umbra viri) and *Specul. juris aleman.*, ch. 305, sections 13–14, in Schilter, *Thesaurus antiq. teuton*, 2:180 (Spilluten und allen den die gut fur ere nement … den git man ainz mannez schatten von der sunnen. Das ist also gesprochen: vuer in icht laidez tut, daz man in bezzern sol, der sol zu ainer vuende stan da dui sunne anschinet und sol der spilman … den schaten an der vuende an den halz slahen).

5 A law given in 1216, in Magdebourg (Item advocatus civitatis nullius haerediatatem debet accipere praeterquam histrionum, joculatorum et advenarum). See *Collection des écrivains d'Allemagne de Meibôme*, 2:377.

6 Given in the civic laws of Gotzlar (Onechten luden und spelluden den gifft men drittich schillinge Luttiker pennighe to bote de der stadt gesind sint; se sint och ane wergeld). See *Anciennes lois municipales de la ville de-Gotzlar*, article 10.

7 Lyndesay G. Langwill, *The Waits* or *Waits, wind band [and] horn* (Hinrichsen, 1952), 171.

8 Grove, 7:809 (daz neylige sacrament geben und tun solle alse andern kristen luten … ungehindert irs pfiffens).

9 *Zunft, Glide* (from *Gelten*, 'to be worth') and *Bruderschaft* in German, *confrérie* in French, and *corporación* in Spanish.

European musicians probably had no knowledge, but rather on the guilds of the other medieval crafts. All around them the minstrels could see examples of other professions which had managed to achieve for their members social acceptance, legal protection, and integration into urban society through their guilds. In addition the minstrels saw the opportunity to provide for the welfare of its sick and retired members, as well as the framework for limiting performance to its members—thus creating still a wider exclusion of the wandering musician.

The Speelmanskapel (chapel of the guild of musicians), Belgium, fifteenth century
Photograph by Marc Ryckaert / CC-BY

The earliest minstrel guild in the real sense of the word was the *Nicolai-Brüderschaft* of Vienna, which was established in 1288 and can be said to be the direct ancestor of the Vienna Philharmonic. The first minstrel guild in France was the *Confrérie de St. Julien des ménestriers*, chartered in 1321 by thirty-seven minstrels, of whom eight were women. St. Julian was their patron saint and they soon built both their own chapel and a hospital for older members.

As the better minstrels became more and more successful in establishing themselves as resident musicians in the cities and courts during the later Middle Ages, the true minstrel of the earlier tradition was at the same time being gradually thought of as an undesirable. Already in 1284, in England, one reads of a proclamation against 'Westours, Bards, Rhymers, and other idlers and vagabonds.'

By the fifteenth century there was evident concern among the established musicians to protect the playing opportunities, and consequent rewards, for themselves and to forbid the participation of the wandering musician. One can see this, for example, in an order the king's minstrels in England secured, which appointed a committee of minstrels,[10] to control the performance of minstrels thoughtout the realm, with the exception of the County of Chester.[11] The order noted,

> Whereas many rude husbandmen and artificers of England feigning to be minstrels and some of them wearing the King's livery and so pretending to be the King's minstrels collect in certain parts of the realm great exactions of money of the King's lieges by virtue of their livery and art and though they be unskilled therein and use divers arts on working days and receive sufficient money thence, they fare from place to place on festivals and take the profits wherefrom the King's minstrels and other skilled in the art of music and using no other labours or mysteries should live.[12]

There were some attempts at forming guilds to protect the free-lance musician, notably the charter granted in 1469 by Edward IV to the 'Fraternity of Ministrels of England.' But even this guild discriminated against the wandering musician, noting that the competition from such a minstrel with the 'real minstrels causes decay in the art, and neglect of agriculture.'

Under increasing pressure from these royal, municipal, and guild ordinances, the minstrel who carried on the medieval tradition of wandering freely from town to town could no longer sustain himself and the institution barely survives the fifteenth century. It seems sad, perhaps, to think that he who produced nine-tenths of all medieval literature should in the end be thought of only as a vagabond and beggar.[13] Thinking of the Middle Ages as a whole, this wandering minstrel was probably much more influential than it will ever be possible to document. As Wangermée points out,

[10] William Langton, Walter Haliday, William Maysham, Thomas Radcliff, Robert Marshall, William Wykes, and John Clyff.

[11] In 1380 it is said, the Earl of Chester and his troops were besieged by the Welsh. The Earl sent out a call for help and his constable, Roger Lacy, gathered together all the 'fiddlers, players, cobblers, debauched persons, both men and women' at the Chester fair and made the rescue. As a reward, Lacy was given perpetual control over such persons. He passed this authority on to one, Dutton of Dutton, and his heirs. A Dutton in mid-seventeenth century annually held a kind of mock court over his minstrels, featuring a procession to the chapel where he heard 'a set of loud (wind) music (playing) a solemn lesson or two.'

[12] Henry A. F. Crewdson, *The Worshipful Company of Musicians* (London: Knight, 1971), 26–27.

[13] Duncan, *The Story of Minstrelsy*, 212, quotes one who observed, 'the first musicians were gods; the second, heroes; the third, bards; and the fourth, beggars.'

These, then, were musicians who have left scarcely any concrete evidence of their activity, an activity which was, for all that, intense and, in relation to the mass of inhabitants of a city, perhaps played a part more important than that of musicians educated in the learned art of counterpoint.[14]

But we must not mourn the passing of the genuine minstrel for it also reflects the fact that his more proficient colleagues had now found permanent, respectable employment as members of the court and civic wind bands discussed below. The independent minstrel is dead, but the true wind ensemble is born.

[14] Wangermée, *Flemish Music*, 182.

PART III

Wind Ensembles in the Medieval Church

10 *The Intolerance of the Church*

PERHAPS THE ORIGINAL BAN ON INSTRUMENTAL MUSIC in the early Christian Church came as a question of security, rather than of conscience. During the period of persecution the services were held in secrecy, an environment not conducive to instrumental music of any kind.[1] Indeed, in the New Testament no references to the use of musical instruments in the actual service can be found; the only references to instruments are in regard to secular customs.[2]

Another objection of the early Church to instrumental music lay in the fact that they saw the performers of such music, the jongleurs, as undesirables. Not only was he a homeless, uneducated itinerate in the eyes of the Church, but the entire class of traveling entertainers had developed reputations, in many cases no doubt justly earned, unsuitable to participation in the church service. Honorius of Autun, in his *Elucidarium*, asks,

> Do the jongleurs have any hope? None. Because they are from the bottom of their hearts the ministers of Satan.[3]

Even as late as the thirteenth century, Conrad of Zurich included them in a category with evil-doers and prostitutes.[4]

In addition to the very thought of association with these unsavory characters, the instrumentalists, a Church dedicated to the celebration of the glory of God and fighting to eliminate pagan elements from the lives of the faithful could hardly afford the inclusion of popular music.[5] Augustine was among those who argued strongly against the 'intrusion of affective elements and subjective feelings' into the service.[6]

Thus, from about 370 AD, instrumental accompaniment was not permitted the early Christians.[7] But the laws of the Church are sometimes difficult to keep and, judging by the stream of interdictions which begin in the eighth century, one must believe that this policy was not strictly observed.

For example, in the year 789 bishops, abbots, and abbesses were forbidden to keep 'ioculatores' and in 791 the Council of Aquileia ruled,

[1] The significance of this can be observed by anyone who visits Salzburg, where a chapel can be seen carved inside a mountain of solid rock by the early Christians in an attempt to achieve secrecy.

[2] See Matthew 9:23; 6:2; 24:31; and 11:17; Luke 7:32; I Corinthians 13:1; 14:7–8; and 15:52; Hebrews 12:19; I Thessalonians 4:16; and Revelation 18:22; and 14:2.

[3] Jacques Paul Migne, *Patrologiae cursus completus, series latina*, 172, col. 1148.

[4] Edmond Faral, *Les Jongleurs en France au moyen âge* (Paris: Champion, 1910), 27.

[5] The church's identification of the instruments as pagan can be seen in a martyrology of 397 AD which cites the power of the *tuba* (here perhaps a folk trumpet) to exorcise evil. Quoted in Grove, 6:296.

[6] Augustine, *Confessions*, 10:33.

[7] Georges Kastner, *Les Danses des morts* (Paris, 1852), 147.

All the worldly honors to which the people of this age and the princes of the earth are accustomed, such as hunting, secular song, endless and immoderate rejoicings ... should not be part of the way of life of the servants of the Church.[8]

The Council of Tours in 813 warned priests to avoid the 'immodesties of dishonest actors and their obscene amusements.'[9] To even give a donation to these wandering entertainers was considered tantamount to robbery of the poor. Such interdictions continued for centuries.[10]

The Church at once found itself faced with a rather difficult theological dilemma: Having taken this stand against instruments in the service, how does one explain their constant appearance in the Old Testament? In the famous Psalm 150, for example, the Jews were exhorted to praise God with various musical instruments. How could God encourage this evil usage among his chosen people?

Most early Church writers circumvented this problem by taking these references to be mere symbols. Thus the writer known as Pseudo-Athanasius wrote, regarding Psalm 57:8 ('Awake, my harp and lyre!'), 'the harp is the soul, the lyre is the body.'[11] Augustine's interpretation of the famous, 'Praise the Lord with cymbals, praise him with loud cymbals,' in Psalm 150:5, is even more imaginative:

> Cymbals touch each other in order to play and therefore some people compare them to our lips. But I think it better to think of God as being praised on the cymbals when someone is honored by his neighbor rather than by himself.[12]

The exegetical School of Antioch, which treated the Old Testament more as an historical document than a symbolic or allegorical book, had particular difficulty with this question. Thus, Theodore of Cyrus (d. ca. 460 AD) becomes almost anti-semitic in his attempt at giving an historical flavor to his interpretation of the Jew's use of instruments.

> If old Levites used those instruments in the Temple of God to praise Him, not because it pleased Him ... Once it happened, however, He tolerated it, wishing to take them from the error of idolatry. Since they were fond of play and laughter, and since all this sort of thing took place in the temples of the idols, He allowed it, thus to lead them, and by the smaller evil avoid the greater.[13]

[8] Quoted in Goldron, *Minstrels and Masters*, 18.

[9] Ibid.

[10] See M.B. Bernhard, *Notice sur la Confrérie des Joueurs d'Instruments d'Alsace* (Paris, 1844), 5, fn. 4, for the original texts for similar interdictions by Brême (1292), Köln (1307), Salzburg (1310), and Strasbourg (1306, 1310, and 1345) church officials.

[11] James W. McKinnon, 'Musical Instruments in Medieval Psalm Commentaries and Psalters,' *Journal of the American Musicological Society* 21, no. 1 (Spring 1968): 7.

[12] Ibid.

[13] Ibid.

These arguments, as we shall see, could not forever hold back the charms of music.

11 *Toward Acceptance of Instrumental Music by the Church*

ONE INFLUENCE which helped prepare for instrumental music in the church was the gradual acceptance of the organ. The organ begins to appear in Western Europe as early as the seventh or eighth century AD, but before the thirteenth century remained imperfect and noisy. One might imagine the sound produced by the organ in Winchester, described by the deacon, Wulstan, ca. 963, which required the services of 'seventy strong men labouring with their arms to drive the wind up.'[1]

By the twelfth century the organ, but not other instruments, was accepted in some churches as we can see in the treatise, *Ars Musica*, by Gilles de Zamore.

> And of (the organ) alone the church has made use of in various kinds of singing ... other instruments being commonly rejected because of the abuses of the Jongleurs.[2]

But it would be many years before the enthusiasm was general, even for the organ. One reads, for example, in the *Nürnberger Liederbuch* (fifteenth century), 'When too much is made of the organ, the people do not like it.'[3]

Gradually, however, this form of instrumental music became irresistible, giving other instruments a precedent. But the organ played an even more important role from the standpoint of the history of the wind ensemble: the very *sound* of the organ—so much like a wind band in texture that most of the individual pipes are named for wind instruments—must have helped to prepare the way psychologically for the acceptance of the 'real' wind ensembles.

Another important factor in the gradual progress toward the acceptance of instrumental music in the church can be seen beginning in the thirteenth century. As the minstrels themselves, some church leaders now begin to make some ethical distinction among the professions, finding some more acceptable than others.[4] Thus St. Thomas Aquinas (1225–1275) wrote that the profession of an *histrio* is not in itself unlawful. It was

[1] Quoted in Duncan, *The Story of Minstrelsy*, 31.

[2] Quoted in Martin Gerbert, *Scriptores ecclesiastici de musica sacra potissimum* (Saint Blaise, 1784), 2:388.

[3] Leo Söhner, *Die Orgelbegleitung zum Gregorianishcen Gesang* (Regensburg: Pustet, 1936), 27.

[4] This seems to have been a period of moderation in general with regard to the attitude of the church. Perhaps it was due in part to such people as St. Francis of Assisi (1181–1226) who was himself a troubadour in his youth and named his Minorites *ioculatores Domini* and sent them singing over the world. (Chambers, *The Mediaeval Stage*, 1:46.)

ordained for the reasonable solace of humanity, and the *histrio* who exercises it at a fitting time and in a fitting manner is not on that account to be considered a sinner.[5]

A more explicit classification of minstrels was made by Thomas de Cabham (d. 1313), an early Archbishop of Canterbury. Writing at the end of the thirteenth century, he first

Above: Jan van Eyck (1390–1441), two panels from the top row of the Ghent Altarpiece, 1432, Museum Saint Bavo Cathedral, Ghent

[5] *Summa Theologiae*, 2.2, quaest. 168, art. 3.

cites two classes which are damnable: those who wear horrible masks, or entertain by indecent dance and gesture, and those who follow the courts of the great and amuse by satire and by raillery. Some are distinguished by the use of their instruments, but some sing wanton songs at banquets and are also damnable. However, those who sing of the deeds of princes, and of the lives of the saints, these—on the authority of Pope Alexander—may be tolerated.[6]

During the thirteenth century one also begins to see frequent payments, or food and shelter, to minstrels for performances in the individual monasteries and priories, particularly in those of the Augustinian and Benedictine orders.[7] One attractive story says that in 1224 a Benedictine house in England received with joy two visitors assumed by their dress to be minstrels. When it was discovered that they were only visiting friars, they tossed them out! By the fourteenth century such accounts begin to show payment for ensembles of minstrels, as one can see in the payment records of the Durham and Thetford Priories in England. In 1374 and 1375, for St. Cuthbertum Day, the Durham Priory made a payment to twelve minstrels for their performance.

Certain folk traditions which must have included performance by wind players in ceremonies connected with church property were increasingly difficult for the Church to control at the local level. Such a case was dancing, which was in the Middle Ages part of almost every civic celebration and must have included winds. The Council of Avignon declared in 1209 that on the eve of important religious festivals,

> there should not be, in the churches, any of this theatrical dancing, these immodest rejoicings, these meetings of singers with their worldly songs, which incite the souls of those who hear them to sin.[8]

Similarlily in 1212 the Council of Paris ruled,

> Gatherings of women for the purpose of dancing and singing shall not be granted permission to enter cemeteries or to tread on consecrated gound ... Nuns will not set themselves at the head of processions which sing and dance on the grounds of churches and their chapels ... for according to St. Gregory it is better to plough and to dig on the Sabbath than to conduct these dances.[9]

[6] *Penitential*, quoted in Chambers, *The Mediaeval Stage*, 1:59.

[7] Chambers, *The Medieval Stage*, 1:56.

[8] Goldron, *Minstrels and Masters*, 19.

[9] Ibid.

Another thirteenth-century interdiction is even stronger, the Council of Bayeux warning,

> Priests will forbid gatherings for dancing and singing in churches and cemeteries, on pain of excommunication.[10]

[10] Ibid.

The continuing negative attitude of these pronouncements suggest that they were not being heeded. Indeed, the craze for dancing which was spreading over Late Medieval Europe in general must have necessitated the Church 'turning its head' from time to time in favor of local traditions. Some German spiritual songs of the fifteenth century portray Jesus as master of heavenly dancing, with behind him a troupe of holy maidens striking drums and playing the flute. In Dubrovnik (now in Croatia) the Church permitted dancing in the cathedral, accompanied by wind instruments, on the eve of the town's patron saint day, St. Blaise, between 1379 and 1456.[11]

[11] Gustave Reese, *Music in the Renaissance* (New York: Norton, 1959), 758.

In another example of local tradition, we see the citizens of Eichstadt rebel in 1237 against an interdict by Bishop Friedrich III and continue their custom of burying their dead with the accompaniment of instruments.[12]

[12] Grove, 7:810.

The quality of ceremonial music heard outside the church must have been another persuasive argument for opening the doors to instrumental music. The reference by Thomas de Cabham, above, to those minstrels 'who follow the courts of the great,' remind one that the secular princes by this time had begun to surround themselves with musicians, making ceremony a prop of authority. The Church, long dependent on pomp to help impress the minds of the medieval townspeople, must have found it difficult to compete with the spectacle of the aristocratic courts. The impressive music heard outside the church must have been an easy victor in the competition for the burger's awe. As one later churchman said, the early church leaders must have wondered why the devil had all the good tunes!

One can understand, then, why the church princes, following the lead of their secular noble colleagues, also began to evidence a desire for the proper ceremonial accouterments. As Goldron reminds us,

It is to be remembered that many senior members of the clergy were at the same time aristocrats and of noble birth. When they moved to their abbeys or to their official palaces they were loth to leave behind them all the trappings of the court. From the time of Charlemagne there is ample evidence of rich and powerful princes of the Church maintaining musicians to add splendor and status to their offices. By the thirteenth century there was scarcely one in Europe who was without his jongleurs.[13]

Thus at least as early as Gregory IX, in 1227, one begins to see wind instruments being called upon by the popes in Rome to help make their coronations as festive as those of the secular kings.

In England, it is possible to document the newly elected thirteenth-century Abbot of St. Albans, John de Hertford, being received, in 1235, in the Abbey with minstrelsy of shawms, 'which we call *burdones*' (sonantibus chalamis, quos *burdones* appelamus) as a Te Deum was sung.[14]

In fourteenth-century England the Bishops of Durham, Norwich, and Winchester all had 'minstrels of honour,' as any secular noble.[15] Even the most austere of all prelates in England, Robert Grosseteste, had a private harpist.

> He louede moche to here the harpe;
> For mannys wyt hyt makyth sharpe.
> Next hys chaumbre, besyde hys stody,
> Hys harpers chaumbre was fast therby.[16]

There is evidence that during the fourteenth century in the German-speaking countries, many church leaders had their private minstrels as well. Salmen points out that the Bishops of Freising, Brixen, Vich, Schleswig, Regensburg, Lüttich, Halberstadt, Hildesheim, Minden, Meissen, Verden und Bremen, Prag, Konstanz and Ölmutz, together with the Archbishop of Köln, all had private musicians by the fourteenth century.[17] In Mainz there are references to 'des piffer' of the Archbishop in 1371 and 1394.[18]

The most complete documentation for this part of fourteenth-century Europe comes from Salzburg. Here the Archbishop Pilgrim von Puchheim (1365–1396) ruled, 'a more worldly than spiritual lord, witty, splendour-loving, enthralled by the arts.'[19] His villa, called the *Freudensaal*, was dedicated

[13] Goldron, *Minstrels and Masters*, 22.

[14] Richard Rastall, 'Some English Consort-Groupings of the late Middle Ages,' *The Musical Quarterly* 55, no. 2 (April 1974): 193.

[15] Chambers, *The Mediaeval Stage*, 1:56, fn. 3.

[16] Percy Manning, *Some Oxfordshire Seasonal Festivals* (London: Nutt, 1897), 150.

[17] Salmen, *Der Fahrende Musiker*, 73, 179.

[18] See Bernhard, *Notice sur la Confrérie*, 6–7; and J. Laurent, *Aachener Stadtrechnungen aus dem XIV Jahrhundert* (Aachen, 1866), 396.

[19] Grove, 16:437.

to poetry, music, and conversation and was one of the most important salons in Europe. He maintained 'trumetterey' in addition to other instruments. His resident composer, the famous Hermann, Monk of Salzburg (ca. 1350–1410, the first poet–musician to write in German), has composed two- and three-part wind ensemble pieces, labeled, *ist gut zu blasen*. These compositions are among the very earliest of all extant wind ensemble works.[20]

References for fifteenth-century ensembles maintained by the German church leaders usually provide a clue to the instrumentation. Frequently they are referred to as *pfiffer*, after the Italian usage, meaning a shawm ensemble. Such private ensembles can be documented for the Bishops of Kostentz (1449), Tryer (1452), and Würzburg (1433–1434).[21] A similar ensemble performed in the Pfarrhause in Gonobitz in 1487.[22] Additional fifteenth-century references include a trombone ensemble of the Bishop of Trient, which performed in Nürnberg in 1436,[23] and the 'minstrels' of the Archbishop of Köln, who appeared in London in 1402.[24]

The acceptance of wind ensembles by these church leaders for their personal use, for whatever the reason, was an important stage in the movement toward the acceptance of instrumental music in the service itself. This point is well summarized by Nanie Bridgman:

> Thus we are not surprised to find such a figure as the great fifteenth century politician–churchman, Savonarola, using wind music to help in the indoctrination of his flock. We see him, in the court-yard of his monestary, organizing simple citizens in rounds, hand in hand, singing their *Laudes* to the sound of trumpets and wind instruments ("Piffari"). It, was this acceptance and employment by the Church itself in the late fifteenth century which made possible the glory of Gabrieli in the following century.[25]

Whenever these church princes gathered together, in one of the great church councils, they brought their wind players. If they did not maintain such an ensemble, as in the case of the Pope, they hired them for these occasions, so as not to be overshadowed. Thus, for the Council of Florence in 1438, the Pope made his entrance with trumpets, drums, and shawms.[26]

[20] These works exist in the *Spörl Liederbuch*, now called the *Mondsee Wiener Liederhandschrift* (A:Wn Mss.2856).

[21] Salmen, *Der Fahrende Musiker*, 176.

[22] (Tibijs aliquando diversis fistulis maioribus scilicet et minoribus cecinerunt), see Hellmut Federhofer, 'Beitrage zur altern Musikgeschichte Karntens,' in *Carinthia* (145), 1955, 377.

[23] Salmen, *Der Fahrende Musiker*, 163.

[24] James Hamilton Wylie, *History of England under Henry the Fourth* (London, 1884), 4:236.

[25] Nanie Bridgman, 'Fêtes italiennes de plein air au Quattrocento,' in *Hans Albrecht in Memoriam* (Kassel: Bärenreiter, 1962), 37.

[26] Vladimir Féderov, 'Des Russes au Concile de Florence,' in *Hans Albrecht in Memoriam* (Kassel: Bärenreiter, 1962), 30 (Trompeten und Trommeln und Schalmeien, wie nach Bebrach, und so wurde es auch von Kardinalen, Erzbischofen und Bischofen in ihren eigenen Kirchen gepflegt).

The greatest church conference of the Middle Ages was the Council of Constance (1414–1418). Here, in one of the most historic gatherings of European history, assembled no fewer than three popes (John XXIII of Rome, Gregory XII, the Avignon pretender, and Benedict XIII, who was a creation of Ludwig of Bavaria), five Patriarchs, thirty-three Cardinals, forty-seven Archbishops, fifty-three hundred priests, three hundred noblemen, and fifteen hundred knights. The primary purpose of the council was to deal with the problem of the three popes and also to try to suppress the growing Hussite movement in Bohemia.

Such a great church gathering must have also been very festive in character, for it is said sixty-three thousand people traveled to this village of seven thousand persons! One report said that it was so crowded there were five hundred accidental drownings in the lake.[27]

The number of participants must have varied during the four-year period, but one can assume that at all times there must have also been a very large number of wind players gathered here from throughout Europe taking advantage of the opportunity to share literature and techniques. A number of eyewitness accounts confirm this. One reports that during the first five months of the council there were three hundred and forty-six 'pfifer, prussuner und spillut.'[28] Another observer records four hundred and twenty 'ioculatores, hystriones, fistulatores' (minstrels, actors, and flutists) and still another account mentions five hundred.

> Item spillüt, prusuner, trummeter, pfiffer, singer, giger vnd allerhand spillüt, der varent funf hundert vnd dar bi.[29]

One of the officials reported seventeen hundred musicians, 'prusuner, pfifer, fidler und allerlay spillüt,' an estimate which no doubt covers the entire span of the conference.[30] Even the pope from Rome arrived with a shawm and trombone ensemble, although they may have been newly hired for the occasion as one observer who heard them said they played in 'wild discord.'

> prosuner und pfiffer, die ymer me dar prosonten und pfiffen zu wilderstrit.[31]

[27] Ernest F. Henderson, *A Short History of Germany* (New York: Macmillan, 1916), 1:208.

[28] M. Schuler, 'Die Musik in Konstanz während des Konzils 1414–1418,' *Acta Musicologica* 38, no. 2/4 (Apr–Dec 1966), 163; and Joseph Riegel, *Die Teilnehmerlisten des Konstanzer Konzils* (Freiburg, 1916), 74ff.

[29] Richard Fester, 'Die Fortsetzung der Flores temporum von Reinbold Slecht,' *Zeitschrift für die Geschichte des Oberrheins* (Stuttgart: 1894), 132; Anton Henne von Sargens (ed.), *Die Klingenberger Chronik* (Gotha, 1861), 193; and Otto Carl August Zur Nedden, *Quellen und Studien zur oberrheinischen Musikgeschichte im 15. und 16 Jahrhundert* (Kassel: Bärenreiter-Verlag, 1931), 53.

[30] Ulrich von Richental, *Ulrichs von Richental Chronik des Constanzer Conzils*, Michael Richard Buck, ed. (Tüblingen, 1882), 215.

[31] Ulrichs von Richental, *Das Konzil zu Konstanz* (Otto Feger, ed., Konstanz: Starnberg, 1964), 252.

All the accounts mentioned thus far have been concerning the use of small wind ensembles as part of the personal regalia of the church princes. When wind music first began to be used by the Church itself as part of its ritual it seems to have been outdoor music, for processions. It is easy to see this now as a logical first step, official church instrumental music, but not yet inside the church building.

Already after 1000 AD, one reads in the *Chronicle of Mont Saint Michel* (Paris) of a wind ensemble of horns, flutes, and shawms played by minstrels in a pious procession to the celebrated Abbey.

> Ci1 jugleor l'a ou il vunt,
> Tuit lor vi'eles traites unt;
> Laiz et sonnez vunt v'ielant.
> ...
> Cors et boisines et fresteals
> Et fleutes et chalemeals[32]

[32] Quoted in Edmund A. Bowles, 'Musical Instruments in the Medieval Corpus Christi Procession,' *Journal of the American Musicological Society* 17, no. 3 (Autumn 1964): 256.

In 1264, Pope Urban IV instituted the festival of the Corpus Christi, with which musical instruments always seem to be associated. Held the first Thursday following Trinity Sunday, it was created to be a parade, with clergy, musicians, lay and civic organizations participating. Numerous accounts of this festival through the following years mention wind players or minstrels. In Malines (now Belgium) in 1334, the minstrels were given gifts of wine and pairs of gloves following the procession. In Heidelberg, in 1469, an ensemble performed on trombones, trumpets, and numerous shawms.[33]

[33] Ibid., (Mit schellenluten, glockenglangk, Pusaum, trumeten, pfiffen vil …).

Another regular church procession was held to celebrate the Festival of the Virgin Mary. In 1406, in Utrecht, twenty-six musicians were hired for this procession.[34] A reference to this festival procession in Frankfurt a. M., in 1467, carries the interesting mention of 'muted' trumpets (gedämpten Drompten)![35]

[34] Édouard Georges Jacques Gregoir, *Notice historique sur les sociétés et écoles de musique* (Antwerp, 1869), 16. A miniature from this period (Christine de Pisan, *Oeuvres poétiques*, Mss 9231, fol. 51v., in the Royal Library, Brussels) pictures such a procession with three shawm players, two trumpeters and a rare player of the drum.

[35] Ehmann, *Tibilustrium*, 36.

The actual use of wind instrument ensembles *inside* the church may have first come with the medieval drama, discussed below. Certainly the appearance of wind ensembles in the church building must date from the time such ensembles begin to represent secular princes. No aristocratic marriage or baptism from that time could be held without the nobleman's accompanying musical troupe.

Documents mentioning noblemen appearing with their personal ensembles in the church are extant from about the fourteenth century. The Prince of Wales's vigil before he was knighted in 1306, in England, was accompanied by a large band of trumpets and shawms. One eyewitness, Matthew of Westminster, recalled that it was so loud that when the choir entered with their 'shout of praise' they could not be heard.[36] In 1386, in a church in Ghent, trumpets and clarions were heard performing after the sermon by Duke Philip the Bold.[37]

According to most authorities, it was Philip the Good, of Burgundy, who set the precedent of employing non-clerical musicians for the first time in his chapel.[38] In any case, when one reads that during the marriage ceremony of his successor, Charles the Bold, with Margaret of York, in 1468, an ensemble of shawms and trombones performed a motet and a chanson, it is clear that a new attitude on the part of the church is now established.[39]

The first church official to plea for the use of wind instruments may have been Jean Gerson, canon at Notre Dame who wrote in ca. 1390 that although only the organ was normally used in the church, and rarely the trumpet, he would like the admissibility of players of bombardes, shawms, and the large and small cornemuse.[40]

By the fifteenth century the use of wind ensembles in the church in Western Europe appears to have been generally accepted, although in some towns this seems to have been limited to special occasions. In Bologna there were such appearances by members of the Concerto Palatino, a wind ensemble, in St. Petronio.[41] In the Low Countries there appears to have been a tradition by which the town wind band performed for the first Mass read by a new priest. One finds a payment document from Leiden, in 1412, for example, which reads,

> Payment to the pipers (shawms), because they accompanied us to the offering of the two first masses.[42]

In many towns the use of the additional wind instruments was perhaps found only on the great church festival days, as one can see in the civic records of Ghent.

[36] Quoted in Rastall, 'Some English Consort-Groupings', 194.

[37] Edmund A. Bowles, 'Haut and Bas: The Grouping of Musical Instruments in the Middle Ages' in *Musica Disciplina* 8 (1954):134.

[38] George van Doorslaer, 'La Chapelle musicale de Philippe le Beau,' in *Revue Belge d'archéologie et d'histoire de l'art*, 4:159.

[39] Olivier de la Marche, *Mémoires* (Paris, 1885), 3:152ff. G. Thibault, 'Le Concert Instrumental au XVe Siecle,' in Jean Jacquot, ed., *La musique instrumentale de la renaissance,* (Paris: Editions du Centre National de la Recherche Scientifique, 1955), 31, suggests some specific chansons which might have been performed on this occasion. Iconography of the fifteenth century begins to reflect the wider acceptance of instruments. For example, the Beauchamp window in St. Mary's Church, Warwick (England), has stained glass panels designed in 1447 which show an angelic wind band of single and double horn pipes, cornett, and keyboard types.

[40] Ellies du Pin, ed., *Joannis Gersonii opera omnia*, 4.

[41] Grove, 3:3. Fragments of music used on these occasions survive in the church archives.

[42] *Stadsrekeningen van Leiden*, ed. A. Meerkamp van Embden (Amsterdam: Müller, 1913–1914), 1:270 (... Den pipers gheghevens, dat zi met ons ghinghen tot 2 eersten missen te offeren ...). A similar payment can be found in these records for 1429 (ibid., 2:291).

... item paid to Pieter de Keyser and his companions because they trumpeted (trombone) and piped (shawm) at New Year ... during all holy days, at Christmas, at Easter, and at Pentecost.⁴³

Ehmann cites such examples of winds participating in the special feast day celebrations in the fifteenth-century German cities as well, including Luzern (1431), Munich (1450), and in Saxony (1481).⁴⁴

Such regular appearance suggests the possibility of the wind ensemble being used in choral support. Indeed, Tinctoris mentions in his *De Inventione et Usu Musicae* the use of 'tibicinibus adiuncti tubicines' in choral support in the Cathedral of Chartres.⁴⁵

One may perhaps assume that it was in this role of choral support that accounts of wind ensembles performing in the Mass itself exist from the fifteenth century. Already in 1390 one reads of a Mass being sung in the abby of St.-Aubert, in France, by 'moult braves chantres et flûteurs musicaux.'⁴⁶ Civic

43 Ghent Municipal Archive, financial accounts for 1413–1414, fol. 46. (Item pieter de keyser en zijn ghesellen van dat zij trompten ende pepen ter Jare doemen ... in aler helighe daghe, in kerstadaghe in paeschdaghe en in tsinxen daghe ...), quoted in Keith Polk, *Flemish Wind Bands in the Late Middle Ages* (PhD diss., University of California, Berkeley, 1968), 73.

44 Ehmann, *Tibilustrium*, 36, 150. Luzern (1431), the Stadtpfeifer are required 'an gewissen Feiertagen in der Frühe sowie an den Vorabenden der hohen Kirchenfeste eine halbe Stunde auf dem Rathausturm blasen'; Munich (1450), a local physician, Sigmund Gotzkircher counted in this year no fewer than twenty feast day celebrations, 'cum tubis et tympanis et organis et fistolatoribus et aliis instrumentis ... (note continued)

Altar wall of the Carafa Chapel showing wind instruments, by Filippino Lippi (1457–1504), ca. 1489–1491

pay records in the Low Countries reveal the same practice. In Leiden, in 1412, the 'pipers & trompers' were paid to accompany the 'Heilich Sacrament.'[47] In Ieper such payments were made to wind players in 1409 and 1452.

> Cakaerd, van dat hy speilde voir theleghe sakrement met eere muse, xij s.
>
> ...
>
> Joris Van den Casteele, die hier speilde voor tsacrement metten ministreulen van binnen, xl s.[48]

Finally, there is a reference to the King of Denmark's wind ensemble making a guest appearance in a service in Nördlingen, in 1444 (des kungs von Tennmarck pfeiffer in der messe).[49]

There are also accounts of what appears to be brass ensembles playing with the organ during the fifteenth century. Ehmann cites such examples in Dresden (1404), Werden a. d. Ruhr (1427), and in Paris (1424). He suggests that perhaps they performed a chorale as a cantus firmus to the organ.[50] In this regard one is reminded of the handful of extant compositions, such as the Dufay *Gloria ad modum tubae* (Gloria, in the manner of a trumpet), which have instrumental parts playable on the medieval trumpet.[51]

---

44 (cont.) ... musicalibus et cum cantoribus, cum clericis et laycis,' performing; and Saxony (1481), a payment to 'den Trommettern geben zum Nawen Jar als sie zu Nacht am Nawen Jarstag meyn gn. hern angeplassen haben, nach alder gewonheyt gibt man yedem 20 gr.'

45 Emile Haraszti, 'Les Musiciens de Mathias Corvin et de Beatrice d'Aragon,' in Jean Jacquot, ed., *La musique instrumentale de la renaissance*, 57.

46 'Mémoriaux de l'abbe de St-Aubert,' in *Archives historiques du Nord de la France* (1844), 5:539. A later French miniature, ca. 1450, in the *Book of Hours* of Etienne Chavalier, painted by Jean Fouquet, pictures an ensemble of three slide trumpets, two large shawms, a bagpipe, and an organ; cited in Vivian Safowitz, 'Trumpet Music and Trumpet Style in the Early Renaissance' (PhD diss., University of Illinois, 1965), 32.

47 Embden, *Stadsrekeningen van Leiden*, 1:245.

48 Quoted in Vander Straeten, *La Musique*, 4:132, 4:134.

49 Salmen, *Der Fahrende Musiker*, 168.

50 Ehmann, *Tibilustrium*, 40, 156–157. Dresden (1404), 'Nota man gebit den blesern chore dreyen inglichen alle iar 6 gr. Das sie der grossen orgel mit flise warten sullen und blasen ezu desin nachgeschrebin festen'; Werden a. d. Rohr (1427), 'bleseren upp der orgeln'; and Paris (1424), 'wie wenn es Gott ware und man spielte auf Orgeln und Trompeten.'

51 See Safowitz, 'Trumpet Music and Trumpet Style,' 141ff.

12 *Wind Instruments in the Medieval Church Drama*

THE GREAT TRADITIONS OF GREEK AND ROMAN DRAMA died with those civilizations and was reborn with the *ludi* of the medieval village festivals. The village festival had, of course, a very pagan character as they were born out of the most primitive instincts, such as the observations of the changing seasons. The most ancient of the summer festivals must be the fertility celebrations of May Day, which had its basis in the myth of the marriage of heaven and earth, resulting in the showers which fertilize the crops.

No doubt a strong heathen quality was at the heart of these celebrations and when one considers how rare such amusements were for these toilers of the soil, it may be assumed that the general behaviour surrounding them provided the Church with text for many a sermon.[1] Bishop Grosseteste of Lincoln, in England, classed these village plays during the thirteenth century together with drinking bouts, ram-raisings and other athletic contests, as performances which no Christian should attend; actors were automatically excommunicated.

But Bishop Grosseteste and his kind represent the reformer, while many parish priests took a more moderate view. Perhaps sensing that the new religion could not immediately cleanse the peasant of eons of pagan tradition, they sought to regulate through participation, rather than to ban. Thus, one of the oldest extant plays of modern European literature, the 'Representation of Adam' (twelfth century), is written in French, but bears stage directions in Latin. It was a natural step for the priest to become a part of the village play. The Mass itself was a dramatic spectacle of course, but even as early as the eleventh century there were kinds of church drama acted out inside the cathedrals as part of the observance of the major holy days.[2] Gradually, from the twelfth century, these kinds of sacred drama were performed outside the church as well as they were becoming too elaborate. The medieval scholar, Bowles, reviews this early transition.

[1] In his *Dialogue agaynst light, lewde, and lascivious Dancing* (London, 1583), the Puritan author, Christopher Fetherston, says he has 'hearde of tenne maidens which went to set May, and nine of them came home with childe.'

[2] Brander Matthews, *Development of the Drama* (New York: Scribner, 1921), 115.

It was during the twelfth century that liturgical drama gradually outgrew the confines of the church and the limits of its service. The length of these plays, their use of the vernacular, the encroachment of various worldly elements, and the subject matter that transcended or shifted the focus from the liturgy drove them out into the cathedral square, where they were performed under the brow of the church facade, itself a drama in stone. The growth of plays with large casts, scenery, and complex staging demanded so much for their performances by way of personnel, organization, direction, and financing that the laity was pressed into service and medieval drama became a communal affair. With this influx such secular performers as minstrels and jongleurs were introduced. Staging was accomplished under the aegis of guilds and confraternities, which were devotional in aim ... However, the plays continued to be supervised by the clergy and their scholars, and priests and monks supplied the texts. By the end of the fourteenth century these dramatic presentations were widespread, particularly in the environs of Paris.³

By the fourteenth century the church drama and the village *ludi* had joined together to become the literature of the medieval 'mystery' (stories set within the time frame of the Bible)⁴ and 'miracle' (post-Biblical) plays.

The day of a performance would begin with a trumpet fanfare, called *le cri du jeu* in French, or 'banns' in English.

> Now, mynstsrell, blow up with a mery stevyn!⁵

For performances concurrent with major feast days, a procession with the sacrament might also precede the play. From fourteenth-century France we have a description of such a procession.

> The Thursday following this Pentecost week, all the citizens and craftsmen of Paris held a great celebration: some came in rich costumes of superior workmanship, others in new dress, on foot and on horseback, each guild as prescribed, above the isle of Notre Dame, to the sound of trumpets, small drums, buisines, tambourines, and nakers, with much merriment and making a lot of noise, and with very handsome mysteries.⁶

The actors also marched from their lodging to the stage accompanied by these wind bands. An account from Paris (1496) speaks of the actors following the sounds of 'trompetes,

---

3 Edmund A. Bowles, 'The Role of Musical Instruments in Medieval Sacred Drama,' in *The Musical Quarterly* 45, no. 1 (January 1959): 70–71. Much of the material used here is taken from this work.

4 A miniature by Jean Fouquet, ca. 1470, pictures a performance of the Mystery play, *The Holy Apollo*, and shows three slide trumpets, two shawms, and a bagpipe performing (French Hours Book of Etienne Chevalier, Musée Condé, Chantilly, Mss. 71, see image opposite page).

5 Joseph Quincy Adams, *Chief Pre-Shakespearean Dramas* (Boston: Houghton Mifflin, 1924), 244.

6 Jules Marie Édouard Viard, ed., *Les grandes chroniques de France* (Paris, 1837), 1:xlviii. (trompes, tabours, buissines, timbres et nacaires)

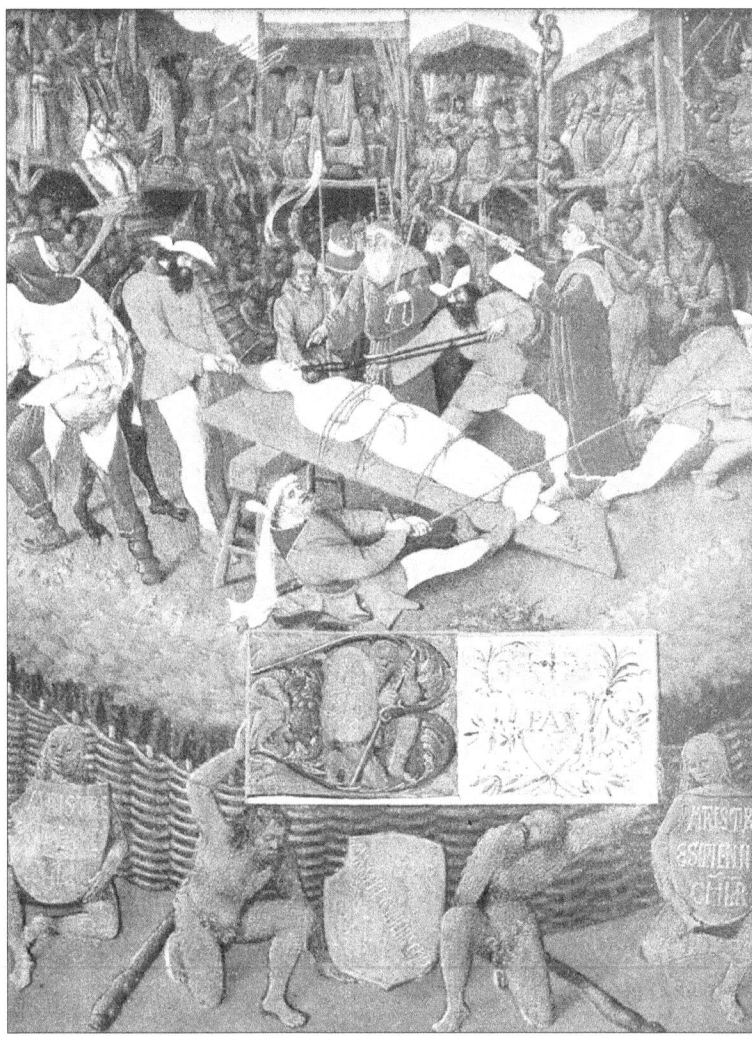

Jean Fouquet's depiction of a performance of the Mystery play, *The Holy Apollo*, shows three slide trumpets, two shawms, and a bagpipe performing (upper left).

clerons, bussines, orgues, harpes, tabourins' and other loud and soft instruments.[7] A similar German example, from ca. 1490, reads,

> Thus the characters are first solemnly led to their places with musical instruments and the blaring of trumpets.[8]

The performance itself was begun in France with minstrels playing fanfares[9] and on occasion fanfares seem to have been played between speeches.

> After this speech the two horn players come forward and blow for the third time.[10]

[7] Achille Jubinal, *Mystères inédits du XV siècle* (Paris, 1920–1934), 5:198.

[8] Richard Froning, *Das deutsche Drama des Mittelalters* (Stuttgart, 1891), 340. A miniature of a German theater scene, ca. 1410, shows a shawm and trumpet playing (Paris, National Library. Mss. lat. 7907 A, fol. 2v).

[9] Bowles, 'The Role of Musical Instruments in Medieval Sacred Drama,' 71.

[10] In the 'Alsfelder Passionsspiel,' quoted in Richard Heinzel, *Beschreibung des geistlichen Schauspiels im deutschen Mittelalter* (Hamburg, 1898), 83.

Within the context of the dramatic structure itself there was a rather consistent use of specific instruments with specific characters, events, places, and kinds of plays. Stage depictions of heaven and Christ were always accompanied by 'soft' music, for the most part string instruments. Many other situations, however, called for wind instruments. Shepherds, in Nativity plays, as an obvious example, usually appeared with recorders.

> Willingly and quickly I'll go (to Bethlehem), but I shall take my recorder (flaiot) with me, which I will play to comfort the little babe, who is God and lord of the whole world.[11]

[11] Gustave Cohen, *Le théatre à Paris et aux environs à la fin du XIV siècle* in *Romania*, 38:591. A French miniature from the same date pictures a theater scene with accompanying shawm and trumpet players (Paris, Bibl. de l'Arsenal, Mss. 664, fol. lv).

One scene for which the 'loud' (wind) instruments were always needed was the representation of the Last Judgment. In the English play, *Judgment Day*, ca. 1430, God speaks:

> In erthe I see butte synnes seere
> Therefor myne aungellis will I sende
> To blawe ther bemys that all may here
> The tyme is comen I will make ende.[12]

[12] Adams, *Chief Pre-Shakespearean Dramas*, 200.

In Greban's Passion, *Signes de la fin du monde*, an angel blew,

> A frightening horn (boisine), dreadful, dismal, and woeful, will be heard near and far.[13]

[13] Frédéric Godefroy, *Dictionnaire de l'ancienne langue française* (Paris, 1881), 1:755.

In the German *Spiel von jüngsten Tag*, an ensemble of angels played.

> Then they blow on the four horns with determination.[14]

[14] Heinzel, *Beschreibung des geistlichen Schauspiels*, 83.

Bowles suggests that there was an important symbolic relationship in using wind instruments in connection with these scenes of the last judgement.

> Wind instruments were indicative of life and resurrection to the early ecclesiastical writers, since the wind producing their sounds was analogous to *flatus*, or breath. This was scripturally based, since breath was a symbol of life in Genesis and of the resurrection in II Kings.[15]

[15] Bowles, 'The Role of Musical Instruments in Medieval Sacred Drama', 81, fn. 68.

Hell itself was often depicted by an earthen 'mouth', augmented with sulphurous fumes and real fire made from burning brandy. The sounds, or 'music' for Hell and the devil seem to have been made from percussion instruments, barrels filled with stones, etc.[16]

As might be expected, any scene calling for military or battle scenes call for wind instruments. Royalty, as in life, appeared with the 'loud' wind instruments. In the *Mystère de Saint Louis* (1472) a scene depicts the investiture of the son of a sultan.

> Play, minstrels and trumpeters so that your sound reverberates everywhere. Make merry, get together and cry with joy: sing, dance, and everybody act with complete gaiety and happiness.
> (Stage direction: The trumpets, minstrels, drums, and all available instruments should sound)[17]

This rich usage of instrumental music in the sacred drama suggests to some that there was more use of instruments in the church service itself than most history texts would suggest. Safowitz summarizes this viewpoint.

> The similarity between the description of instrumental participation with the organ in the Church and the orchestra of the religious drama might offer a clue to the instruments which were tolerated in the Church in the later middle ages. Certain music historians have been reluctant to consider that such a connection might exist, but ... one would suspect that the preference for loud (wind) instruments in the plays extended to the music within the Church walls ... and was eventually applied to the liturgical music.[18]

The documentation given in the previous pages prove his hypothesis is quite correct. These appearances of wind ensembles in the actual church services of the fifteenth century set the stage and made possible the further development which resulted in the extraordinary Italian church music for wind instruments of the sixteenth century. For the moment, the parishioner could finally, after fifteen centuries, fully appreciate Psalm 98:6:

> With trumpets and the sound of the horn
> Make a joyful noise before the King, the Lord!

[16] A miniature, ca. 1410, *De l'institucion des gieux qui s'appellent sceniques*, from the Jean de Berry collection (Philadelphia Museum of Art, Mss. Collins 45.65.1, fol. 26) shows two shawms(?) and a rare percussion instrument in a theater iconography.

[17] Bowles, 'The Role of Musical Instruments in Medieval Sacred Drama,' 79.

[18] Safowitz, 'Trumpet Music and Trumpet Style,' 33–34.

PART IV
The Civic Wind Band

The Civic Wind Band

DURING THE MIDDLE AGES many towns in Western Europe built great encircling walls for security. As night approached, even with the gates closed, security remained a primary concern for now in a town without lights there was fear of human predators, rouges, and especially fire—which could destroy the entire town.

It is from these same concerns that the towers were built along the walls and with them comes an important civic employee, the watchman. By the thirteenth century the larger towns had great numbers of these towers; for example, Milan had one hundred and twenty and Frankfurt one hundred and forty.[1] Kastner believes the origin of these towers can be found earlier in the Middle Ages in portable towers which could be moved with armies for lookout purposes.[2]

Some of these towers also had a large bell suspended at the top which served as a means of communicating signals, thus one also finds bells in the medieval civic towers for the same reason.

It is thought that sometime in the late twelfth century the practice began of placing wind instrument players, trumpet-types at first, in the towers, from which we can date the beginnings of official civic music in modern Europe. As opposed to the mere bell-ringer, a musician could give a much more precise signal. For example, whereas the bell-ringer could announce the outbreak of a fire, the musician, by a recognizable short fanfare, could at the same time indicate the location and severity of the fire. While on duty he could also, as we shall see, provide a number of other valuable civic functions, from musically announcing the time of day (important especially at night, when one could not see the town clock) to warning lovers of the approach of dawn.[3]

This civic musical watchman went under the name, in English, which described what he did mostly: 'wait.' The word can be traced to several ancient languages, from Anglo-Saxon, 'Wacian,' to Icelandic, 'waka,' to old German, 'wahta,' or 'wahte' (modern German, 'Wachter,' means watch or guard).

[1] Edmund A. Bowles, 'Tower Musicians in the Middle Ages,' in *Brass Quarterly* 5 (1962): 91.

[2] Kastner, *Manuel Général*, 80ff.

[3] Wangermée, *Flemish Music*, 179, adds, 'In Germany, France and the Low Countries, many songs present this personage who warns lovers of the coming of dawn: "die wachter blaest sinen horen" say those songs which, in French, are called *chansons d'aube*, aubades, songs of dawn.'

The Norman–French could not pronounce the 'W' and so the word became 'Guet' or 'Gaite,' and for centuries a morning salutation was 'bon-gaite.'

One of the earliest references to this musician–watchman is found in an early thirteenth-century treatise, *De Naturis Rerum*, by Alexander Neckham, an English Abbot.

> Let there also be watchmen (Waytes) on guard making a loud noise and din with their horns.[4]

One of the most famous anecdotes about these tower musicians concerns a lonely trumpeter in Cracow[5] who faithfully blew a warning of the approach of the Tartar hordes in 1241. In the middle of his fanfare, a Tartar arrow pierced his throat and the fanfare was left unfinished. Until the present day the watchmen of Cracow have performed this unfinished fanfare in his honor.[6]

As the reader will see in the following pages, these watchmen–musicians, as paid civic employees, were gradually called upon to assist with other routine civic duties. One such duty was to accompany the civic announcer as he informed the citizens of important news.[7] To help impress, by example, the citizens, he also played as prisoners were paraded through the streets to the whipping post with chamberpots hanging from their necks[8] and accompanied prostitutes to their public flogging.[9]

By the end of the thirteenth century these civic musicians also began to perform a wide range of civic entertainment functions. Foremost among these was the official town banquet held in honor of visiting dignitaries.[10] They also performed for the common citizens at fairs or for dances in the town square.[11]

The transition from the original watchman to the musician performing a wider range of functions was made possible in part by the improvements in the instruments themselves, through new metallurgical techniques, new alloys, etc. Soon one reads of towns replacing the old buisine, a relic of the crusades, with a more modern trumpet. The town of Dijon, for example, petitioned the Duke of Burgundy in 1425 for permission to use a trumpet because,

---

[4] Quoted in Joseph Bridge, 'Town Waits and their Tunes,' *Proceedings of the Musical Association* 5 (1927–1928): 65. (Assint etiam excubiae vigiles (veytes) cornibus suis strepitum et clangorum facientes)

[5] According to Salmen, *Der Fahrende Musiker*, 172, Cracow already had ten 'Stadtpfeifer' in the year 1390.

[6] The fanfare is reproduced in Stephen Mizwa, *Nicholas Copernicus* (New York: Kosciuszko Foundation, 1943), 73. Cracow today still employs six tower trumpeters, now graduates of the local music schools. Each day one of them climbs the dark, stone spiral staircase, and then four stories of wooden ladders in the five hundred year old tower. The contemporary tower watchman has a television set, a heater, and a hot plate to cook soup. If he stays on the job for forty years, the city promises to retire his trumpet to a local museum!

[7] Examples of early iconography which pictures this function can be found in *Histoire de Charles Martel* (Brussels, Royal Library, Mss. 7, fol. 18v.) and in the Jean Chartier, *Chronique du temps Charles VII* (Paris, National Library, Mss.fr. 2691, fol. 95v, see picture opposite).

[8] Three musicians can be seen playing during an execution, ca. 1475, in a painting (Nr. 198) now in the John and Mable Ringling Museum of Art, Sarasota, Florida. An account of trumpets and shawms playing as prisoners are marched through the streets can be found in Hugh Baillie, 'A London Gild of Musicians, 1460–1530,' *Proceedings of the Royal Musical Association* 83 (1956–1957), 16.

[9] An example of a trumpet player playing for such a flogging can be seen in the Jean Froissart, *Chroniques*, ca. 1468–1469, now in the Berlin, Staatsbibliothek, Depot Breslau 1, Mss. Rehd. 3, fol. 44.

Musician accompanying the town herald (Jean Chartier, *Chronique du temps Charles VII*)

many lords and foreigners make fun of the horn because it is degrading; and it would be a much greater honor for the town to have a trumpet rather than a horn.[12]

During the fifteenth century another conversion takes place with the introduction of the slide trumpet, which also seems to be concurrent with the arrival of three-part instrumental music. The development and improvement of the shawm also must have helped increase the opportunities for performance by the civic musician. This instrument had also been used in the tower from an early date and was, in fact, known for a time in England as the 'wayte pipe.'

[10] In Lille in 1489 one reads of a rather unusual example of three-part trumpet music for such a banquet. See A. de la Fons-Mélicocq, 'Les ménestrels de Lille,' in *Archives historiques et littéraires du nord* (1885), 58ff.

[11] An early English public dance was accompanied by 'loude cry of shallys (shawms).' See John Lydgate, *Prilgrimage of the Life of Man*, ed. F. J. Furnivall (London, 1905), 387.

[12] O. Longeron, 'La trompette d'argent,' in *Mémories de la Commission des antiquitiés de la Côte d'Or* (9, second series), 92.

What do we know of the music these multi-part civic wind bands performed? Because so few fifteenth-century manuscripts are extant and because most iconography pictures the wind players without music, most scholars have assumed the players only improvised.[13] There is some evidence, which will be given below, which suggests that these wind bands did play from music on occasion. Perhaps it is best to think of this question in terms of the function of the music performed, rather than in terms of the abilities of the players. There must have been many kinds of events for which improvised music was not only traditional, but logical and practical. The basse-dance is a well-documented example of the extraordinary abilities of these wind bands to perform with improvisation in more than one voice.[14] On the other hand, it is difficult to believe that the performance of multi-part chansons and motets in banquet and tower concerts, not to mention the church, were accomplished without some form of written music.

Another factor which may have delayed the performance of music as we know it today, reading from music and the concept of rehearsal, which follows automatically, lies in the concept and function of music itself before the fifteenth century. This idea is brilliantly reviewed by Huizinga.

> Art in those times was still wrapped up in life. Its function was to fill with beauty the forms assumed by life. These forms were marked and potent. Life was encompassed and measured by the rich efflorescence of the liturgy: the sacraments, the canonical hours of the day and the festivals of the ecclesiastical year. All the works and all the joys of life, whether dependent on religion, chivalry, trade or love, had their marked form. The task of art was to adorn all these concepts with charm and colour; it is not desired for its own sake, but to decorate life with the splendour which it could bestow. Art was not yet a means, as it is now, to step out of the routine of everyday life to pass some moments in contemplation; it had to be enjoyed as an element of life itself, as the expression of life's significance. Whether it served to sustain the flight of piety or to be an accompaniment to the delights of the world, it was not yet conceived as mere beauty.[15]

Therefore, when the civic wind bands of the fifteenth century began to give brief concerts from the towers, in the public squares, and as part of civic banquets, an historic moment had occurred in the history of western music. Not only were these the first real concerts, but they represented the first small step toward music as an art and not a mere craft.

[13] The best explanation for the lack of actual original wind ensemble music before 1500 lies not in the performance practices but in the delay in the development of printed music. After all, what would we know about even the later Renaissance music of all kinds if only the extant manuscripts were available today?

[14] Polk, *Flemish Wind Bands*, devotes the larger part of his study to the investigation of what these actual improvisation methods might have been.

[15] Johan H. Huizinga, *The Waning of the Middle Ages* (New York: Doubleday Anchor, 1954), 243–244.

13 Civic Wind Bands in Italy

If one considers the important role which wind music played during the Roman Empire, it should be no surprise that it is in Italy that one finds some of the oldest accounts of civic wind music of the modern era. Although accounts are by no means continuous, an occasional reference, as for example by San Girolamo in 379,[1] hints at the possibility that the traditions of music for civic celebrations and ceremonies may actually have linked these two periods.

The earliest musical institution of modern Italy can be dated to an occupation of Milan by the Franconian King, Conrad II (1024–1039). In 1037, Aribert, Archbishop of Milan, seeking to organize the resistance of the town's people, created a civic symbol called the *carroccio*.[2] This was a large wagon which contained an altar, the civic flag, and at the rear eight trumpeters who played a fanfare to assemble the people. The priests, on the wagon, read a field mass and gave the last rites for those killed in the resistance against the Franks. The trumpeters, who carried the rank of officer, performed another fanfare at the end of the service, to renew the fight. It was, writes an Italian author,

> a curious emblem of superstition and faith, of popular poetry and military discipline, of fantastic images of religion and the nation; a wagon of victory and later of peace around which you would fight with energy and die with enthusiasm.[3]

In peace time the *carroccio* was used for important civic celebrations. One sees it, for example, when the Queen of Sicily visited Milan on 7 October 1268, and the civic band of Milan (*tamburi, ciaramelle e trombe*) performed seated upon it.[4] Several other cities in Italy also had these movable civic wagons, in particular Venice and Florence.[5]

References to Italian civic wind music in the twelfth century are still very rare. Definite indications that such organizations existed include a reference to the performance of civic 'trombe e i corni' in Milan in 1121[6] and one from Genoa, where already in 1180 a visitor reported 'jogleurs, chanteors e

[1] See Alessandro Vessella, *La Banda* (Milan: Istituto Editoriale Nazionale, 1935), 34–35.

[2] Gottfried Veit, *Die Blasmusik* (Innsbruck: Verband Südtiroler Musikkapellen, 1972), 21.

[3] Romualdo Bonfadini, 'Le origini del Comune di Milano,' in *Albori della Vita Italiana* (Milano, 1897).

[4] Bernardino Corio, *L'Historia di Milano volgarmente scritta* (Padoa, 1646), 251. In the earliest records no specific definition can be made for 'tromba, trombettieri, tombetti, or trombatta.' The 'ciaramella,' or 'cennamella,' was a pre-shawm reed instrument. See Vessella, *La Banda*, 33, 69.

[5] Filippo Bonanni, *Gabinetto armonico pieno d'istrumenti sonori indicati* (Rome, 1722).

[6] Corio, *L'Historia di Milano*, 57.

troubadours' in residence.[7] A notarized document from 1213 converts the service of twenty-four musicians from the court of Monferrato to municipal duty.[8]

An early writer, Froissart (1333–1400), heard this band in person. Traveling there in 1390 with French and English troops under the leadership of the Duke of Burgundy, he reported the welcoming ceremonies.

> Great beauty and great pleasure there was to see the ... banners, pennants, richly decorated with the arms of the city, flying in the wind and resplendant in the sunshine, and to hear the trumpets and clarions (trompettes et des claironceaux) resound and other minstrels performing their craft on bagpipes, shawms and drums (pipes et de chalummelles et de naquaires), so much that the sounds and the voices caused the sea to vibrate throughout.[9]

For the thirteenth century there is sufficient evidence to establish the fact that some cities had regular paid civic bands. In Florence, for example, a civic document dated 8 February 1232 says the band should have both summer and winter uniforms in order that they can represent the city in an honorable manner.[10] There are several extant mid-thirteenth century documents from Florence relative to the hiring of additional trumpets for duty in the civic militia.[11] By the end of the thirteenth century one can find an extant contract, dated 1291, for the engagement of six trumpets (*sei tubatores*) for the city.[12] It is also in the thirteenth century that one finds for the first time a kind of minstrel guild established in Florence, the 'La Filarmonica dei Laudesi.'[13]

For most of the fourteenth century the civic wind music in Florence seems to have been primarily performed by trumpets. There is a document from 1339 relative to the employment of ten trumpets; another regarding nine trumpets in 1351; and a contract in 1358 for six trumpets, a *naccherino* and *cennamellai*, to be paid one lire for each month of service.[14]

Near the end of the fourteenth century the civic music of Florence seems to have undergone dramatic growth, for between 1386 and 1390 a re-organization occurred creating three separate ensembles.[15] First there was the *pifferi*, a shawm ensemble of three players. This ensemble was primarily musical and provided music for important civic occasions and was on call daily to play at the city hall (*Palazzo*). The second

[7] Grove, 7:204.

[8] Ibid.

[9] Jean Froissart, *Les Chroniques*, in *Historiens et Chroniqueurs du Moyen Age* (Bruges, 1963), 714.

[10] Giuseppe Zippel, *I Suonatori della Signoria di Firenze* (Trento, 1892).

[11] Vessella, *La Banda*, 37.

[12] Grove, 7:205.

[13] Zippel, *I Suonatori della Signoria di Firenze*.

[14] Emanuele Repetti, *Compendio Storico della città di Firenze, sua comunità diocesi e compartimento fino all'anno 1849* (Firenze, 1849) and Vessella, *La Banda*, 41.

[15] Keith Polk, 'Civic Patronage and Instrumental Ensembles in Renaissance Florence' (unpublished), 4ff. Professor Polk, after his brilliant studies on the bands of the Low Countries, has now taken on the 'uncatalogued, chaotic riches of the Florentine archive.' I am indebted to him for this ever generous sharing of his wealth of knowledge.

ensemble consisted of six trumpets, the *trombetti*. They represented the glory of the city, performing for the reading of announcements and proclamations, etc., and were expected to serve in battles. The third ensemble was called the *trombadori* and were paid less. Their instrumentation and function is not entirely clear, but they seem to have consisted of wind and percussion instruments, used perhaps for entertainment purposes.

In Siena, the earliest document which mentions the employment of civic 'tabatores e tamburelli' is dated 1262.[16] It says the band was to accompany the city fathers when they left the city hall and were to perform for all civic celebrations, banquets, etc. The players were given clothing, housing, and a monthly salary based on the amount of performance. The purchase and care of the instruments was the responsibility of the players.

These records indicate that the average number of players in the Siena civic band during the thirteenth century was five, but the number grew to nine by the beginning of the fourteenth century. Documents from 1309 and 1310 promise to purchase new clothes for the civic 'trombatori, cianamella e tamburello' once a year and also imply the beginning of an educational program to train new players under the direction of the mayor. These players were also given food and housing and were not permitted to associate with former friends or visit their families, an isolation which was perhaps intended to mark the exclusive honor of being permitted to serve the city.

In the Republic of Pisa, a document of 1324 discusses a civic band of four trumpets, 'nacchere e cennemella.' They were paid four lire per month with an allowance of ten lire for clothing. If they failed to wear their official red gowns they were subject to a fine. One of their duties, outlined in this document, was to wake, dress themselves, and parade around the public square before the ringing of the bells, to announce the new day. If they failed to do this, they were also fined.[17]

A similar role was expected of the civic band in Bologna, ca. 1336. Following an old tradition, the nine trombetti, 'gnaccarino' and piferi were to play each day at three o'clock in the morning.[18] Civic wind bands in Bologna can be documented back to an ensemble called 'trombe e de trombette' which played as civic announcements were read.[19]

[16] Vessella, *La Banda*, 39.

[17] Zippel, *I Suonatori della Signoria di Firenze,* and Francesco Bonaini, *Statuti inediti della città di Pisa* (Firenze, 1870), 2.

[18] Antonio di Paolo Masini, *Bologna perlustrata* (Bologna, 1649). (all'usanza antica di Bologna, cioe alle hore tre di notte).

[19] Grove, 3:184.

For Perugia one finds an actual contract from 1342 for the eight members of the civic band, called 'Trombadore del Commune de Peroscia.'[20] The contract calls for the players to always be at the service of the city and sets fines of twenty-five *libre di danaro* if they fail to do so. They are to have horses only at their own risk and danger. Their silver trumpets belong to the city and must be returned when requested; these instruments are to be played exclusively for the public and not for their own private use, at the risk of a fine of ten *libre di danaro*. Finally, there is an interesting comment that players were to perform at the usual civic banquets, etc., but also in the public square for the joy of the public. Failure to do this resulted in a fine of twenty *soldi di danaro*.

[20] Vessella, *La Banda*, 44–45, gives the names of these players.

In Lucca a similar contract exists, dated 21 September 1308, for the 'trombetta et tubatores lucani communis.' One who heard this band during the arrival ceremonies for an official visitor in 1325 speaks of the air being 'filled with the sounds of bells and trumpets.'[21] By 1377 this band had five *trombetti*, one *tubatore*, and two *nactarini*, the latter replaced by four *tamburini* in 1391.[22]

[21] Antonio Mazzarosa, *Atti e memorie della R. Accademia di Lucca*, 3.

[22] Vessella, *La Banda*, 44.

There were no doubt smaller towns which could not afford a regular civic band, but hired players only as needed for important civic occasions. Such an example was perhaps Arezzo, which set aside three hundred lire per year for hiring 'nacchere, trombe e cennamelle.'[23]

[23] Ibid., 42.

One can see how important these early civic wind bands were, from the perspective of the town government, in a document dated 1395 in the civic archives in Treviso.

> Item: the above said lords, the consuls and the 18 (councillors), being in the above said palace which is the dwelling and habitation of the consuls and of the leaders, by right of their office resolved that, out of the funds of the community of Treviso, money should be given to Pietro di Bartolomeo Boldrani herewith, in order that he could buy a trumpet and learn to play it: for the presence of artists increases the honor of the whole community [!]; and the said Pietro would then be able also to give evidence of his skill, and thus serve the community. Furthermore; he is above all a very poor person, and so to provide for him mercifully is an act of charity acceptable both to God and to the saints. So it was arranged that he should be given one florin, which he should at once have from the funds of the said community for his legitimate expenses.[24]

[24] Quoted in Don L. Smithers, *The Music and History of the Baroque Trumpet before 1710*. (London: Dent, 1973), 75–76.

During the fifteenth century a great period of growth occurs in the Italian civic bands, both in size and purpose. Now many of these bands carry the title of 'Concerti,' a name which the reader will see in a later volume will carry the wind ensemble tradition through the Baroque to the foundation of *Harmoniemusik* in the Classic Period.

In fifteenth-century Florence, despite vast amounts of civic funds spent on defense, these ensembles continued to grow and flourish. The pifferi ensemble now had four regular members, although a city statute of 1415 specified ten.[25] Beginning with the employment of a German-speaking shawmist in 1401, a strong preference for foreign musicians now characterizes this ensemble. In fact, the trombonists, now members of the pifferi ensemble, were German-speaking during the entire fifteenth century. One of these, Master Augustine of Augsburg, who served in Florence from 1489 to 1493, may have been the same person who appears later in the wind band of Maximilian I.[26] This preference for German-speaking musicians in the Florence wind band can also be seen in the use of a German word, *musizierten* (modern German, *musizieren*, 'to perform music'), in a civic document from the end of the fifteenth century. Now the pifferi ensemble of three shawms and two trombones, as well as the ensemble of six trumpets, are required to play every Sunday at the city hall, in addition to the usual processions and ceremonies.[27]

During the fifteenth century one sees the pifferi (shawm) ensemble as a separate civic band throughout Italy. In Siena, in 1423, there were on civic payrolls seven trumpets, four pifferi and a 'naccherino.'[28] By the end of the century the band was known as the *Concerto di Palazzo* and remained in existence until the fall of the republic. Vessella gives the instrumentation for this band in 1487 as ten trumpets, four pifferi, trombone, and 'nacchere.'[29] Another large fifteenth-century civic band can be found in Lucca, the *Concerto della Signoria di Lucca*. There there were no fewer than seventeen players, four pifferi, nine trumpets, three trombones, and a 'tabatore.'[30]

The shawm ensemble (*bifari*) also appears in Perugia during the fifteenth century and these players are required to play not only for official civic occasions, but 'for the enjoyment of the public.'[31] This language signals the beginning of public concerts in the modern meaning. The most famous of such con-

[25] Polk, 'Civic Patronage,' 16; Grove, 6:647.

[26] Polk, 'Civic Patronage,' 17.

[27] Luigi Cellesi, 'Documenti per la storia musicale di Firenze,' in *Rivista Musicale Italiana* 34 (1927): 285.

[28] Vessella, *La Banda*, 40.

[29] Ibid.

[30] Ibid., 44.

[31] Ibid.

certs in the fifteenth century were found in Bologna, which had begun the century with three shawms, eight trumpets, and a drummer (*naccarino*). By the end of the century, ensembles of eight shawms and eight trombones and cornetti gave daily concerts of an hour duration before the city hall.[32]

It is possible that such daily concerts by civic wind bands were more wide spread at this time, for a similar reference by an eyewitness from Turin describes an hour-long concert from a tower or arcade of an official building.

> Ma che alegrezza se alde tutto il zorno de quel pifari de la signoria che sona in cima a un pergolo del palazzo un'ora de longo![33]

Among the most important civic celebrations in Italy were those of the patron saint of each city, a combined religious and civic observance. In Florence this festive occasion fell on 23 June and one fifteenth-century eyewitness reports that the processions, balls, and banquets turned the area into a paradise of music and joy. On the first day of the celebration, statues and relics of the saint were carried in solemn procession to the Church of San Giovanni to the sound of shawms and trumpets. On the second day offerings were similarly taken to the church with 'great pomp.'[34] In a similar ceremony the civic trumpets and drums of Lucca celebrated the Feast of San Regolo.[35]

There were also regional festivals inaugurated by the local aristocracy on behalf of the citizens. For example, in 1472 the Duke of Ferrara began a celebration called *dell'andare alla ventura*, held the night before Ephiphany. The gentlemen of the city, led by the duke himself, filled the streets with singing 'all'improvviso' and accompanied by a 'small orchestra of wind instruments.' Carrying torches, they went from door to door begging 'ventura,' that is to say a great amount of poultry, cheeses, and wines, which they ate at the end of the procession.[36]

The great city-states like Venice often had celebrations of a political nature which reached vast proportions. An allegorical procession in Venice on 12 April 1495, was organized to celebrate a new treaty between the Republic of Venice, Maximillian of Austria, Ferdinand of Spain, the Duke of Ferrari, and the Pope. The various fraternal orders of Venice, those of the *scuole*, as well as the various trade guilds, joined with civic

---

[32] Lodovico Frati, *La vita privata di Bologna* (Bologna: Zanichelli, 1900), 189.

[33] Andrea Calmo, *Lettere*, ed. Vittorio Rossi (Turin, 1888), 331.

[34] Cesare Guasti, *Le Feste di San Giovanni Battista in Firenze* (Florence, 1884), 7. A miniature from 1403 shows the town officials in a torch procession in Perugia, led by two trumpets and a timpanist (Perugia, Biblioteca Comunale Augusta, Mss. 973, fol. 2).

[35] Luigi Nerici, *Storia della musica in Lucca* (Lucca, 1880), 182.

[36] Antonio Frizzi, *Memorie per la storia de Ferrara* (Ferrara, 1847), 91–92. No doubt wealthy middle class persons also had small wind ensembles among their servants. A manuscript (Vienna, National Library, Ms. Ser. nov. 2644, fol. 104) which belonged to a prosperous tradesman, named Ceruti, in late fourteenth-century Verona, includes a picture called 'Hygienic Dance' and shows two shawms and a bagpipe player playing in a private home for a dance.

officials to participate in the parade.[37] They carried officials in elaborate chairs, a model of the School of Saint Giovanni with forty chandeliers, a fountain with flowing perfumed water, and an enormous paper map of the world. The church officials carried the cross, sheltered by a canopy of gold, and relics: the foot of Saint Paul and the head of Santa Barbara.[38] This parade must have looked very much like the one pictured in a painting of the following year by Gentile Bellini, *Procession in the Piazza*.[39] Pictured here are a total of ten wind players of trumpets, shawms, and sackbuts, dressed in the uniform of the doge, whose wind band usually numbered six during the fifteenth century.

[37] Minstrel guilds began in Italy in the early thirteenth century. Early guilds included, in addition to the one in Florence mentioned above, fourteenth-century ones in Bologna and Lucca, according to Edmund A. Bowles, 'Musical Instruments in Civic Processions during the Middle Ages,' *Acta Musicologica* 33, no. 2/4 (Apr–Dec 1961): 156.

[38] Bridgman, 'Fêtes italiennes,' 36.

[39] These annual processions in Venice can be documented to one in the thirteenth century which included six trumpets and six pifferi marching immediately behind the flag of the republic. See Vessella, *La Banda*, 36.

Left: Detail from the middle right of *Procession in the Piazza*, by Gentile Bellini, showing ten wind players.

The civic bands, who would have always played a role in great processions such as those described, probably found their most rewarding musical experience in the official civic banquets where they would have been heard in an environment more approximating a concert. A civic welcome in Florence in 1459, extended to Galeazzo Maria Sforza, first provided a dinner in his honor at one of the private country estates of the Medici family, where one heard music by the 'soft' instruments, harps, viols, etc.; however, when the official civic banquet was held to honor the young Sforza, it was the music of shawms and the sackbuts which began to sound.

> ... pifferi d'l trombone
> cominciaro a sonare ...[40]

[40] Otto Gombosi, 'About Dance and Dance Music in the Late Middle Ages,' in *Musical Quarterly* 27, no. 3 (July 1941): 293.

Not all civic occasions were so formal in nature, of course. One reads that in Florence trumpet and shawm bands played for the yearly carnival.[41] In the city of Udine, where civic shawm players can be documented to 1379, the civic appearances included horse races and archery contests.[42]

[41] E. Elsner, *Untersuchungen der instrumentalen Besetzungspraxis der weltlichen Musik* (Leipzig, 1925), 21ff.

[42] Grove, 19:308.

As in the rest of Europe, the Italian civic band members found a regular source of extra income by performing for weddings of the wealthy middle-class businessmen. In Italy one finds an unusual documentation in the form of paintings on *cassoni*, large chests given to the brides by their parents. One such *cassone*, illustrating the story of Aluceius and Lucrezia, shows the wedding party dancing in the street, before a large palace, to the music of four shawms.

A more famous example is the *cassone* for a bride of the Adimari family, painted in 1450 by an unknown artist.

> Five couples are dancing underneath a baldachin in front of the open loggia of the palace. The Baptistery of Florence is shown in the background. The group is dancing the *chiarenzana*, the much loved wedding dance of the early Renaissance. The bride and bridegroom form the last couple. The former can easily be identified by her headgear of peacock feathers. The musicians, who are provided with three shawms and a slide trumpet, are seated at the left, one of them—a shawm player—reaching out for a cup of wine. They are men in the service of the city-republic of Florence, as is indicated by the fact that their instruments are decorated with its banner.[43]

[43] Gombosi, 'About Dance,' 291–292, which includes a reproduction of this painting. A miniature from Padua, ca. 1390, showing the exchange of rings in a civic ceremony pictures two timpani, two shawms, two trumpets, and a bagpipe (Dublin, The Chester Beatty Library, Hs. W 76A, fol. 113v.).

The civic musicians were also hired by students who had obtained the doctorate to celebrate their new title. A Bologna statute of 1405 speaks of the trumpets being ready for the ceremonies and indicates they are to be paid more if on horseback. A later statute, of 1436, indicates the candidate can not have trumpet music, but that the newly created doctor could leave the cathedral with four trumpets. A list of payments for such a ceremony in the same year includes the four trumpets and three shawms.[44]

[44] Nan Cooke Carpenter, *Music in the Medieval Universities* (Norman: University of Oklahoma Press, 1958), 35–37. A similar statute exists from Padua in 1331.

14 *Civic Wind Bands in England*

CIVIC WIND BANDS IN ENGLAND began, as elsewhere, out of a concern for security. This is clearly evident in the oldest extant reference to this tradition, an order issued by King Henry III.

> ... but for a full remedy of enormities in the night ... in the yeere of Christ 1253 Henrie the third commanded Watches in Cities, and Borough Townes to be kept, for the better observing of peace and quietnesse amongst his people.[1]

[1] John Stowe, *Survey of London* (London, 1618), 158.

Only a single wind player, serving as the 'watch,' or 'wait,' appears to be mentioned until the end of the thirteenth century. Until then it seems that at least part of the responsibility for maintaining this watchman–musician rested with the person who lived nearest the watch point, as a London civic statute of 1296 suggests.

> (Each gate of the city is to be) shut by the servant dwelling there, and that he shall have a wayt at his own expense.[2]

[2] Alan Ross Warwick, *A Noise of Music* (London: Queen Anne Press, 1968), 33.

Perhaps a more significant form of payment to early wait musicians was the granting of the use of land in exchange for wait service. Already in the period of Henry III (1216–1272) one finds a record of 'Simon le Wayte' who held a virgate of land at Rockingham during his tenure as 'castle-wayte.' A similar musician, 'Gilbert the Wayte,' was paid in the same fashion during the reign of Edward I (1272–1307). Examples of this form of payment can be found during the subsequent four hundred years.[3]

[3] Langwill, *The Waits*, 171.

In addition to London, extant records suggest that by the fourteenth century more civic wind bands were now founded, including Leicester (1314), Exeter (1362), and York (1369). While the details of the specific duties of these bands are almost non-existant, it may be assumed the wait responsibility was their main function. A fourteenth-century Romance, *Kyng Alysaunder*, suggests that in addition these musicians were also performing for civic banquets.

When theo table was y-drawe, Theo Wayte gan a pipe blawe.[4]

    One of the traditional occasions for which there are frequent later references regarding the London Waits was the annual Lord Mayor's Procession. When King John, in 1215, granted a charter to the city and recognized the appointment of a mayor, he stipulated that the mayor present himself before the court. Until 1251 the mayor, together with the leaders of the city and representatives of the craft guilds (called 'Companies,' or 'Corporations,' in England), accomplished this by horse, hence the term 'Ridings.' By the fourteenth century this had evolved into a ceremonial occasion of a very festive nature. On such occasions the city hired additional musicians, from among the minstrel class, to augment the official city waits. Thus the Court Minute Book for 1369 lists payment to nine minstrels for playing and for their hoods and drink at the Lord Mayor's Day.[5] The craft guilds also began to hire minstrel bands at an early date to represent them in this parade. Apparently the rivalry was such, and minstrels so numerous, that the Court of Common Council in 1409 ordained that henceforth minstrels would no longer be permitted to ride before any company except the Mayor, and then only three bands at most.[6]

    Some of the more prosperous guilds seem to have had their own wind bands, as can be seen in the purchase by the Goldsmith Company, in 1391, of trumpets, clarions, a shawm, a bombard, a 'large shawm,' and a bagpipe. Their records for this year also indicate payment to four minstrels who had their own instruments. Another annual celebration in fourteenth-century London was Guild Day, when all the guilds employed minstrels for the procession. An eyewitness to this parade in 1396 observed horns and clarions.[7]

    By the fifteenth century London had a nine-member civic wind band and Dublin had eight members, however the standard size seems to have been six. In this century many more bands appear, including Beverly in Yorks (1423), Cambridge (1484), Canterbury (1492), Chester (1484), Colchester (1469), Coventry (1423), Darlington (1457), Dartford (1494), Doncaster (1457), Dover (1492), Kingston-on-Hull (1429), Maidenhead (1450), Maidstone (1492), Northampton (1493), Norwich (408),[8] Nottingham (1463), Salisbury (1409), Sandwich (1492), Shrewsbury (1437), and Southhampton (1433).[9]

---

[4] Ibid.

[5] Maurice Byrne, 'Instruments for the Goldsmiths Company,' in *The Galpin Society Journal* 24 (July 1971): 63.

[6] Ibid., 64.

[7] Paul Meyer, *La Manière de langage qui enseigne à parler et à écrire le Francais* (Paris, 1873, but written in 1396), 392 (Les corneours et clariours se comencent a corner et clarioner tres fixt.).

[8] A single Wait can be documented in Norwich as early as 1288 (Grove, 7:811).

[9] Langwill, *The Waits*, 181; and Walter Woodfill, *Musicians in English Society: From Elizabeth to Charles I* (Princeton: Princeton University Press, 1953), 293ff.

It was during this century that civic bands began to appear in uniform dress. As early as 1409 it was ordered that all musicians in the Lord Mayor's Procession in London should wear hoods of the city's colors, red and white.[10] Considering the lively competition which existed between cities in so many areas of life, one can imagine that each civic band was eager to outdo the others in the splendor of its regalia. Thus, in 1442, the London Waits petitioned the Lord Mayor and aldermen to be allowed a livery like waits in other towns.[11] In this case the aldermen agreed and the band appeared in blue gowns, red caps and silver collars with entwined letters 'S' (*Spiritus Sanctus*), and finally a silver badge bearing the arms of the city.[12] The Norwich Waits in 1435 wore cloaks of blue stamell cloth, and robes.[13] The beautiful silver chains, with civic arms, which so many of these civic wind bands wore are in some cases preserved in local museums. An early example, dating from 1476, can be seen today among the Exeter city regalia.[14]

As the civic bands began to appear in a broader range of activities, one begins to see more civic rules and regulations in their behalf. In the case of the Coventry civic Wait band, which numbered four members in 1423, one reads of an early instance of the designation of a leader.

> The Trumpet schall have the rule of the wayte and of them be Cheffe.[15]

In Liverpool, the chief was called 'Captain of the Waits,' while in Norwich he was termed, 'Headman.' In York the chief wait wore a tattered or pinked cap, a badge of some antiquity, the origin of which has not been discovered.[16]

In Coventry, one reads that in 1458 the town fathers appointed a kind of tax collector to accompany the wait band for the purpose of raising the funds for their support.

> Hit was ordyred yt an honest man in every ward should be assyned by ye Meir (Mayor) to go wt ye Wayts, to gader their wages quarterly at the petition of ye Wayts then beying.[17]

Besides these wages the Coventry Waits were also given food (horse meat!). However small their pay must have been, one contemporary chronicler noted, 'Observe that in those dayes they payd there mynstrells better than thyre preistes.'[18]

[10] Unsigned article, in Crewdson, *The Worshipful Company of Musicians*, 168.

[11] Ibid.

[12] Warwick, *A Noise of Music*, 36.

[13] Bridge, 'Town Waits,' 75.

[14] Langwill, *The Waits*, 176.

[15] Bridge, 'Town Waits,' 75.

[16] Ibid.

[17] Ibid., 80.

[18] Duncan, *Story of Minstrelsy*, 99.

One must assume that these forms of pay did not satisfy the Coventry Waits for they took it upon themselves to seek additional requests from nearby religious houses. In a civic order of 1467, they are instructed not to extend this search beyond the immediate town.

> Also it ye wayts of yis Cite it now be and hereaft to be shall not pass yis Citie but to Abbott's and Priors within ten myles of yis Citie.[19]

[19] Bowles, 'Tower Musicians,' 94.

This form of travel to gain donations from their performance was a common means of securing additional money. Having the opportunity to travel in the livery of the city identified the waits as law-abiding musicians and freemen, as opposed to the vagabond musicians.

By mid-fifteenth century, many cities still expected the wait band to perform some form of the old watch duty. In Dublin, an order of 1457 required a rather demanding night shift from its eight town waits.

> ... to perambulate the city nightly from curfew to five in the morning ... for which they would receive ... four pence of every hall and three pence of every shop within the city bounds.[20]

[20] Smithers, *Baroque Trumpet*, 117–118.

In London a similar order of 1454 requires the waits to make these nightly walks for the purpose of preventing robberies, but also for the recreation of the people.[21] One account of 1484 mentions that the London 'Wayts' serenaded the local citizens and businessmen on Christmas Day with carols.[22] Perhaps this indicates a changing of attitude toward these musicians, in any case, by the sixteenth century their function will be predominantly musical in nature.

[21] Woodfill, *Musicians in English Society*, 45.

[22] Paul Murray Kendall, *Richard the Third* (New York: Norton, 1955), 365.

The principal form of entertainment in which waits were expected to participate was the official civic celebration. In fifteenth-century London the Lord Mayor's Procession was still the most important annual event, now however it had become a parade on the river. Thus the wind ensembles hired by the various craft guilds now rode in boats rather than on horse. The Grocers' Company, for example, in 1435 authorized payment to,

> ... the handys of John Dodyn for mynstrelles ... amending of Baneris and hire of barges for ... goyng be watir to Westminster.[23]

The degree of attention which was focused on this annual event can be seen in 1483 when a dispute between two rival guilds, over which of their barges should have precedence in the water procession, actually resulted in 'bloodshed and loss of life.'[24] The mayor, of course, was represented each year by the London Waits.

Another cause for civic celebration occurred with any official appearance of a member of the royal family. Thus when the young Prince Edward arrived in Coventry, in 1474, he was received by the local town waits together with a variety of other musicians.

> With mynstralley of the Wayts of the Citie, with mynstrales of harpe and Dowsemeris, with mynstrealey of harpe and lute, by the Childer of Issarell syngyng, by ij knyghts armed with mynstralsy of smal pypis, and mynstraley of orgonpleyinge.[25]

A similar reference can be found in a work published in 1440, *Romance of Sir Eglamour*.

> grete lordys were at the Assent;
> Waytys blewe, to mete they wente.[26]

As in other countries, the civic waits were able to obtain a wide variety of other temporary performance opportunities to augment their income. In England they were hired frequently during the fifteenth and sixteenth centuries to provide music for the theater and on occasion even as substitute actors. In Shrewsbury, for example, an account for 1483 records payment of fifteen shillings,

> For the livery of the Common histriones called the waytes of the town.[27]

[23] Warwick, *A Noise of Music*, 21.

[24] Ibid., 22.

[25] Stevens, *Early Tudor Court*, 238.

[26] Langwill, *The Waits*, 172.

[27] Bridge, 'Town Waits,' 81.

15 Civic Wind Bands in the Low Countries

THE LOW COUNTRIES, while not yet a nation in the modern sense, were highly developed on the civic level before the sixteenth century. In many of these cities one can see considerable activity by the town wind band (*stad pijpers* or *scalmeyers*) in the fourteenth and fifteenth centuries.[1]

The average size of these bands before the sixteenth century was four players, under regular contract. Some cities had bands of larger or smaller sizes depending on the influence of economic and political fluctuations, as is the case today. Certainly it was a rare exception, even for a prosperous city, that Ghent had under contract in 1430 no fewer than sixteen trombones, three trumpets, and eighteen shawms (*pijpers*)![2]

At the end of the fifteenth century the combination of the military costs of the struggle against Maximilian I and the depression in the weaving industry, due to competition from England, combined to cause particularly hard times for the civic bands. Some towns which had just increased their number of players to five, such as Ghent and Bruges, now reduced them again to four. While many of these towns eventually recovered during the sixteenth century, some never did. Ieper today has only half the population it had in 1350!

The basic instrumentation of the four-member band was two shawms, a bombard or tenor shawm, and a sackbut as contra-tenor. What I identify as the sackbut, was called *tromper* in the actual town records of this century.[3] It seems clear, here, that a slide instrument was being described, although earlier in the fifteenth century it may have been a slide-trumpet.[4]

A three-member band would drop one of the shawms; when more than four players were used, it was the lower parts which received the additional support, which perhaps reflects the movement toward a darker, lower sound as would be preferred in the Renaissance.

Until about 1480 instrument purchases by the towns are almost exclusively shawms, bombards, or sackbuts. After this time purchases begin to include recorders, crumhorns, and cornetts. The professional civic bandsman was, of course,

[1] Much of this material is taken from Keith Polk's *Flemish Wind Bands*, and a paper, 'Ensemble Instrumental Music in Flanders, 1450–1550,' both unpublished.

[2] C. Snoeck, 'Notes sur les instruments de musique en usage dans les Flandres au moyen âge,' in *Compte Rendu de la Féderation Archéologique et Historique de Belgique* (1896), 276.

[3] Polk, *Flemish Wind Bands*, 41.

[4] References such as the famous description of a wind band by Johannes Tinctoris, in *De Inventione et Usu Musicae* (1487) leave no doubt regarding the existence of the trombone instrument. The true trumpet also existed, but was used apart from the town band. Many later writers, due to the similarity of *tromper* with *trumpet* have mistranslated this term.

expected to be able to play all of these instruments. Thus, when Joos Zoetens, a member of the Ghent civic band was contracted in 1493 to take on two apprentices, the contract read that he must teach them 'shawms, flutes, and other instruments.'[5] This versitility allowed the band to appear, as for example at a banquet concert, with enough instruments to create variety in texture from composition to composition.

It seems logical to assume that the town bands in the Low Countries began, as elsewhere, with the civic watchmen. They appear frequently in the town records of the early fourteenth century, but the practice may be older than the surviving documents.[6] These early wind players were expected to sound their instruments in case of fire or at the approach of the enemy. Since in this respect they were only as good as their eyes, one is not surprised to read that in Mechlin these players were given eye examinations, in addition to musical trials, as part of the auditions to fill vacancies.[7] By 1400–1413, Mechlin had two trumpets, four shawm players, and a drummer playing fanfares on the hour from the four cardinal points of the compass, from the highest church tower, as the town slept.[8] This surrogate clock-chime duty reminds one that the wind players of Ghent were also responsible for the lubrication of the town clock while they were in the tower and were given extra funds to purchase oil for this purpose.[9]

By providing so many services in the tower, not to mention those given on the ground, these wind players achieved a valued status. In Bruges, in fact, they were required to swear an oath not to quit the town's service for a specified term, to prevent their being hired away by a rival town or aristocrat.[10]

To help protect the players' rights, guilds were founded in the fourteenth century in most major cities. The oldest of record in the Low Countries is the minstrel guild of Bruges for which records date from 1292. The patron saints for some of these guilds were: St. Job, in Brussels and for Flanders; St. Job and St. Marie-Madeleine, for Brabant; St. Gilles, in Liege; and St. Cecile, for Hainaut.[11]

By the fifteenth century these civic wind bands had become more valued for their contributions to the broader range of civic entertainment and the watch duty was given over to separate trumpet players. One important appearance was in the civic processions (*Ommegang*) which were part of all important

[5] Polk, 'Ensemble Instrumental Music,' 17.

[6] Documents are extant which describe watch musicians in Bruges in 1310, in Mechlin in 1311, and in Antwerp's oldest surviving civic document, dated 1324. See Grove, 7:811.

[7] Raymond Joseph van Aerde, *Musicalia: Notes pour servir à l'histoire de la musique, du theatre et de la danse à Malines* (Malines: Dierickx-Beke, 1925), 4, 14.

[8] Ibid., 10.

[9] Ghent Municipal Archive, 'Financial Accounts, 1447–1448,' fol. 451v.

[10] Aerde, *Musicalia: Notes*, 4, 14.

[11] Vander Straeten, *La Musqiue*, 1:16; 4:79.

civic celebrations. The earliest reference to an *ommegang* performance, in Mons in 1342, indicates the trumpet and shawm players rode horses in the procession.[12] The fifteenth-century versions of these processions were more elaborate and cities would spend considerable sums of money to employ visiting bands or individual minstrels to help. One of the best known of these was one held each August in Termonde. Already in 1405 seventeen separate bands, totaling sixty musicians, participated in the procession and played concerts before the city hall. In 1477 seventy-one visiting musicians participated, including the civic wind bands from Ghent, Brussels, Mechlin, Antwerp, and Aelst, not to mention an ensemble of twenty-eight bagpipers.[13]

Mechlin also employed numerous visiting musicians for its annual Procession of Peace, held regularly from 1368 and apparently one of the most colorful of its kind (in 1436 one saw elephants and camels). In 1385 the procession included thirteen trumpeters and eighty-four minstrels and in 1414 there were twenty-four trumpeters and fifty-eight shawms. In 1418 the city fathers hired no fewer than two hundred and fifteen '*spellieden, pijpers*,' and '*snaerspeelders.*'[14] The Mechlin town band itself seems to have played from the tower, leaving the marching to the guests.

The arrival of a royal visitor required the town band not only for welcoming duties but for the inevitable official banquet. An early account describes the Count of Flanders visiting Ieper in 1326 and being met by the mayor and six minstrels.[15] A royal visitor traveling with trumpets of his own was often met by civic trumpeters as a gesture toward his rank. Thus, in 1476, when the Duke of Burgundy visited Ghent his six trumpeters were joined by twenty-four from the city in the welcoming ceremonies.[16]

More formal aristocratic occasions called for even greater participation by civic wind players. When Philip the Good traveled to The Hague for the marriage of Philippe de Courcelles, in 1432, he heard not only the minstrels of all the attending nobles, but the civic wind bands of Campen, Utrecht, Harlem, Leyde, and Delft.[17]

One imagines these welcome ceremonies as a profusion of signal-like trumpet calls coming from all directions, but an occasional remark by an eyewitness suggests that some-

[12] Ibid., 4:247.

[13] Wytsman, *Anciens airs et chansons populaires de Termonde*, quoted in Vander Straeten, ibid., 4:198.

[14] Ernest Closson, *La facture des instruments de musique en Belgique* (Brussels: Huy, Degrace, 1935), 65ff.; Bowles, 'Tower Musicians,' 160.

[15] Lambin, *Messager des Sciences* (1836), 186.

[16] Jacques du Clerq, *Mémoires*, ed. J.A. Buchon (Paris, 1838), 111.

[17] Jeanne Marix, *Histoire de la Musique et des Musiciens de la Cour de Bourgogne sous le règne de Philippe le Bon* (Strasbourg: Heitz, 1939), 29.

times perhaps it was a bit more organized, and perhaps even rehearsed. A reception in Ghent, in 1385, for the Duke and Duchess of Burgundy after the Battle of Tournai, included a performance by a large ensemble of wind instruments. One who heard this performance describes it as an ensemble which played together and was enjoyable to hear.

> les trompettes, clarons et ménestreuls de toutes manières d'instruments commencerent à jouer et sonner tout à une fois que c'estoit chose plaisante et mélodieuse à ouyr.[18]

[18] Kervyn de Lettenhove, 'Fragment inédit de Froissart,' in *Bulletin de l'Académie royale de Belgiques* (1868), 25:57.

Another musical clue in descriptions of ceremonies in which both the trumpets and the civic band performed is found in the choice of verbs used by the early scribes. Nearly always the trumpets are said to 'blow' (*gheblasen*) while the shawms are said to 'play' (*ghespeelt*).[19]

[19] Vander Straeten, *La Musique*, 4:127.

For many civic wind bands of the fifteenth century, the banquet concert, the short performance for the guests at the end of the banquet, not the 'dinner music' during the meal itself, was as close to the modern meaning of the word 'concert' as they ever came. For such an event the repertoire was still mostly transcribed vocal polyphony. A typical example was the performance of the Brussels civic band at a banquet for Philip of Burgundy (son of Maximilian I) in 1495 of 'various chansons.'

> Assavoir aux ménestreurs de la ville de Bruxelles, pour don que mondit seigneur leur en a fait pour une fois quant aujourdhuy ilz ont joué de leurs instrumens devant sa table plusieurs chansons de musique.[20]

[20] *Archives generales du royaume*, quoted in Vander Straeten, *La Musique*, 4:159–160.

Bruges was a city with a long tradition of concerts by the town band. Already in 1350 this organization was giving regular concerts in the main town plaza in front of the statue of the Virgin Mary.[21] A fifteenth-century contract for the city band goes into interesting detail regarding the band's concerts.

[21] Désiré van de Casteele, *Annales de la Société d'Emulation pour l'Étude de l'Histoire et des Antiquitiés de la Flandre* (Bruges, 1868), 64.

> Each of them are obligated to play at the front of the old hall at the customary place on all Sundays and Holy Days at 11:00 before noon and at 6:00 in the evening from Easter to *Baefmesse* (Feast of St. Bava, held on October one), and from *Baefmesse* to Easter at 3:00 in the afternoon; they are to play two chansons (liedekens) or motets (moteten) at each performance; each performer is to appear in livery and sign the work book.[22]

[22] Louis Gilliodts-Van Severen, 'Les ménestrels de Bruges,' in *Essais d'Archéologie Brugeoise* (Bruges: Imprimerie de L. de Plancke, 1912), 2:111.

Another very interesting document, from the civic accounts of Bruges for 1484–1485, suggests that perhaps not all references one reads of these bands performing 'motets' or 'chansons' were necessarily references to transcribed music. In this case, the city paid one of the priests of the cathedral to compose motets specifically to be played by the town band.

> Betaelt heer Casin de Brauwer, priester ende cantor van den Kinderen van Sint-Salvators, voor zyn salaris van den moyte by hem ghehadt van ghestelt ende ghemaect te hebben, ten diverschen stonden, zekere motetten, omme die by den menestruelen van deser stede ghespeelt te werdene.[23]

In addition to accounts of concerts before the city hall, there are references to concerts in the market place, which of course was another focal point for the people of the town. The *Chronik von Antwerpen* reports regular evening concerts by the six-member civic wind band (*Stadspeelieden*) in the main market place.[24] A similar account of concerts by the Mechlin band speaks of their performing overtures (*overijssche*) in the market place.[25]

The opening of the annual town fair was yet another occasion which demanded the appearance of the civic band. In one account, the opening of the fair in Bergen-op-Zoom, in 1499, this appearance included music of a concert nature.

> The singers, organist and city pipers sang certain motets during the night.[26]

A document from 1481 tells us that the Bruges wind band was paid to play every evening, '*tout la durée de la faire,*' and similar mention is frequently found for the Mechlin band.[27]

[23] Quoted in Vander Straeten, *La Musique*, 4:99.

[24] Leo Philips Maria de Barbure de Wesembeek, 'La musique à Anvers aux XIVe, XVe, et XVIe siècles,' in *Annales de l'Académie Royale d'Archéologie de Belgique* (Anvers, 1906), 243.

[25] Aerde, *Notes*, 24.

[26] Korneel Slootmans, 'De Hoge Lieve Vrouwe van Bergen-op-Zoom,' in *Jaerboek van de Oudheidkundige Kring de Ghulden Roos* (25), 212.

[27] Désiré van de Casteele, 'Préludes historiques sur la Ghilde des ménéstrels de Bruges,' in *Annales de la Société d'Emulation*, 3e série (Bruges, 1868), 3:65ff.; and, Aerde, *Notes*, 17–72.

16 Civic Wind Bands in France

ONLY A VERY FEW REFERENCES to civic wind music in France can be found from before the fourteenth century. These include only an occasional name, such as a minstrel called Eude, from twelfth-century Beauvais and a passing mention of musicians in the 1295 tax roll in Paris.[1]

[1] Grove, 2:326; 7:205.

By the fourteenth century minstrel guilds appear, such as the one in Marseilles which performed polyphonic compositions for voices and instruments and accompanied the civic secular and mystery plays.[2] There is extensive documentation for the minstrel guild in Paris, which will be discussed below. The formation of these guilds, early in the fourteenth century, suggests a richer and far earlier tradition than the surviving records.

[2] Ibid., 11:705.

Some of the earliest records of civic wind music deal with the watch, or tower music, during the fourteenth century in Paris and Marseilles.[3] The importance of this duty in Paris can be seen in a Parisian police document of 1372 which, in hope of guarding against false alarms, made 'unofficial' trumpet playing after the curfew hour a crime—weddings were excepted.

[3] Ibid. A miniature from ca. 1460–1470 in France shows a tower musician performing on a rather primitive horn-type instrument (Chantilly, Musée Condé, Ms.fr. 1363, fol. 8).

By the fifteenth century this duty seems to have become more ceremonial in character, with the Bishop riding the watch on horse, accompanied by clarions, trumpets and other instruments.

> Maistre Jehan Balue, evessque d'Evreux, fist le guet de nuit parmy ladicte ville, et mena avecques lui la compaignie dudit Joachin Rouault, avecques clerons, trompetes et autres instrumens sonnans, par les rues et sur les murs.[4]

[4] Jean de Roye, *Journal de Jean de Roye connu sous le nom de chronique scandaleuse*, ed. Bernard de Mandrot (Paris, 1894), 1:53.

In 1418, one 'knight of the watch' in Paris never went on duty without his own personal wait band. To frighten potential muggers, he would walk the streets with two or three minstrels 'playing loud instruments' (wind instruments) walking before him.

> Il y avait alors à Paris un chevalier du guet nommé Messire Gautier Rallart, qui ne se rendait jamais au guet sans se faire précéder de deux ou trois ménétriers qui jouaient très fort, ce qui paraissait très étrange au peuple et lui faisait dire qu'il semblait annoncer aux malfaiteurs: "Fuyez, car je viens!"[5]

[5] *Journal d'un bourgeois de Paris* (Paris: le Monde en 1018), 50.

In France one also reads of civic trumpets being used to accompany the town crier in his rounds of making official announcements. Thus, in Paris in 1418, to announce the armistice between England and France, the crier was accompanied by 'quatre trompes,' and also six minstrels, who were no doubt shawm and trombone players.[6]

[6] Ibid., 114.

Civic wind players must have appeared at all civic celebrations and processions. The earliest such reference, from 1391, seems to speak only of trumpets and drums.

> Quae guidem processio facta in dicta villa cum omnibus mimmis, tam cordarum grossorum instrumentorum "tromparum et taborellorum."[7]

[7] Auguste Bottée de Toulmon, *Dissertation sur les instruments de musique in Memoires de la Société des antiquaires de France* (Paris, 1844), 69.

One of the oldest French civic parades was the Procession of Our Lady, in Lille, dating from 1270. An early fourteenth-century account speaks of a procession of archers, crossbowmen, and cannoneers, accompanied by the civic 'trumpet' players and grotesquely dressed clowns. Each guild was present, with various insignia, together with city officials richly dressed in robes and fur, the clergy and members of the monastic orders with shrines and relics. At the end of the procession were all the visiting minstrels.[8]

[8] Léon Lefebvre, *Histoire du théâtre de Lille* (Lille, 1907), 1:38.

Official visits to a major city demanded the kind of pomp only the city trumpets could provide. Thus when the Duke of Bedford entered Paris in October 1424, preceded through the streets by his own four trumpeters, it was said he was received, 'as if he were God.'[9] The clergy greeted him at Notre Dame, singing hymns 'so pure.' There were players of organs and trumpets and all the bells were ringing.

[9] Bowles, 'Musical Instruments in Civic Processions,' 151–152.

> les chanoynes de Notre-Dame le receurent à la plus grant honneur, en chantant hymnes et louages que ilz peurent, et jouait-on des sorgues et de trompes; et sonnoient toutes les cloches.[10]

[10] *Journal d'un bourgeois de Paris*, ed. Alexandre Tuetey (Paris, 1888), 200.

When the Duke of Orleans returned from his visit to England, on 24 January 1448, he was welcomed by the 'loud minstrels' and allegories were performed upon twelve specially built scaffolds.[11] Similarily, when Louis IX visited Orléans in 1461, he passed two scaffolds on which were a wind band (haut ménestrels) and a children's chorus, singing with an organ.[12]

Actual documentation of French 'concert' activity by the wind bands is very rare. However, such references as the following ones are so similar in nature to those found in other countries that one may assume it was a broader tradition. In Lille, in 1480, one reads of a trumpeter, no doubt a slide instrument, and three minstrels, who are probably shawms, performing a typical daily duty of performances from the town tower.

> … tous le jours, au matin, à la cloche du jour et au vespre … sur le belfroy, bein et notablement à l'honneur de la ville.[13]

[11] Bowles, 'Haut and Bas: The Grouping of Musical Instruments in the Middle Ages,' in *Musica Disciplina* 8 (1954): 130–131.

[12] Yvonne Rokseth, *La musique d'orgue au XVe siècle et au début du XVIe* (Paris, 1930), 42.

[13] Alexandre de la Fons-Mélicocq, 'Les ménstrels de Lille,' in *Archives historiques et littéraires du Nord* (1885), 5:62.

Confrérie de St. Julien

On 14 September 1321, the day of the Festival of Saint-Croix, thirty-seven minstrels (male and female), led by a court minstrel named Pariset, presented to the Provost of Paris a document of eleven by-laws from which one dates the beginning of the minstrel guild of Paris. By 1331 they had constructed a chapel and hospital in the rue St. Martin, a building which apparently existed until the late eighteenth century.[14]

The original by-laws were aimed at attempting to restrict all public music in Paris to members of the guild. The fact that the first of these by-laws refers to 'the science and music of minstrelsy,' suggests that the profession had much earlier roots in Paris. Much of this document deals with the ethics of playing contracts: one may not leave an engagement to take another until the first one is finished; once one is contracted to play a particular job, one may not have another minstrel take his place—unless he is ill or in prison; and if one is hired to play for a wedding, one can not—on the side—also contract to be the head cook or to supply food, nor deprive any third person of their commission.

[14] A reproduction of a painting of this building can be seen in José Subirá, *Historia de la Música* (Barcelona, 1947), 600.

There were some restrictions on advertizing: one may not walk through the streets of Paris advertizing his availability, rather potential customers should be directed to the guild headquarters. This was perhaps aimed more at visiting, foreign minstrels than toward guild members themselves.

The by-laws also discuss the subject of apprenticeship. An apprentice may not accept a performance without his master's knowledge and the apprentice who is caught playing in a tavern is expelled.[15]

These statutes were extended several times to reflect the changing profession. A new statute in 1372 exempts minstrels from having to play 'serenades' at night, unless they are inside, in order to protect them from robbers. In 1395 a statute reveals singers (mouth-minstrels, as they are called) have been admitted into the guild. It forbids them, however, to sing songs which satirize the pope, king, or any of the great men of France, under penalty of prison with bread and water!

Further new statutes in 1407 go into more detail regarding the control over new members, in particular the apprentices. A young candidate had to go to the home of one of the members, 'masters,' to sign a formal contract. In theory, the apprentice program lasted six years and concluded with the performance of a *chef-d'oeuvre*. In practice, this period was usually shorter, especially in the case of the son of a current member of the guild. While there seems to be little evidence that many persons failed this apprentice program, the purpose of it is clear—to control the number of members.[16]

The leader of the guild was called the 'king' of the minstrels. The title itself, for the leader of a guild, can only be understood in the sociological perspective of this feudal and monarchial era. Moreover, in some ways he exercised powers like a king: he had the right to judge without appeal, he was the last resort in all that concerned the exercize of the craft, and he levied fines for offenses against the laws of the guild and controlled the apprentice program. The first of these 'kings' was Robert Caveron, 'roy des menestsreuls du royaume de France.' He was succeeded by Lorenz de Caveron (1349), Copin du Brequin (1357), and Jean Portevin (1392).

[15] Marie-Bernard Bernhard, 'Recherches sur l'histoire de la Corporation des Ménétriers ou Joueurs d'Instruments de la Ville de Paris,' in *Bibliothèque de l'Ecole chantes* (April, 1842), 24–27 (contains the original text of the 1321 by-laws).

[16] François Lesure, *Musique et Musiciens Francais du XVI Siècle* (Genève: Minkoff Reprint, 1976), 129ff.

Once each year a great procession was held to celebrate Epiphany. On this joyous occasion, the 'king' seems to have actually played the part of king. A document of 1367 speaks of the purchase of a 'crown' for the king to wear on 'le jour de la Tiphaine au roy des menestrels.'[17]

[17] Bernhard, 'Recherches,' 20.

17 *Civic Wind Bands in the German-Speaking Countries*

ALL MUSICIANS are familiar with the great German civic wind music of the seventeenth century, the Stadtpfeifer compositions of Pezel and Reiche. We are familiar with this period only because it is the first music of its kind for which we have extensive documentation, but actually it was the logical climax of a long period of German art. Even if the Stadtpfeifer activity of the earlier centuries is less familiar to us, it is possible that it was even more important to the development of German musical tradition than that of the seventeenth-century period.

> For a long time the former significance of the so-called Stadtpfeifers has been lost. In earlier times they played a great role and were often the only ones who carried the art of German music.[1]

While the extant evidence of early civic wind activity in Germany is very fragmentary, it does suggest a state of development surprisingly early. Already in the twelfth century, for example, an extant police statute from Mulhouse (then German-speaking) limits the number of wind players which can be used for private weddings at six.

> Zu der kockzyd sal man nicht mer hahn danne sechs spylmann dy tencze und reygin machin.[2]

According to Salmen, both Hamburg and Breslau had established four-men civic wind bands in the thirteenth century.[3] In Köln the street which is today called *Nächelsgasse*, was named *platea joculatorum*, already in 1231.[4]

Such civic wind players were the elite representatives of a broader number of minstrels who had begun to settle in the German cities, forming civic bands and guilds during the thirteenth century. It is at this same time that one finds increasing legal restrictions against the wandering minstrel in Germany.[5]

The Nuremberg Stadtpfeifers, ca. 1449, playing for the butchers' guild dance at the annual Schembart Carnival.

[1] Clemens Meyer, *Geschichte der Mecklenburg-Schweriner Hofkapelle* (Schwerin, 1913), 2.

[2] Marie-Bernard Bernhard, *Notice sur la Confrérie des Joueurs d'Instruments d'Alsace* (Paris, 1844), 5, fn. 2.

[3] Salmen, *Der Fahrende Musiker*, 89. During the fifteenth century the civic minstrels of Hamburg were under the direction of the council pastrycook!

[4] Ehmann, *Tibilustrium*, 8. Today's *Altgrabengässchen* was formerly known as *spilmannsgazze*.

[5] Arno Werner, *Vier Jahrhunderte im Dienste der Kirchenmusik* (Leipzig: Carl Merseburger, 1932), 200–201.

The Nicolai-Brüderschaft of Vienna, founded in 1288, has been mentioned above.[6] Lübeck also had such a fraternity in the thirteenth century, the *Marienbrüderschaft der Musicanten und Spielleute zu St. Catherinen*. The guild formed in Gdańsk (Danzig) during the fourteenth century was no doubt typical: it defined privileges for the members, established a seven-year apprenticeship program, and permitted itinerant minstrels to remain in town only two weeks.[7]

These guilds were ruled by an internal hierarchy, led by a *Comes joculatorum* (Lübeck, 1316), *spilgraf* (Regensburg, 1320, and Vienna, 1354), or *Pfeiferkonig* (Strasbourg).[8] This 'king,' or 'count,' and his minstrels celebrated a special holiday, *Jahrestag*, each year.[9]

From the fourteenth century one finds references to larger civic wind organizations, especially among the prosperous trading cities of the North. Bremen and Brandenburg had six and eight civic wind players already in 1303.[10] These, however, must have been somewhat unusual; more typical were the three- and four-member bands, such as those in Zwickau (1348), Nürnberg (1377), and Dortmund (1363).[11] Both the Nürnberg and the Dortmund references are from the oldest extant civic records dealing with civic music in those towns.

By the fifteenth century, the civic wind band had stabilized at three shawms and a sackbut or slide-trumpet. Such four-member civic wind bands can be documented in fifteenth-century Köln, Basel, and Freiburg.[12] Wealthy cities had even larger ensembles, as for example Bremen, which had seven to ten players; Halle, which had six players in 1482; and Lübeck, which had nine players in 1454.[13] The civic wind band most familiar to the modern reader is of course the one in Leipzig, yet extant documents permit the dating of this organization only from 1479. Leipzig added a fourth regular player at the end of the fifteenth century. While they all received free lodging from the city, there seems to have been some irregularity in their weekly pay, for a document of 1499 promises once again that they shall have their forty Groschen each week![14]

One may assume that one of the oldest duties of the early German civic wind players was the watch duty, as we have seen in the other countries of Western Europe. One of the oldest civic documents of Lübeck refers to the appointment of such a tower musician in 1280.[15] Civic records in Bremen men-

---

[6] Ehmann, *Tibilustrium*, 28, quotes some of the original 1288 charter.

[7] Grove, 7:207.

[8] Grove, 7:811; Lesure, *Musique et Musiciens Français*, 138.

[9] Josef Sittard, *Zur Geschichte der Musik und des Theaters am Württembergischen hofe* (Stuttgart, 1890), 1:2. Sittard, 1:321ff., quotes the complete by-laws of a fifteenth-century guild from this area of Germany.

[10] Salmen, *Der Fahrende Musiker*, 89.

[11] Salmen, ibid; Grove, 7:811 and 3:579; Rudolf Schroeder, *Studien zur Geschichte des Musiklebens der Stadt Dormund* (Emsdetten: Lechte, 1934), 3.

[12] Fritz Ernst, 'Die Spielleute im Dienste der Stadt Basel im Ausgehenden Mittelalter,' in *Basler Zeitschrift für Geschichte und Altertumskunde*, vol. 44 (Basel, 1945), 88–111; Karl G. Fellerer, 'Mittelalterlichen Musikleben der Stadt Freiburg im Uechtland,' in *Freiburger Studien zur Musikwissenschaft* (Regensburg, 1935), Ser. ii, 3; Hans Moser, 'Zur Mittelalterlichen Musikgeschichte der Stadt Köln,' in *Archiv für Musikwissenschaft* (Rildesheim, 1964), 137.

[13] Salmen, *Der Fahrende Musiker*; Bowles, *Musikleben*, 13.

[14] R. Kade, 'Die Leipziger Stadtpfeifer,' in *Monatshefte für Musik-Geschichte* (Leipzig, 1889), 194.

[15] Grove, 7:811.

tion a wait trumpet in 1339 and Köln purchased three trumpets and '*2 cornibus trompettis*' for this purpose in 1372.[16] The tower musicians in Frankfurt were required in 1362 to perform 'Watch, Entertainment and Signals.'[17]

During the fifteenth century the importance of having a musical watch for fires is evident in the extant civic documents. A contract for the tower musicians in Dortmund in 1444 gives their primary responsibility 'to sound the alarm.'[18] In Köln a civic ordinance of 1452 states that the watch musician at the outbreak of fire must first play his trumpet and then ring the fire bell. During the night he was to perform hourly, to serve as a clock and perhaps to make certain he stayed awake. Almost identical civic duties were expected in Dresden during the fifteenth century.[19] A civic statute for Weissenfels in 1483 requires the tower musicians to perform every hour during the day and every fifteen minutes during the night, which perhaps indicates a brief musical signal to give the time of day. In addition they were to play *Abblasen* at seven or eight in the morning, at eleven or noon, at three, and at eight or nine o'clock in the evening.[20]

It was also during the fifteenth century that the duties of the civic wind band broadened. Freiburg, which in 1414 had only five tower musicians, had by 1474 shawms, a trumpet and drum for tower duty, entertainment at civic celebrations and marching with the town militia.[21] One of these new duties was the welcoming of visiting nobles, as one can see in a typical example when the civic trumpet ensemble and the shawm ensemble of Aachen performed for Friedrich III when he entered the town in 1454.[22] Marix, in her chronicle of Philip the Good's trip through Germany, Switzerland, and Austria in 1454, documents the performance by civic wind players in virtually dozens of towns of all sizes.[23]

Perhaps it was to represent the city with the greatest degree of splendor that the appearance of more formal uniforms was required by the towns. In Frankfurt the players wore, in 1362, 'rich blue tunics' with the city coat of arms.[24] Three of the actual uniforms issued to the Köln wind band in 1446 can be seen today in the treasury room of the city hall.

Accounts of performances of a 'concert' nature, other than the *Abblasen* references, are more rare than in the literature of the other countries. A fifteenth-century statute in Basel

[16] Smithers, *Baroque Trumpet*, 122; Moser, 'Stadt Köln', 155.

[17] Caroline Valentin, *Geschichte der Musik in Frankfurt-am-Main* (Frankfurt: Völcker, 1906), 14, 17.

[18] Schroeder, *Studien zur Geschichte*, 5 (Die Wächter auf dem Statthurme bliesen Lärm). A miniature from ca. 1425 shows a tower watch-musician in Nurnberg (Nurnberg, Statsbibliothek, Mss. 317.2, fol. 6).

[19] Grove, 5:615.

[20] Werner, *Vier Jahrunderte*, 275.

[21] Fellerer, 'Mittelalterlichen', 77–87.

[22] Carl Hegel, ed., *Die Chroniken der deutschen Städte* (Leipzig, 1864), 364ff.

[23] Marix, *Histoire de la Musique*, 66–73.

[24] Valentin, *Geschichte der Musik*, 42.

requires the civic wind band to perform a typical 'Sunday concert' found in the other cities of Europe. Here the musicians were to play every Sunday after the sermon and in the evening on the *Rheinbrücke* (bridge), as well as when the civic dignitaries gave banquets in the civic hall.

> Alle Sonntag nach der predig uff dem richthusz unnd nachdem nachtmal uff die Rimprug, unnd wan man uff der Herrenstuben mol hat, und ab tisch pfiffen.[25]

It was probably sometime during the fifteenth century that the tradition of playing chorales from civic towers at specific times during the day began in Germany. An early account from Basel (1410) indicates the city employed four wind players who made rounds through the streets of the city, while another group played from the St. Martin's tower at times designated by the city.

> Item zum ersten sol man verschaffen und innen by iren eiden beitten den wechttren, souff die wacht blossen, by dag uff zuo blossen und am morgen by dag ab zoo blossen, order am morgen ein wenig spetter in dag, den die stett wer den gewonsich am morgen gewunnen, wen man ab der wachtt god.[26]

In return for performing these official duties the Stadtpfeifers were given fixed salary contracts (*salarium fixum*) and often expenses for instruments. On New Year's Day they were given donations and they were exempt from taxes.[27] All of this still did not enable them to live sufficiently well, which is why the control of the outside, private, performances for weddings, etc., was so rigidly controlled by the guilds. The municipal authorities helped reserve this source of extra income for the Stadtpfeifers, as can be seen in numerous statutes in the thirteen and fourteenth centuries.[28] In Weissenfels, in 1483, the tower musicians had exclusive rights to all secular banquets.[29]

Some of the municipal regulations suggest that rather large wind bands were sometimes used for private weddings, as one can see in a Bremen statute of 1303 which limits the number to eight. A similar regulation in Munich (1322) permits a maximum of eight musicians for the weddings of the more wealthy citizen, four for the less affluent, and only two for the poorer

[25] Karl Nef, 'Die Stadtpfeiferei und die Instrumentalmusiker in Basel,' in *Sammelbande der Internationalen Musikgesellschaft* 10, no. 3 (Apr–Jun 1909): 396.

[26] Ernst, 'Die Spielluete', 88–111.

[27] Grove, 18:242.

[28] See Grove, 7:204–205, for examples from Strasbourg (ca. 1200), Brunswick (1227), Hamburg (1286), and Nördlingen (1300).

[29] Arno Werner, *Städtische und fürstliche Musikpflege in Weissenfels* (Leipzig: Breitkopf und Härtel, 1911), 35.

townsfolk.[30] A somewhat more detailed regulation from Köln (1439) states that on the evening before the wedding one may hire no more than four musicians and they must be paid one mark each. On the wedding day itself, again the limit is four musicians, but now they must be paid two marks for a whole day and one mark for a half-day. No musician should accept more than one wedding per day.[31]

There is little documentation before the sixteenth century to reveal the nature of the fines assessed against those Stadtpfeifers who broke the municipal statutes governing their professional lives. For the serious offender, perhaps the musician was subjected to something similar to the device which one can see today in the torture tower (*Folter-tor*) in Rothenburg-on-the-Tauber. It has a heavy iron collar which was fixed to the poor wretch's neck and to this collar was attached an iron imitation of a musical instrument with a mouthpiece which fits just under the chin. The bad musician's fingers were held down over six finger holes by means of a metal bar, which fastens down tightly. Probably he was then chained to a post in a public square!

[30] Grove, 7:204–205.

[31] Moser, 'Stadt Köln', 156.

The Nuremberg Stadtpfeifers, ca. 1519, playing for a dance by the city's butchers' guild at the Schembart Carnival.

In the German-speaking regions which are today Czechoslovakia and northern Hungary, one finds mention of wind players as early as the fourteenth century. For example, a civic payment in Schemnitz for 1365 lists payment to the '*fistulatores*.'

Payments may be found for all the usual functional performances, such as a payment in Bardiov, of seven Gulden from the city treasury, for the welcome given the Kaiser in 1433, by a lute player and the civic trumpeters. More unusual is a payment to a travelling minstrel in 1450 by the city of Kremnitz of a 'Red Gulden,' which was the equivalent of twice the weekly salary of the civic trumpeter. In this case, perhaps the city fathers were impressed by this musician's companion, a bear!

> Item: am montag nach Francisci (October 5) dem herren Daniel das her geben hot dem pfayfer mit dem bern rot fl 1.[32]

The instruments which appear most in the civic pay records in this region are the recorder, shawm, horns, cornett, and even as late as the seventeenth century, the bagpipe. In Kremnitz, in 1464, a watch trumpeter was paid thirty-six Denar weekly, which was the same pay as a forest ranger. The jailor was paid fifty-three Denar; the executioner, sixteen Denar; and the regular civic worker, eighteen Denar, which allows one an opportunity to compare civic values. By the end of the fifteenth century, the trumpeter had his pay increased to fifty-four Denar.[33]

[32] Ernest Zavarsky, 'Beiträge zur Musikgeschichte der Stadt Kremnitz,' in *Musik des Ostens* (Kassel: Bärenreiter, 1963), 119.

[33] Ibid.

PART V
The Medieval Court Wind Band

The Medieval Court Wind Band

THE FASCINATION WITH THE WIND INSTRUMENTS heard during, and brought back from, the crusades helped begin a new relationship between winds and the aristocracy in the West. Rapidly the many ceremonial possibilities of instrumental music came to be appreciated, as traced by Harrison:

> The early use of trumpets and drums in the West was for heralding the ceremonious movements and occasions of royalty and high nobility. The particular instrument of heralds was the high-pitched clarion, while the long trumpet (busine) seems to have been played at such court events as tournaments and banquets. With the increasing use of the imperious sound of clarions to punctuate events of high social ritual, players of these instruments became indispensable to the entourage of persons of high rank. They and the trumpeters were the most highly regarded and the best paid of the growing new class of 'minstrels'—properly so called because they were paid members of the retinue (ministerium) of great personages. Playing individually or in groups—in contrasts to the earlier competitive individualism of jongleur and harper—the *ministralli*, a term that included heralds, trompours, nakerers, harpers, pipers, tabourers, etc., formed themselves into guilds. They thus became the *organized* keepers and transmitters of an unwritten repertory and the art and craft of playing it.[1]

[1] Frank L. Harrison, 'Tradition and Innovation in Instrumental Usage 1100–1450,' in *Aspects of Medieval and Renaissance Music*, ed. Jan LaRue (New York: Norton, 1966), 325.

During the late fourteenth century there was a great development of courtly wind music which, together with similar developments in civic wind bands, forged the wind band into an internationally identifiable ensemble with its own unique repertoire of multi-part music.

Accustomed as we are to large ensembles consisting of a relatively few different instruments which are doubled many times over, it is sometimes startling to read in early literature of large ensembles apparently consisting of one each of very dissimilar instruments. Already in 1155 one reads of the court musicians, in *Roman de Brut*, by Wace, performing on vielles, rotes, harps, panpipes, lyres, dulcimers, shawms, hurdy-gurdies, psalteries, trumscheits, cymbals, and the citharas.

> Mult ot a la cort jugleors
> Chanteors, estrumenteors,
> Mut poissies oir chancons,
> Rotruenges et noviax sons,
> Vie leurs de lais et de notes,
> Lais de vieles, lais de rotes,
> Lais de harp et de fretiax,
> Lyre, tympres et chalemiax,
> Symphonies, psalterions,
> Monocordes, cymbes, chorons.[2]

[2] Bowles, 'Haut and Bas,' 117. Several additional examples may be found here.

This impression can still be found in some fifteenth-century literature, as for example in the *Buke of the Howlate*, written in Scotland.

> All thus our lade thai lovit, with lyking and lysh,
> Menstralis and musicianis, mo than I mene may.
> The psaltery, the sytholis, the soft sytharist,
> The croude and the monycordis, the gittyrnis gay;
> The rote, and the recordour, the rivupe, the rist,
> The trumpe and the talburn, the tympane but tray;
> The lilt pype and. the lute, the fydill in fist,
> The dulset, the dulsacordis, the schalme of assay;
> The amyable organis usit full oft;
> Claryonis lowde knellis,
> Portatius and bellis,
> Cymbaclanis in the cellis,
> That soundis so soft.[3]

[3] Henry G. Farmer, 'Music in Medieval Scotland,' *Proceedings of the Musical Association* 54 (1929–1930): 77.

Extensive as this list is, the author says there were even more ('mo than i mene may')! The variety was so great that one can easily share the bewildered reaction by John Lygate, a monk of St. Edmunds, that perhaps no one could know them all.

> Eke Instrumentys high and lowe
> Wel mo than I koude knowe,
> That I suppose, there is no man
> That aryght reherse kan
> The melodye that they made.[4]

[4] Quoted in Bowles, 'Haut and Bas,' 117.

It is important for the reader to remember that he has been reading literature, not historical reporting, and such quotations tend only to supply a catalog of the known instruments. The real ensemble usage of these instruments was quite different.

Court documents, much literature, and eyewitness accounts all, in discussing medieval ensembles, made a clear distinction between the 'loud' ensemble (*haut*, *stark*, and *alta*) and the 'soft' ensemble (*bas*, *bajo*, and *still*). It was the loud ensemble which was the pure wind ensemble, consisting usually of members of the trumpet, trombone, shawm, horn, bagpipe and percussion families. The soft ensemble consisted of the families of flutes, recorders, lute and keyboards. The choice was purely functional, not aesthetic, as pointed out by one of the greatest scholars of medieval music: loud music for outdoors and large palace rooms and soft music for smaller rooms.[5]

An early didactic poem which does observe accurately the common usage, is the anonymous *Echecs amoureux* of ca. 1375. In defining the loud ensemble it also correctly associates the medium with the aristocratic dance.

> Whenever that they were fain to dance
> And frolic, gathered in a crowd,
> The dancers called for music loud—
> It was this that always pleased them best,
> And ever added to their zest.
> One could hear each instrument
> That sounded forth its merriment.
> Trumpet, tabor, drum and bell
> Cymbals (which played so well)
> Cornemuse and shawm
> And horns that they did loudly blow.[6]

This same poem lists flutes, cromornes (doucaines?), rebec, rote, etc., as soft instruments employed when 'less noise' is desired and which are pleasing for the appropriate entertainment.

This distinction is widely documented during the fifteenth century. The chronicler of the household of Philip the Good of Burgundy, for example, reports,

> The Duke had six loud minstrels, who carried the arms of the prince and were counted (paid more?) as trumpets, the Duke had four players of soft instruments similarily counted.[7]

[5] Heinrich Besseler, 'Alta,' in *Die Musik in Geschichte und Gegenwart*, ed. Friedrich Blume (Kassel-Basel: Bärenreiter-Verlag, 1949), 1:378. Also, Grove, 12:348.

[6] Curt Sachs, *World History of the Dance* (New York: Norton, 1937), 287.

> Et quant il vouloient danser
> Et faire grans esbattemens,
> On sonnoit les haulz instrumens,
> Qui mieulx aux dansez plaisoient
> Pour la grant noise qu'ilz faisoient
> La peuist on oir briefment
> Sonner moult de renuoisement
> Trompez, tabours,
>   tymbrez, naquaires,
> Cymballes (dont il n'est
>   mes guaires),
> Cornemusez et chalemelles
> Et cornes de fachon moult belles.

[7] Olivier de la Marche, quoted in Bowles, 'Haut and Bas,' 119.

Johannes Tinctoris, in his treatise, *De Inventione et Usu Musicae* (ca. 1487), identifies the loud wind band by the Italian equivalent of the French *haut*, or loud.

> For the lowest contratenor parts, and often for any contratenor parts, to the shawm players (tibicines) one adds brass players (tubicines) who play very harmoniously upon the type of instrument which is called trompone [sic] in Italy, *sacqueboute* in France. Together it is called *alta*.[8]

[8] Quoted in Richard Rastall, 'Some English Consort-Groupings,' 193.

18 *The Wind Band in Medieval Courtly Life*

THE FUNCTION OF THE WIND BAND, or 'loud' ensemble, in the later Middle Ages seems to have been very consistent throughout Europe. These instruments are to be expected, of course, in any sort of welcoming ceremony for the aristocratic world. In a typical account, concerning the visit of Charles the Bold of Burgundy to the Emperor, Friedrich III, in 1473, an eyewitness reports,

> About a mile before the city, with great pomp, the Archbishop and all the knights of the city welcomed him. Each had a great multitude of trumpets, which drew up before him and played. The Duke offended the Emperor by having his trumpets proceed (before the Emperor's).[1]

Contrary to an old musicological myth that only wind instruments played 'table music' (*tafelmusik* rather often being synonymous with wind music in modern historical writings), it was the soft music which was used for private dinner music. One writer said the predilection for soft music for dinner was because it helped digestion!

> Encore est chose convenable que tu aies des ménestreux a bas instrumens pour aucune recreation, faisant digestion de ta personne royale après les conseils et travaux de la royale majesté.[2]

Wind bands *did* play for the great state dinners and banquets at court, which of course were held in larger rooms requiring music consisting of 'more noise.' In addition, a state banquet was an occasion rich in protocol, beginning with a musical 'call to dinner' by the wind instruments.

> In kinges court, as it is lawe
> Trumpes in halle, to metes gan blawe.[3]

> And after that, on scaffold highe a-lofte
> The Noyse gan, lowde and no thing softe
> Both of trompetis and of clariouneris.[4]

> They wenten to the dyner, the whole company
> With pipis and with trompis and othir melody.[5]

[1] Quoted in George Lauterbeck, ed., *Regentenbuch des Hochgelerten weitberumbten Herr Georgen Lauterbecken, Fürstlichen Brandenburgischen Rahts ...* (Frankfurt am Main, 1579), 148. Many examples of iconography picture such a scene during the fifteenth century. A typical example, a miniature showing the entrance of Charles VI and the Duke of Burgundy into Paris in ca. 1460, pictures the four trumpets of the king preceding him (Paris, National Library, Ms.fr. 6465, fol. 417, see image below).

Entrée de Charles V à Paris après le sacre de Reims, by Jean Fouquet

[2] Quoted in Bowles, 'Haut and Bas,' 137.

[3] Eugen Kolbing, ed., *Amis and Amiloun* (Heilbronn, 1884), 84.

[4] John Lydgate, *Troy Book*, ed. Henry Bergen (London: Kegan Paul, Trench, Trübner, 1906), 57.

[5] Frederick James Furnivall, ed., *The Tale of Beryn* (London: Kegan Paul, Trench, Trübner, 1909), 117.

This first 'noise' was called in France, *Corner l'eau*, which reminds one that it was also the custom for the guests to wash their hands in perfumed water before eating.

> Trompers tromped to the mete
> They weschen and went to sette.⁶

[6] Leslie Frank Casson, ed., *The Romance of Sir Degrevant* (London: Oxford University Press, 1949), 44.

When the guests were seated a soldier would yell, 'a la viande,' the meat course, and the musicians would often accompany with music the entrance of the food from the kitchen. A typical miniature from the early fourteenth century shows the Dominican monk, Ludolf von Sachsen of Strassburg, seated at the table with two shawm players and a slide-trumpet playing as the first course was served.⁷

[7] Chicago, Newberry Library, Mss. 40, fol. 43.

During the meal the musicians would continue to play and to announce, musically, each new course of food.

> Which mynstrallis pipen and trumpen … whan he goith to mete and at ech course of seruyce at the table and whan he risith fro mete.⁸

[8] Quoted in Bowles, *Musikleben*, 46ff., together with much of this material on courtly life. Additional examples of iconography include another miniature showing two shawms and slide-trumpet (Brussels, Royal Library, Mss. 8, fol. 33v.), another picturing three shawms (Paris, Bibl. de l'Arsenal, Ms.fr. 5073, fol. 148.), and one showing three trumpets from the period of Philip the Good (Paris, National Library, Ms. fr. 12574, fol. 181v, see image at left).

Repas des noces d'Arus et de la fille d'Olivier, by Loyset Liédet (1420-1479), showing three trumpets playing from the balcony during a banquet.

Wind bands were also a basic part of all courtly entertainments, including the masquerades (a kind of court ballet with allegorical scenes, masks, and disguises) and the mummer's play. The latter, in England, included a prologue, the drama, and a finale in which characters in grotesque masks appeared to gather contributions.

Foremost among all outdoor entertainments in the Middle Ages was, of course, the tournament, joust or tilt. In a typical tourney, the knights themselves would fight mock battles related to some allegorical story, take prisoners and exact ransom as in a real war. Indeed, if there were a practical purpose for these events it was to train one for actual combat.[9] But these tournaments were probably not thought of as military training at the time, rather they were life itself—a kind of three-dimensional personification of the coat-of-arms and all that it represented. Thus one can understand the comment by the fourteenth-century aristocrat, Gaston Phébus, that the nobles were only interested in three things: 'd'une en armes, l'autre en amours et l'autre est en chasses.'[10]

The wind music at these tournaments was, in the same way, functional but also an aural symbol of the aristocrat as well. Very much like the twentieth-century American football music, the medieval musicians performed as the combatants entered the field, again with each extraordinary hit of the lance, and finally as the winner was celebrated.[11]

Numerous passages in early literature and examples of iconography suggest that the usual music for the tournaments was provided by trumpets and percussion instruments.

> Pusaunen und prummen,
> pawcken und trumen
> slug man da, das er erhal.
> Da ward grosser freuden schal.[12]
>
> Trummen unde busin
> hôrte man dâ hellen[13]
>
> Wyth coronals stef and stelde
> Eyther smyt other in the scheId
> Wyth greet envye.
> Har shaftes breke asonder,
> Har dentes ferthe as thonder
> That cometh out of the skye;

[9] I call this 'training,' but on occasion these tournaments got out of hand, as in Neuss, in 1240, when sixty knights were killed!

[10] Bernard Nabonne, *Gaston Phébus, seigneur de Bearn* (Paris: Corréa, 1936), 77.

[11] Kastner, Manuel Général, 79.

[12] Heinrich von Neustadt, *Apollonius von Tyrland*, ed. Samuel Singer (Berlin: Weidmann, 1906), 282.

[13] Heinrich von dem Türlin, *Diu Crône*, ed. Gottlob Heinrich Friedrich Scholl (Stuttgart, 1852), 688ff.

> Taborus and trompours
> Herawdes, good descoverou(r)s,
> Har strokes gon descrye.[14]

[14] Maldwyn Mills, ed., *Libeaus Desconus* (London: Oxford University Press, 1969), 132.

> The trumpeing and the tabouringe
> dede to gider the knightes flinge.[15]

[15] Eugen Kölbing, ed., *Arthour and Merlin* (Leipzig, 1890), 256.

Sometimes, however, a larger band of more instruments seems to have been present.

> Up gon the trumpes and the melodie,
> and to the liste's ride the compagnie
> ...
> Ther maystow seen devysing of harneys
> so uncouth and so riche, and wroght so weel
> of goldsmithrie, of browding, and of steel;
> the sheeldes brighte, testers, and trappures;
> gold hewen helmes, bauberks, cote-armures;
> lordes in paraments on hir courseres,
> kinghts of retenue, and eke squyeres
> ...
> Yemen on fote, and communes many oon
> with short staves, thikke as they may goon;
> pypes, trompes, nakers, clariounes,
> that in the bataille blowen blody sounes.[16]

[16] Geoffrey Chaucer, 'The Knyghtes Tale,' in *Complete Works*, ed. Walter William Skeat (Oxford: Clarendon, 1924), 4:72.

> To tornay that tide
> with trump and with naker
> and the scalmus eclere.[17]

[17] Casson, ed., *The Romance of Sir Degrevant*, 64.

One source comments on the size of the wind band, 'more than three pairs' of trumpets and timpani, and says that the result was louder than thunder.

> Menestrelz, trompes, naquaires
> y avoit plus de troys paires,
> qui si haultement cournoyent,
> que mons et vaulx resonnoyent.
> ...
> Lors menestrelz liement
> cournoient, hairaux crioent,
> Lances brisent, cops resonnent,
> etces menestrelz haut sonnent
> si qu'on n'oist Dieu tonnant.[18]

[18] Christine de Pisan, 'Le livre du duc des vrais amants,' in *Oeuvres poétiques*, ed. Maurice Roy (Paris, 1896), 3:79ff, 89ff. Typical iconography of the fifteenth-century tournament include a miniature showing two straight trumpets and one slide-trumpet performing (Brussels, Royal Library, Mss. 9017.), a miniature showing musicians signaling the end of the 'battle' (Paris, Bibl. l'Arsenal, Ms.fr.5074, fol. 65), and one in which trumpets are playing for a tournament which has turned into an uncontrolled 'free-for-all' (Paris, National Library, Ms.fr. 2692, fol. 67v, 68, see image, *La mêlée,* on opposite page).

La mêlée (The Fray), ca. 1488–1489

Another aristocratic preoccupation was hunting and already in the fifteenth century the hunt made use of specific musical signals. In France the notation was centered in the rhythmic values: a *vois* was a note; a *mot* was a tone or call; the *menée* was a fanfare; the *moot* was a whole-note; the *trout*, a quarter-note; and *trourourou* was an eighth-note.[19] A fifteenth-century English translation of a contemporary French hunting treatise says,

[19] Bowles, *Musikleben*, 86.

> You ought to blow after the unharboring two moots. And if your hounds do not come to your will as quickly as you would like, you ought to blow four moots to hasten the company to you, and to warn the company that the hart is unharbored (dislodged). Then you ought to recheat on your hounds (call back from the wrong scent). And afterwards, when they are gone ahead of you, you ought to call in the manner as I shall tell you, you ought to blow "trout, trout, troutoutout, trout, trout trourourourout, trourourourout, trourourourout."[20]

[20] Guyllaume Twici, *L'art de vénerie*, trans. Alice Dryden (Northhampton, Mass.: W. Mark, 1908), 23.

The hunt usually began witb three long blasts, which signaled the unleashing of the dogs.

> He with his hatheles on hyse horsses weren. Thenne thise cacheres that couthe cowpled hor houndez, vnclosed the kenel dore and clade hem theroute, blew bygly in buglez thre bare mote.[21]

[21] J.R.R. Tolkien and Eric Valentine Gordon, eds., *Sir Gawain and the Green Knight* (Oxford: Clarendon, 1925), 35.

The members of the court wind bands also had to accompany their aristocrats to the field of battle. An eyewitness to the Siege of Valenciennes in 1340 reports hearing bagpipes, nakers, shawms, and two kinds of trumpets.[22] According to the same chronicle, the English maintained wind bands on their naval ships during battle.

> en grant nruit et en grant noise de trompes et de nakaires et de tous manieres de menestrandies.[23]

A German chronicle of the fifteenth century also speaks of wind bands on the battle field.

> etlich mit pauken bestellt; disselben pfiffen und pauckten dem fussvolck auf.[24]

[22] Jean Froissart, *Oeuvres*, ed. Kervyn De Lettenhove (Brussels, 1867), 3:150, 195. (Muses, calemelles, naquaires, trompes et trompettes)

[23] Ibid., 195.

[24] Bayerische Akademie der Wissenschaften (München), Historische Kommission, *Die Chroniken der deutschen Städte vom 14. bis 16. Jahrhundert* (Leipzig, 1864), 3:248.

19 *The Wind Band and the Medieval Dance*

ONE OF THE CHIEF INDOOR PLEASURES of the late medieval aristocrat was dancing. The most important dance of the late fourteenth and fifteenth centuries was the basse-dance (from *basse*, meaning 'low,' a solemn dance with gliding steps) and virtually every scholar seems to agree that the wind band provided the music for this dance. Gombosi, for one, states,

> music for the court dance proper ... came to be confided more and more, during the course of the fifteenth century, to the *haults menestrelz*, to the players of the "loud-sounding" wind instruments. The other group, that of the "low" instruments, is now mentioned very rarely.[1]

The ensemble which is first associated with this dance seems to have been shawms and the bagpipe, the latter being preferred because of its ability to play a sustained melody.

> In such accord and such a soune of bombarde and of clarioun with cornemuse and schalmele.[2]

Soon the ensemble appears with the slide-trumpet replacing the bagpipe.

> Men danste den hofdans bi manieren met trompen ende met scalmeyen.[3]

> ... trumpers and trumpetes, lowde shallys and doucetes.[4]

During the late fifteenth century, as suggested by Tinctoris, the sackbut may have replaced the slide-trumpet.[5]

The reason why the wind band became indispensible to the basse-dance can be understood in how the dance itself was organized. 'Basse-dance' was only a general term, which represented four different dances, each differing in tempo, meter, and in the actual steps.[6] The basse-dance music, when notated at all, was notated only in one form. It was the play-

---

[1] Otto Gombosi, 'About Dance,' 291ff. See also, Tinctoris, *De Inventione*; Besseler, 'Alta'; Eileen Southern, 'Basse-Dance Music in Some German Manuscripts of the 15th Century,' in *Aspects of Medieval and Renaissance Music*, ed. Jan LaRue (New York: Norton, 1966), 738; Harrison, 'Tradition and Innovation'; Rastall, 'Some English Consort-Groupings'; and Bowles, 'Haut and Bas,' 130–131.

[2] John Gower, *The English Works of John Gower*, ed. George Campbell Macaulay (Oxford: Oxford University Press, 1901), 358ff. Iconography which shows the bagpipe included in the dance wind ensemble includes Paris, National Library (Ms.fr. 1665, fol. 7), Brussels, Royal Library (Ms. 11187, fol. Iv.), and Vienna, National Library (Hs. s.n. 2644, fol. 104).

[3] Reinaert, 'Willems,' in *Altniederländische Schaubuhne*, ed. August Heinrich Hoffman von Fallersleben (Breslau, 1834), 196.

[4] John Lydgate, *Reson and Sensuallyte*, ed. Ernst Sieper (London: Kegan Paul, Trench, Trübner, 1901), 1:146.

[5] See also, Wangermée, *Flemish Music*, 161.

[6] The *piva*, the fastest dance, in 6/4 or 4/4; the *saltarello*, called *pas de Brabant* in France and *alta* or *altadanza* in Spain, was in 3/2 or 6/4; the *guaternaria* or *saltarello tedesco* in 2 x 2/2; and the *bassadanza* proper, in 2 x 3/2.

ers themselves who transformed the tune, extemporaneously, into the appropriate meter and tempo for the particular dance requested.

> We can now understand why the favorite dance orchestra of the 15th century consisted of two or three shawms and a slide trumpet. There is no other combination of instrmnents that better answered the requirements of a polyphonic *bassadanza*. The slide trumpet obviously blew the theme, the single tones of which had to be heard very clearly, since the steps had to correspond to them. The rich figuration of the counterparts could not have been better performed than by the shawms, which were able to play rapid passages and had a peculiar nassal timbre that contrasted sharply with the sound of the slide trumpet.[7]

Two points should be stressed. First, the wind band music for this dance was clearly polyphonic and multi-part in character, not unison. Second, the improvisation which lay at the heart of the performance provides the answer why so little actual music has survived. Virtually all of what has survived is only the slide-trumpet part, the tune.[8]

An outdoor dance which was also associated with the wind band was the 'round' or 'choral' dance.[9] This association can be seen in the German poem, *Trojanischer Krieg*, by Fuctrer.

> No fairer choral dance
> Was seen, afar or nigh around.
> Within a ring the dancers wound
> About, without the ring a few.
> The drummers beat, the pipers blew,
> Their music did direct the stride.
> Lightly the dancers did the glide
> And afterwards the leap.[10]

There were also some regional dances which were associated with wind bands. One, for example, was the *moresque*, an Italian masked dance, which was accompanied by 'pifferi e tamburini.' The chronicler, Molinet, mentions a drum (*tambourin*) playing in the *style* of a moresque, which suggests a specific role in this dance by the percussion.[11] On the other hand, it may have been that a folk percussion instrument was used in this dance, for during the wedding celebrations of Constanzo Sforza and Camilla of Aragón, in Pesaro, in 1475, an 'strumenti rusticani' joined with the '*pifferi*' in playing for this dance.[12]

---

[7] Gombosi, 'About Dance,' 301.

[8] The most famous example of extant basse-dance tunes, all notated in breve-note values, is the extraordinarily beautiful manuscript called *Basses Danses de Marguerite d'Austriche* (Brussels, Royal Library, Cabinet des Mss, Nr. 9085). Manfred F. Bukofzer discovered one manuscript in which the upper, improvised, parts exist; this can be seen, in part, in his *Studies in Medieval and Renaissance Music* (New York: Norton, 1950), 199.

[9] An example of iconography, ca. 1460, which shows a round dance in a garden with two shawms and a bombard playing can be found in the National Library, Paris (Ms.fr. 19153, fol. 7, see image below).

[10] Quoted in Sachs, *World History of the Dance*, 283.

> Ez wart nie schöner reige
> gemachet von deheiner schar,
> sie wunden sich dan unde dar
> und brachen sich her unde hin.
> man horte luten under in
> tamburen, schellen, pfifen.
> lis uf den füezen slifen
> und dar nach balde springen.

[11] Gombosi, 'About Dance,' 290.

[12] Ibid.

Another regional dance, of which virtually nothing is known, was the *trumpetum*. An early fifteenth-century German treatise mentions this dance as another example of polyphonic wind music.

> Trumpetum and stampania may have two or three parts and wander frequently to the fifth.[13]

[13] University of Breslau (cart. Iv. Qu. 16).

Finally, the most ancient of medieval wind dance bands, the *one*-man band, the pipe and tabor player, seems to have existed as an anachronism by the fifteenth century. Gombosi reports that while iconographic representation is rare by this date, the pipe and tabor is frequently mentioned in literary documents.[14] Even by the early sixteenth century, Castiglione, in his *Il Cortegiano*, described how Madonna Margarita and Constanza Fregosa joined hands and danced a basse-dance while 'Barletto played on his instruments.'[15]

[14] Gombosi, 'About Dance,' 293.

[15] Southern, 'Basse-Dance Music,' 738–739.

20 The 'Lost' Repertoire of the Medieval Wind Band

The enigma of the medieval court wind band's literature is the fact that so little actual music has survived.

> No period in the history of music reveals so deep a rift between musical sources and accounts of musical practice as does the close of the Middle Ages.
>
> …
>
> On the one hand, the musical sources preserve for us only a negligible quantity of purely instrumental music; on the other, the actual existence of this music and its variety are mentioned in practically all chronicles, memoirs, and reports of festivities, and are attested to by numerous pictures.[1]

[1] Gombosi, 'About Dance,' 293.

One category of 'lost' wind band music may well be the vast amount of choral music from before 1500 which has one or more voices notated either without text entirely, or with an incipit of text only. Early historians often went to great lengths to try to create a rational explanation for this body of 'vocal music without text.'[2] Some said it must have all been vocalized and some said the singers all knew the text from memory (in the case of the third volume of the Petrucci publication, this would mean all the singers knowing hundreds of texts in *other* languages!). These kinds of arguments are all so unreasonable that most scholars today have reached the inescapable conclusion: this body of music was intended for instrumental usage and the better wind players, such as those found in courts, could indeed read mensural music. The new Grove, for example, notes that in addition to dance music, 'the minstrels seem to have played the tenor and contratenor parts of the standard three-voice polyphonic chanson of the 14th century.'[3]

[2] The primary reason given why these parts were *not* instrumental is the tendancy of iconography to show singers with music, but instrumentalists without. But can this not be explained better as simply an artistic choice, the artist simply preferring to avoid the clutter? After all, the instrumentalist was identified as a musician by his instrument, while the singer could be identified *only* by showing the actual music!

[3] Grove, 12:348.

One hint that instruments did indeed play these untexted parts may perhaps be found in a handful of extant works such as the famous *Gloria ad modum tubae* by Dufay, which seem to be designating specific instruments. Historians used to consider these compositions as exceptions, but some today believe they are in fact hints of the normal practice.[4] This may perhaps

[4] Emile Haraszti, 'Les Musiciens de Mathias Corvin et de Béatrice d'Aragón,' in Jean Jacquot, ed., *La musique instrumentale de la renaissance*, Paris: Editions du Centre National de la Recherche Scientifique, 1955, s. [35]-59, 56ff.

be confirmed by the fifteenth-century French poet, Martin le Franc (d. 1461). In his *Champion*, he mentions the use of both 'loud' (wind) and 'soft' music by both Binchois and Dufay.

> But I'm told by those who know
> with so fine a melody
> few of them could discant
> as Binchois and Dufay
> For these men a newer way have found
> in music loud and soft
> of making lively concordance
> through feint, pause, and nuance.[5]

[5] Quoted in Grove, 11:728.

Gombosi is a scholar who believes this body of music was indeed accompanied by instruments.

> At all events the consensus still seems to be that such parts without text are instrumental, and the variety of instruments to be found in the 14th and 15th centuries suggests that these were used for playing the accompanied songs which sprang up at very much the same time. The fact that the paintings usually show one instrument of each kind, though occasionally more, confirms similar lists in literary works, and implies that accompanied songs should not employ instruments of the same family as a general rule. The exceptions are trumpets and, more importantly in view of their more developed technique, members of the shawm family.[6]

[6] Gombosi, 'About Dance,' 289.

Reaney also reminds the reader that one medieval writer said that wind and other instruments may be used in the upper octaves of music as early as the thirteenth-century organa.[7] In as much as most instrumental music of the fifteenth century was clearly wind ensemble music, this body of music must be looked upon as a potential representative of a portion of that medium's 'lost' repertoire.[8]

Another portion of the 'lost' wind band repertoire is the polyphonic vocal literature, for it is generally accepted that the first multi-part instrumental performances were transcribed from this source. Froissart, in the fourteenth century, wrote that it was the fashion at a banquet concert to alternate vocal solos with instrumental pieces, probably of this nature.[9] With regard to such transcriptions, one is reminded that Machaut said that one of his ballades could sound equally well performed by an organ, bagpipe or other instrument and in this

[7] Gilbert Reaney, 'The Performance of Medieval Music,' in *Aspects of Medieval and Renaissance Music*, ed. Jan LaRue (New York: Norton, 1966) 707.

[8] A later volume will present the known sources for this body of music.

[9] Quoted in Reaney, 'The Performance of Medieval Music,' 717.

case he was obviously referring to the vocal part.[10] One can only conclude, therefore, that a great deal of additional music must have been considered at least secondarily instrumental.

[10] Guillaume de Machaut, *Musikalische Werke* (Leipzig: Breitkopf und Härtel, 1928), 2:55.

21 Court Wind Bands in England

The Norman Kings

Individual wind instruments can be traced to very remote times in England, as in other countries. Even in the most ancient literature of the language these instruments appear, as for example in the eighth-century, 'Beowulf':

> They away hurried bitter and angry
> The instant they heard the war-horn sing.

Some actual instruments have been found dating from the Danish conquest, one a trumpet more than five feet long.[1]

It is from the brief reign (1016) of Edmund 'Ironside' that we have one of the earliest names of a jongleur, one called Hitardus. Perhaps it was as Edmund fled, after having lost England to the Danes in the Battle of Assandun, that he gave the hills of Chartham and Walworth to

> cuidam ioculatori suo nomine Hitardo[2]

[1] Henry George Farmer, *The Rise and Development of Military Music* (London: William Reeves, 1912), 7.

[2] Chambers, *The Mediaeval Stage*, 1:44.

William the Conqueror

It is with the first of the Norman Kings, William the Conqueror, that the modern history of England begins. In 1066, upon the election of King Harold, William, then Duke of Normandy, claimed the English throne. Pope Alexander II, in support, excommunicated Harold and sent William a diamond ring said to contain a hair from the head of St. Peter. Thus, at age thirty-nine, William set out to conquer England.

It is said that his ships on their way to England 'resounded with music.'[3] Among the jongleurs accompanying William was one called Taillefer, who's speciality, in addition to music, was throwing his sword high into the air and catching it by the hilt. He begged William to allow him to lead the army into the famous ensuing Battle of Hastings and it is remembered he did so singing heroic songs of Roland, Charlemagne, and Roncesvalles.[4] Taillefer in the process killed the first two Englishmen, but then an English arrow stilled his song.

[3] Farmer, *Military Music*, 7.

[4] Wace (d. 1170), *Roman de Brut*, quoted in Chambers, *The Mediaeval Stage*, 1:43.
> Taillefer, ki mult bien chantout,
> Sor un cheval ki tost alout,
> Devant le duc alout chantant
> De Karlegaigne et de Rolant
> Et d'Oliver de des vassals
> Qui morurent en Rencevals.

William was an unusually brutal man, even amongst early kings. He laid such destruction upon Northern England that it did not fully recover until the nineteenth century.[5] He was also responsible, however, for some notable architectural achievements, including the Tower of London and the Abbaye aux Hommes at Caen, in France. To help rebuild the Winchester Cathedral, William agreed to allow Bishop Walkelin to cut all the trees he could cut in three days from Hempage Forest. The good bishop and his yeomen carried off the entire forest in seventy-two hours!

One of William's remarkable achievements was the *Domesday Book* of 1086. This historic survey of land and people identifies one royal jongleur, Berdic, who was given land in Gloucestershire as payment for his services to William. The book similarly lists a female jongleur (*ioculatrix*) named Adelinda, in the service of Earl Roger.[6]

It is likely that the only regular ensemble of wind instruments that William maintained was his royal trumpets. A very interesting reference to these, from the siege of Rochester in 1088, suggests a rather high level of musical organization.

> When Bishop Eudes was forced to surrender, he obtained the king's permission to quit the city with all arms and horses. Not satisfied with this, he further endeavoured to seek the favour, that the king's military music should not sound their triumphant fanfares during the capitulation. But William angrily refused, saying that he would not make the concession for a thousand gold marks. So, when the rebellious Normans marched out of Rochester, they did so with colors lowered, and to the sound of the king's trumpets.[7]

[5] Edward Augustus Freeman, *History of the Norman Conquest of England* (Oxford: Clarendon, 1870), 2:181:

[6] Chambers, *The Mediaeval Stage*, 1:43–44.

[7] Farmer, *Military Music*, 8–9.

William 'the Red' (1087–1100)

William the Conqueror's son, William 'the Red' was a tyrant in his father's image until he was shot while hunting. It was during his brief reign that the First Crusade (1096–1099) occurred. While we have a great deal more information from the Third Crusade, we do know from the Latin chroniclers that William's troops were accompanied by three kinds of instruments of the trumpet family, the *tubae*, *buccinae*, and the *litutii*, as well as 'corni.' The historian, Fulcher of Chartres (d. 1130), who was present, mentions the musician, Evrardus Venator, who played *tuba* during the crusade, but was a horn player at court.[8] This reflects an apparently ancient concept that some

[8] Henry George Farmer, 'Crusading Martial Music,' in *Music & Letters* 30, no. 3 (July 1949): 244.

kinds of trumpets were used *only* for war purposes. One wishes the French writer, Michaud, had gone into more detail when speaking of the Crusader's 'sonorous horns, pierced with many holes.'[9] On the distinction between these trumpet types, one can only add an interesting comment made by a writer during the Third Crusade which speaks of the 'resounding note of the *tuba* and the clear and high-pitched *lituui*.'

The Arabic historians give the opposing Saracen military musical instrumentation as trumpets (*anāfīr*, from which the word 'fanfare' comes), horns (*būgāt*), shawms (*zumūr*), timpani (*kūsāt*), drums (*tubūl*), and cymbals (*kāsāt*).[10] Several of these instruments used by the Saracens, especially the percussion instruments, were introduced to the West during the crusades and in time became fixtures of Western military music.

Beyond the instruments themselves, two characteristics of the usage of these instruments made a deep impression on Western military thinkers.[11] First, the Saracens used the instruments not only to give the usual military signals for the conduct of the battle, but also deliberately used the total sound to try to *scare* the enemy. Second, the Western leaders were impressed with the organization of military bands according to the rank of the officer in charge. The Sultan Baibar (d. 1277) had a military band of sixty-eight players, consisting of twenty trumpets, forty timpani, four shawms, and four drums. The chronicler of the Third Crusade, Joinville, says when the Sultan's band played the noise was so loud that those standing near could not hear themselves speak. A divisional general was permitted a band but no timpani. Lesser officers were permitted bands of eight or sixteen players, according to the number of men under their command.[12]

[9] Ibid.

[10] Ibid., 243.

[11] One soon sees the influence in literature as well. A fourteenth-century novel, *Alexander the Great in Arabia*, mentions the bells and great drum.
> Quyk he dooth his
> bemen blowe,
> an hundreth upon a rowe.
> His chymbe-bellen he
> dooth rynge,
> and dooth dasshe
> grete tabourynge.

Smithers, G. V., ed., *King Alisaunder* (London: Oxford University Press, 1952), 1:105.

[12] Farmer, 'Crusading Martial Music,' 248.

Henry I (1100–1135)

Henry, another son of William the Conqueror, was a rather peaceful ruler, fighting only one battle, at Tinchebrai, in 1106, during which he lost not a single knight. The name of only one of Henry's jongleurs is known today, but he, Rahere (d. 1144), must have been a very accomplished and successful jongleur. He renounced secular music, became a monk, and gave the money he had accumulated for the purpose of building St. Bartholomew's Hospital in London.

The Plantagenet Kings

Richard I, 'Coeur de Lion' (1189–1199)

In Richard I one finds a genuine musician–king. In one of the most famous of all medieval English legends, it is said that when Richard was being held prisoner in an Austrian castle, a fellow Trouvère, Blondel (thought to have been Jehan I, Lord of Nestles), found him because he heard Richard singing a song known only to Trouvères.

It has been said that Richard would never have had the brilliant reputation which he enjoyed in his lifetime, and which has continued until today, if he had not patronized so many jongleurs and poets who in return sung his praises. Even during his long absence, the regent in England, William de Longchamp, imported jongleurs from France to sing to the English people about Richard.[13] We know one of the jongleurs by name, Ambroise, who participated in Richard's coronation in 1189.[14]

We know from a contemporary poem that there were more wind instruments in his court, including bagpipes, trumpet types and drums. The poem describes Richard sitting on a platform, surrounded by his nobles, with the music playing as the food is brought in from the kitchen.

> To Westemenstre they wente in fere,
> Lordyngs and ladys that ther were
> Trumpes begonne for to blowe,
> To mete they went in a throwe.
> King Richard was set on des
> With dukes and eerles, prowde in pres,
> Fro keehene com the fyrste cours,
> With pypes and trumpes and tabours.[15]

It was Richard I who led the most successful of the early crusades, the one known as the Third Crusade (1189–1192). An early scribe tells us that he had both the *tuba* and the *buccina* with him. Upon his arrival in Messina, we are told, he directed that 'at the third day, at the sound of the *buccina*, let them follow me.' Later, in the same city:

> In front came the terrible dragon standard unfurled. Then rode the King. Behind him the clangour of the *tuba* excited the army.[16]

[13] Funck-Brentano, *The Middle Ages*, 192.

[14] Chambers, *The Mediaeval Stage*, 1:49.

[15] Karl Brunner, ed., *Der mittelenglische Versroman über Richard Löwenherz* (Vienna and Leipzig: Braumüller, 1913), 88, 268.

[16] Farmer, 'Crusading Martial Music,' 244.

From the battle of Arsuf (1191) we have some very interesting details of Richard's use of military music. One expects the usual signals, of course, but here there seems to be the implication of a very early use of some form of multi-part ensemble music.

> It had been resolved by common consent that the sounding of six trumpets in three different parts of the army should be a signal for a charge, viz. two in front, two in rear and two in the middle, to distinguish the sounds from those of the Saracens, and to mark the distance of each.
>
> ...
>
> Meanwhile the trumpets blew, and their sounds being harmoniously blended, there arose a kind of discordant concord of notes, whilst the sameness of the sounds being continued, the one followed the other in mutual succession, and the notes which had been lowered were again resounded.[17]

These have been descriptions of Richard's trumpets as used with the land forces, but the organization of his fleet also took into account the need for trumpet signals. An eyewitness explains that the fleet was arranged in a great pyramid, with three ships in the first row, thirteen in the second, fourteen in the third, twenty in the fourth, thirty in the fifth, forty in the sixth, and sixty in the seventh.

> Between the ships and their ranks there was such care in the spacing of the fleet that from one rank to another the sound of a trumpet could be heard, and from one ship to another (in the same rank) the voice of a man.[18]

Richard's crusaders again found a much broader variety of instruments being used on these foreign shores. Roger of Wendover (d. 1236) mentioned that Richard was met at Acre, in 1191, by the 'shrill sounds of clarions, the braying of trumpets, and the horrid din of horns.'[19] The *Itinerarium* reported the same arrival music as 'trumpae, tubae, tibiae,' and 'tympana.'[20] This reference is quite important as it is the earliest known mention of the cognate form of the trumpet. The instrument is not further identified, but is clearly distinguished from the *tuba*.

A final eyewitness describes for us what it was like to face the attack of these Eastern adversaries with their frightening music.

[17] Farmer, ibid., 245; Farmer, 'Military Music,' 11.

[18] Richard of Devizes, *The Chronicle of Richard of Devizes*, ed. John T. Appleby (London: Thomas Nelson, 1963), 35.

[19] Farmer, 'Crusading Martial Music,' 244.

[20] Ibid.

> They came on with irresistible charge, on horses swifter than eagles, and urged on like lightening to attack our men; and as they advanced, they raised a cloud of dust, so that the sky was darkened. In front came certain of their admirals, as it was their duty, with clarions and trumpets; some had horns, others had pipes and timbrels, gongs, cymbals, and other instruments, producing a horrible noise and clamour. The earth vibrated from the loud and discordant sounds, so that the crash of thunder could not be heard amidst the tumultuous noise of horns and trumpets. They did this to excite their spirit and courage, for the more violent the clamour became, the more bold were they for the fray.[21]

[21] Goeffrey de Vinsauf, *Chronicle of Richard the First's Crusade* (London, 1914; written in 1191), 234–235.

Henry III (1216–1272)

While nothing is known of the music of John (1199–1216), Henry III has been mentioned previously for his order, in 1253, which established the London Waits.

An eyewitness to the marriage of Henry III, in 1236, has left a very interesting description, especially of the trumpet and horn music which seems to have been heard by those present as quite unusual.

> There were assembled at the king's nuptial festivities such a host of nobles of both sexes, such numbers of religious men, such crowds of the populace, and such a variety of actors, that London, with its capacious bosom, could scarcely contain them. The whole city was ornamented with flags and banners, chaplets and hangings, candles and lamps, and with wonderful devices and extraordinary representations, and all the roads were cleansed from mud and dirt, sticks, and everything offensive. The citizens, too, went out to meet the king and queen, dressed out in their ornaments, and vied with each other in trying the speed of their horses. On the same day, when they left the city for Westminster, to perform the duties of butler to the king (which office belonged to them by right of old, at the coronation), they proceeded thither dressed in silk garments, with mantles worked in gold, and with costly changes of raiment, mounted on valuable horses, glittering with new bits and saddles, and riding in troops arranged in order. They carried with them three hundred and sixty gold and silver cups, preceded by the king's trumpeters and with horns sounding, so that such a wonderful novelty struck all who beheld it with astonishment.[22]

[22] Matthew Paris, *Matthew Paris's English History*, trans. John Allen Giles (London, 1852), 1:8.

The brother to this Henry, Richard, Earl of Cornwall, was also King of the Romans. Matthew Paris (d. 1259) described a reception given Richard in Cremona, in 1241, during which the Emperor, Frederick III, of Hohenstaufen, arranged for an elephant to appear in the procession. Upon the elephant were two trumpeters, a drummer, a player on the double-pipes, and the driver, who also played a large handbell.

Edward I (1272–1307)

With the first of the Edwards, one begins to find more specific information of wind instrument activity in the English court.

Edward I had one of the most successful reigns in English history, reorganizing the army (he introduced the long bow), but most important the development of a Parliament. This same grand vision can be seen again at moments of important celebrations. For the ceremonies at Pentecost, 1306, for the knighting of the future Edward II, he assembled minstrels from all parts of Western Europe. For the marriage of his daughter he employed four hundred and twenty-six minstrels!

For the major church feast days he seems to have contributed by hiring additional minstrels. Pay documents exist for the employment of two trumpeters and a nakerer for Trinity Sunday, 1306,[23] and for three minstrels of his sons, for Epiphany of the same year.[24]

According to Rastall, Edward maintained four trumpets as his regular ensemble for daily ceremonial music.[25] If he needed more, as he apparently did for a trip in 1304, he sometimes borrowed them from another noble. During war, these same trumpet players were used for giving signals, such as to assemble the troops, as an eyewitness in 1281 confirms.

> … fist soner ses trompes et ses naquarres pour ralier de ses gens ce qu'il porroit aver.[26]

Edward II (1307–1327)

This Edward was a gentle soul, mostly interested in farming. When he desired to stop the use of torture in the examination of suspects or witnesses, he was immediately reprimanded by Pope Clement V: 'We hear that you forbid torture as contrary to the laws of your land. But no state law can override canon law, our law. Therefore I command you at once to submit

---

[23] Rastall, 'Some English Consort-Groupings,' 180, fn. 7:
Menestralli: … Johanni Garsie, Johanni le Cateloyne trumpatoribus, et Johanni le Nakarer, menestrallis Principis, facientibus menestralciam suam coram eodem apud Neubotel, die Sancte Trinitatis, de dono eiusdem domini ad quatuor capas nigras de secta sibi emendas cuilibet 12.0d per manus proprias 48.0d.

[24] Ibid., 188:
M. Taburr: Martinetto Taburrario, Willelmo et Johanni Trumpariis menestrallis dominorum facientibus menestralciam in presencia corundem in vigilia et die Epiphanie … 20.0d

[25] Ibid., 187.

[26] Frédéric Godefroy, *Dictionnaire de l'ancienne langue française* (Paris: Vieweg, 1902), 5:461.

those men to torture.'[27] Edward also banned football in 1314 because it was a game so violent as to lead to breaches of the peace.

The official household ordinances of 1318 and 1323 require that two trumpet players be available to the king at all times, the latter one reading in part,

> Trompours, Trompetours.
> There shalbe ij trumpeters & two other minstrels, & sometimes more & sometimes lesse, who shall play before the kinge when it shal please him. Thei shal eate in the chamber or in the hal as thei shalbe commaunded; thei shal have wages & robes each according to his estate at the discretion of the steward & thresorer.[28]

Hayes believes there were additional shawm players who appear on the Westminister Feast list without the names of their instruments.[29] Of the trumpet players, payments in 1310 give the names of John de Kenynton and John Scot, accompanied by the the naker player, named Francekinus. Two Welsh trumpeters were visiting at court from 23 July to 1 October 1307, named Yevan and Ythel.[30] Another minstrel, William de Morlee, known as Roy de North, was given a grant of land for his service.[31] Even given the small rooms of some of the castles of this period, these trumpet players were used indoor, as well as for outdoor ceremonial needs. As Rastall points out,

> The trumpeters minstrelsy was not invariably outdoor music. On 20 February, 1311, King Robert, a trumpeter, was one of several minstrels who performed before the king in the house of the Friars Minor at York on the day of the purification of the Countess of Cornwall; the king was again at the house of the York Friars Minor when William Corbet and his companion, trumpeters of the Earl of Arundel, played to him in his chamber on 24 October, 1319; and the same William and Walter the trumpeter were again rewarded for minstrelsy before the king in his chamber in the castle of Devizes on 26 April, 1321.[32]

Finally, there is a miniature of Edward's wedding which shows a trumpeter standing awaiting the end of the blessing in order to play. He appears to be holding a short trumpet, which (if one can trust the artist) may represent the first of the newer instrument which will become the slide-trumpet.[33]

[27] George Gordon Coulton, *Medieval Panorama* (New York: Macmillan, 1944), 379.

[28] Gerald Hayes, *King's Music* (Oxford: Oxford University Press, 1937), 34.

[29] Ibid.

[30] Rastall, 'Some English Consort-Groupings,' 187.

[31] Chambers, *The Mediaeval Stage*, 1:49.

[32] Rastall, 'Some English Consort-Groupings,' 188.

[33] In *Grandes Chroniques de France* (Leningrad, Publitschnaja Biblioteka imeni M. E. Saltykowa-Stschedrina, Ms.fr. F. XIV, 4, fol. 381).

Edward III (1327–1377)

A contemporary said of Edward III, 'his face was like that of a God.'[34] A 'God of War,' perhaps, for he waged war against France for a generation, the cost of which was his general disinterest in domestic affairs, leaving his country in economic and political chaos. But as a military leader he was so successful that he almost completely destroyed France. In his victory at Crecy, in 1346, Froissart wrote that thirty thousand were killed. Edward's success was in his Englishmen's long pikes, against which the French cavalry were helpless. Some date the beginning of the superiority of infantry over cavalry with this battle; artillery was also used here, although with little effect—one eyewitness suggesting its value was limited to its noise.[35]

According to Bowles, Edward had with his army two clarion players, five trumpets, and both the small and large drums during this battle.[36] Following this victory, Edward led his troops to siege Calais. His success there led to that city becoming part of England for the following two centuries. This siege lasted one year and when Edward finally entered the city, the scene was described by Froissart.

> The King mounted his horse, as did the royalty, barons, and knights, they rode forward toward Calais and entered into the city to an abundance of trumpets, tabours, nacaires and buccines.[37]

Chambers also believed Edward's band was of an unusually large size at this time.

> A little later in the reign, between 1344 and 1347, there were nineteen who received 12d. a day in war, when they doubtless formed a military band.[38]

A final picture of Edward at war, engaged in a naval battle with Spain in 1350, is also related by Froissart.

> On embarking, the King gave orders as to the plan of fighting, and then seated himself in the bow of his ship, waiting for the Spaniards. He was dressed in a black velvet jacket, with a beaver hat of the same color, which became him well; and, according to those who were there, he was never more joyous. He made his minstrels play to him, on the horn,

[34] George Gordon Coulton, *Chaucer and His England* (London: Methuen, 1921), 173.

[35] George Sarton, *Introduction to the History of Science* (Baltimore: Williams & Wilkins, 1930), III/i, 38.

[36] Bowles, *Musikleben*, 78.

[37] Quoted in Kastner, *Manuel Général*, 90. Kastner quotes another, unnamed, eyewitness who gives a larger variety of instruments in Edward's military band, 'menestrandiers, de trompes, de tambours, de nacaires, de chalemies et de muses.'

[38] Chambers, *The Mediaeval Stage*, 1:49.

a German dance which "Master John Chandos," who was with him, had brought over from Germany; and he made "Master Chandos" sing with his minstrels, "which gave him great pleasure."[39]

For the 'peace time band' of Edward III we have an extant list of instruments found in the Household Ordinances of 1348:

THE KING'S CLERKES

Trompettes	5
Citolers	1
Pipers [shawms]	5
Taberett	1
Clarions	2
Nakerers	1
Fidelers	1
Waytes	3
Archers on horse	3
Archers on foot	3

There are here two players of string instruments and seventeen of wind instruments, with pay given as 20s. per year. It should be noticed that the ranking is important, which is why I have given the archers. Thus, the trumpets, although paid the same as the other winds, are of the highest rank; all rank above the archers. Even in the time of war, the wind players rank with such people as 'The Kinge's Chaplyns, Espuiers,' etc., above the archers.[40]

From the Issue Rolls in the Pell Office, the records for 1370 provide a few names of the king's wind band members: Arnold le Pyper, Lambekin Taborer, John de Hangston, Havekin FitzLybkyn, Richard Baath, John Prat, John Absolon, John de Middleton, John de Buckyngham, and Nicholas Hanneye.[41]

In general, one can see Edward as a supporter of court music. He sent his bagpipers across the seas to a minstrel school and he supplied his Queen, Philippa, with her own minstrels.[42] An entry in the City Letter Books of 1337 suggests he allowed his musicians to appear at civic events, in order to earn additional pay, 'the minstrels and Palfreymen of our Lord the King.'[43] Another traditional means for the wind players to gain extra pay was to visit the great houses of other members of the aristocracy for performances. One of the great early poems of the

[39] Retold by William Longman, in *The History of the Life and Times of Edward the Third* (London, 1869), 325.

[40] Hayes, *King's Music*, 34.

[41] Ibid.

[42] Chambers, *The Mediaeval Stage*, 1:50.

[43] Crewdson, *The Worshipful Company of Musicians*, 25.

English language, *Piers the Plowman* (1362), by William Langland, suggests that Edward also extended this priviledge to his wind players.

> Clerkus and knyites welcometh
> kynges mynstrales,
> And for loue of here lordes
> lithen hem at festes;
> Muche more, me thenketh riche men authe
> Haue beggars by-fore hem
> whiche beth godes mynstrales.[44]

44 Quoted in Chambers, *The Mediaeval Stage*, 1:41.

One begins to see the lesser English lords also maintaining wind bands at this time. The Earl of Arundel, in 1376, for example, had an entourage which included four shawm players, two trumpeters, and a clarion player with him during the battle of Crecy.[45]

45 Francis William Galpin, *Old English Instruments of Music* (London: Methuen, 1910), 203.

Richard II (1377–1399)

Richard II became king at age eleven. A contemporary said of him, that he was 'seemely of shape and favour, and of nature good enough, if the wickednesse and naughtie demeanour of such as were about him had not altered it ... He was prodigal, ambitious, and much given to pleasure of the bodie.'[46]

46 Raphael Holinshed, *Chronicle*, 3:507.

On the day of his coronation a great procession was held in London. An eyewitness reports:

> Nor did these great guilds lack a large company of clarions and trumpets: for every guild is led by its own trumpeters. Trumpeters had been stationed by the Londoners above the tower in the same street, which had been built in the king's honor, to sound a fanfare on his approach.[47]

47 Thomae Walsingham, *Historia anglicana*, ed. Henry Thomas Riley (London, 1863), 1:331.

As Richard approached the tower, four girls showered his path with golden leaves and imitation gold coins.[48] For the coronation ceremony itself, Richard was represented by eleven state trumpeters, as one knows from an extant order for the preparation of that number of trumpet banners.[49]

48 Bowles, 'Musical Instruments in Civic Processions,' 150.

49 William Jones, *Crowns and Coronations* (London: Chatto & Windus, 1902), 201ff.

If one can judge from the quotation about him by his contemporary, quoted above, Richard enjoyed himself as king. Tournaments were still popular and one can see a tournament scene, showing a slide-trumpet and two timpani, carved on a Worcester Cathedral choir seat from this period.

Mumming was a very popular court entertainment during Richard's reign and there is a surviving account of such an event which occurred in 1377, shortly before Richard's coronation. The 'mummers' were disguised to represent an emperor and a pope with their followers. They rode to Kennington, where Richard lived, entered the hall and invited the prince and lords to play dice. Discreetly, the 'mummers' lost, drank, danced, and departed.

> At ye same tyme ye Comons of London made great sporte and solemnity to ye yong prince: for upon ye monday next before ye purification of our lady at night and in ye night were 130 men disguizedly aparailed and well mounted on horsebacke to goe on mumming to ye said prince, riding from Newgate through Cheape whear many people saw them with great noyse of minstralsye, trumpets, cornets and shawmes and great plenty of waxe torches lighted and in the beginning they rid 48 after ye maner of esquiers two and two together clothed in cotes and clokes of red say or sendall and their faces covered with vizards well and handsomely made: after these esquiers came 48 like knightes well arayed after ye same manner: after ye knights came one excellent arrayed and well mounted as he had bene an emperor: after him some 100 yards came one nobly arayed as a pope and after him came 24 arayed like cardinals and after ye cardinals came 8 or 10 arayed and with black vizards like deuils appearing nothing amiable seeming like legates, riding through London and ouer London bridge towards Kenyton wher ye yong prince made his aboad with his mother and the D. of Lancaster and ye Earles of Cambridge, Hertford, Warrick and Suffolk and many other lordes which were with him to hould the solemnity, and when they were come before the mansion they alighted on foot and entered into ye haule and sone after ye prince and his mother and ye other lordes came out of ye chamber into ye haule, and ye said mummers saluted them, shewing a pair of dice upon a table to play with ye prince, which dice were subtilly made that when ye prince shold cast he shold winne and ye said players and mummers set before ye prince three jewels each after other: and first a balle of gould, then a cupp of gould, then a gould ring, ye which ye said prince wonne at thre castes as before it was appointed, and after that they set before the prince's mother, the D. of Lancaster and ye other earles euery one a gould ringe and ye mother and ye lordes wonne them. And then ye prince caused to bring ye wyne and they dronk with great joye, commanding ye minstrels to play and ye trompets began to sound and other instruments to pipe etc. And ye prince and ye lordes dansed on ye one syde, and ye mummers on ye other a great while and then they drank and tooke their leave and so departed toward London.[50]

[50] London, British Museum (Harleian M.S. 247, f. 172v).

Another manuscript (Harleian, Nr. 433) in the British Museum suggests that Richard was exceptionally generous in his rewards to his musicians.[51] In Rymer's *Foedera*, of 1387, there is a permit granted by Richard to his chief minstrel, 'John Caumz, Rex minstrallorum,' to leave England for a year. Perhaps he left to visit minstrel schools or even to participate in someone's private war. An old ballad of the battle of Otterbourne (1388) says,

> Wherefore schote archars, for my sake
> And let scharpe arowes flee:
> Mynstsrells play up for your waryson (reward)
> And well quyt it shall be.[52]

There are also records of minstrels visiting Richard's court and receiving the customary gifts for their performance. The Issue Roll lists such a payment dated 6 July 1392:

> To two minstrels from the King of Aragon. In money received from them at Nottingham in discharge of 1 pound, 6s.8d. which the Lord the King commanded to be paid them of his gift.[53]

Richard himself was a musician and was praised for his ability by an early chronicle of his life.

> And so playing balades and songs
> Rondeleau and laix
> Very well and beautiful: so it was
> no one left him (when he played).[54]

The economic and political problems left by Edward III caused Richard's reign to be characterized by uprisings, which the young king met with courage. But the seeds of dissent were too deep and Richard was overthrown and placed in a prison at Pontefract where he died, probably murdered, at age thirty-three. He loved books, helped Chaucer and opened schools to everyone for the first time. We remember him for having gained the sympathy of Shakespeare, who wrote of him the immortal lines:

> For God's sake let us sit upon the ground
> and tell sad stories of the death of Kings.[55]

---

[51] The 'impression' of boys for the Chapel Royal seems to have begun at this time. An extant document empowers a John Melynek 'to take and seize for the king all such singing-men expert in the science of music as he could find and think able to do the king's service, within all places of the realm.' Quoted in Duncan, *The Story of Minstrelsy*, 85.

[52] Farmer, 'Military Music', 15.

[53] Hayes, *King's Music*, 34.

[54] Quoted in ibid.
Et si faisoit balades & chancons
Rondeaulx & laix
Tresbien & bel: si n'estoit il que homs lais.

[55] *Richard II*, act 3, scene 3.

Kings of the House of Lancaster

Henry IV (1399–1413)

When John of Gaunt died in 1399, Richard confiscated his property, to the horror of the aristocracy. Gaunt's son, Henry Bolingbroke, raised an army, overthrew Richard, and became king himself, as Henry IV. Henry's brief reign was characterized by constant battle with his enemies, quarrels with Parliament, and his personal tribulations, with leprosy and venereal disease. An early chronicle says he departed to God, 'in great perplexity and little pleasure.'[56]

Early in his reign, Henry had to put down a rebellion by Sir Thomas Blount. Having done this, and wishing to impress the other nobles who might have similar desires, Henry sent his adversaries's heads, slung on poles, before him 'with the music and the sound of the trumpet.'[57] When his ships sailed from Southampton in 1412 to attack the French, his army was accompanied by 'the sound of trumpet and naker.'[58]

A court pay document of 1404 indicates tht Henry maintained a personal ensemble of six players[59] and no doubt these minstrels were among the eight which Henry took with him when he sailed for Denmark, in 1406, for the marriage of his daughter, Philippa, to Eric, King of Denmark.[60]

There is some evidence that Henry supported minstrels long before he was king. A pay document for 1396 carries an interesting reference to a group of minstrels playing on horseback before Henry on New Year's Day and on Epiphany.[61] Another source speaks of Henry traveling abroad with his minstrels in 1390 and 1392.[62] His care of these minstrels can be seen in his orders to clothe them, both from before his reign[63] and to the end of his life. Two months before his death, for example, one finds an order for a suit of clothes for his minstrel, William Bingley.[64]

In addition, there is some evidence that Henry played the recorder. His purchase of '1 fistula nomine Ricordo' in London in 1387 is thought to be the earliest mention of this name in the English language.[65] It is also interesting that he sent three large silver gilt horns as a gift to Count Vertus, in Milan, in 1392, and ordered an ivory garnished horn, overgilded in silver, for himself in 1400.[66]

[56] Holinshed, *Chronicle*, 3:541.

[57] Wylie, *History of England under Henry the Fourth*, 1:107ff.

[58] Ibid., 4:76.

[59] London, Public Records Office, Queen's Remembrancer Wardrobe Account, 95/36. The six minstrels mentioned here were John Clyf, Thomas Norres, William Baldewyn, John Vernage, William Haliday, and John Sendall.

[60] Wylie, *Henry the Fourth*, 2:447.

[61] Duchy of Lancaster Records, Class 28, Bundle 3, Nr. 6; and Wylie, *Henry the Fourth*, 3:328.

[62] Rastall, 'Some English Consort-Groupings,' 189.

[63] Duchy of Lancaster Records, Class 28, Bundle 1, Nr. 2, contains a pay order for 'blod'ray cloth and tanne facings' for the minstrels, William Allgood, William de York, Master John Nakerner, John Bromer, Robert Crakile, and Thomas Trumpett.

[64] Wylie, *Henry the Fourth*, 4:102.

[65] Duchy of Lancaster Records, Class 28, Bundle 1, Nr. 1;. also Wylie, *Henry the Fourth*, 3:325.

[66] Duchy of Lancaster Records, Class 28, Bundle 1, Nr. 3; Public Records Office, Wardrobe Accounts, 45/1.

Henry V (1413–1422)

As a boy, Henry V was said to have a handsome face, thick brown hair, small ears, good teeth and clear hazel eyes. It was said he could run so quick that he could run down the fleetest deer. He was a musician, was fluent in French and could read Latin. One who knew him said that after he became king, 'he was changed into another man, studying to be honest, grave, and modest.'[67]

Immediately after his coronation ceremony, 'the minstrelsy struck up'[68] and the new king was led to his coronation banquet.

> He sat comely and gracious beneath the cloth of estate admidst the noise and whiffling of the waits in their coloured longcloth gowns aloft and the din and clamour of the guests below.[69]

Following the signing of a treaty (9 April 1420), Henry married Catherine, daughter to Charles VI of France at Troyes. The wedding ceremony included the music of 'trompettes et menstrelz du roy d'Engleterre et plusieurs aultres.'[70] After the ceremony a great procession was held. Numerous minstrels came to town to participate, for Henry had had a new gold coin minted and promised one to any minstrel who played in the parade. An eyewitness described this magnificent spectacle with the queen's carriage drawn by

> eight English horses, white as snow, the carriages draped in gilt like the rays of the sun, and in front of the chariot lead a great melody of trumpets, clarions, minstrels, and many other instruments by the hundreds and thousands, and one knows that many players appeared this day because it was ordered that each one of them would receive this day a salut d'or which the king had recently begun to forge.[71]

For Catherine's coronation in 1421 another large wind band, described by an eyewitness as, 'all maner of lowde mynstrelsie' participated.[72] Specially constructed 'giants' guarded the city gates, there were fountains of wine and a great banquet given in Westminster Hall.[73]

[67] Walsingham, quoted in William Stubbs, *Constitutional History of England* (Oxford: Clarendon, 1903), 3:79.

[68] *Antiq. Repert.*, 2:288.

[69] London, Public Records Office, Wardrobe Accounts, 406/26.

[70] Kervyn de Lettenhove, ed., *Le livre des trahisons de France envers la maison de Bourgogne* (Brussels, 1873), 156.

[71] Quoted in Marix, *Histoire de la Musique*, 24.
   Et par, devant ce chariot se dementoit grand melodie de trompettes, clarons, menestres, et de moult d'autres instruments a cents et a milliers, et devez savoir que maint joueur d'instrument y comparu ce jour pour ce qu'il estoit ordonne que chacun d'eux aroit pour ce jour un salut d'or que le roy Henry avoit commence a forger tout nouvellement.

[72] Friedrich Wilhelm Daniel Brie, ed., *The Brut* or *The Chronicles of England* (London: Kegan Paul, Trench, Trübner, 1906), 2:426, 492.

[73] James Hamilton Wylie, *The Reign of Henry the Fifth* (Cambridge: Cambridge University Press, 1914), 3:268.

Henry seems to have maintained a rather large band of minstrels; near the end of his reign, they are given as eighteen and paid 12d. per day.[74] These minstrels performed all the usual duties, such as accompanying the crier who makes the king's announcements[75] and traveling with the king on his voyages.[76]

Henry's brief reign is remembered by all the English-speaking world for his astounding victory over the French in the Battle of Agincourt in 1415. Henry sailed with eleven thousand troops, in more than a thousand ships. In his overwhelming victory, some French historians estimate the English loss at sixteen hundred and the French loss at ten thousand! One of the minstrels who accompanied Henry to this battle wrote that there were eighteen in the band[77] and one who heard them during the battle itself reported, 'drums and nakers beat, horns and pipes brayed, the clarioners and trumpers blew up.'[78]

After the victory, there was a great procession in London, 'with clarionys and all maner of lowde mynstrelsie.'[79] At the city gate two 'giants,' a man and wife, cried out a greeting to the king. There was an allegorical pageant with twelve 'Venerable Apostles and twelve of England's kings,' and a pasteboard castle in which a chorus of girls, dressed in white, danced to tambourines, singing, 'Noel!'

There is a very interesting eyewitness account of regular concerts by Henry's military band during the Siege of Melun (1420). One is reminded that, until the twentieth century, war was a spectator event when one reads that Henry had a house built and furnished for his wife near his tent, just behind the battle lines. Here every day at sunrise and at sunset eight or ten English minstrels of wind instruments gave an hour-long concert.[80]

Henry VI (1422–1461, 1470–1471)

This Henry became king at age nine months. An eyewitness describes the baby lying on a platform during the coronation while the trumpets played.

> All the prelattes wente on procession berynge eche of them a relyk of dyuerse sayntes ... And then he was leyde upon the high scaffold, and that was covered all with red say between the high autere and the quere. And he was set in his astate in the myddes of the scaffold there, beholdynge the people all abowte.[81]

[74] Household Accounts, quoted in Chambers, *The Mediaeval Stage*, 1:50.

[75] For the truce between England and France in 1414, an order provides seven crowns to pay for a copy, six to the herald who proclaimed it, and only one crown to the accompanying trumpets! (Exch. Accts. 186/2).

[76] Wylie, *Henry the Fifth*, 2:5.

[77] John Cliff, of London. See London, Public Record Office, Lord Treasurer's Remembrancer, Misc., Enrolled Accts. 6/11.

[78] Quoted in Wylie, *Henry the Fifth*, 2:156. The French, according to one writer, did not have as many instruments on the field as the English. Jean Le Fèvre, speaking of the night before the battle, said that the French had fifty thousand men, but (with surprise) 'they had there so few instruments to rejoice themselves with.' Quoted in Kastner, *Manuel Général*, 91.

[79] Friedrich Wilhelm Daniel Brie, 'The Chronicles of England,' in *Geschichte und Quellen der Mittelenglischen Prosachronik* (Marburg: N. G. Elwert, 1905), 426.

[80] *Chronique de Enguerrand de Monstrelet* (Paris, 1603; written 1390–1453), quoted in Louis Claude Douët d'Arcq, ed., *Soc. Hist. France* (Paris, 1857), 3:412.

[81] Jones, *Crowns and Coronations*, 210.

The struggle Henry had with his successor, Edward IV, is called the War of the Roses, Lancastrian red and Yorkist white. Edward won and became king in 1461, then Henry won and returned as king in 1470. Edward won again, murdered Henry and secured his family in power. Neither king was king in power or character; both were at the mercy of other forces. Henry was mad; Edward was fat and indolent.

Henry had twelve minstrels by 1455 and we know one was called a 'wait' and six were trumpeters.[82] The king's minstrels may have had some difficulty keeping their ranks full, for one reads in 1456 that they were empowered to force into service any 'young men of comely appearance, trained in the art of minstrelsy.'[83]

During this period when 'minstrel' usually meant a player of wind instruments, the minor nobles who had taken on so much power during the reign of the incapable Henry had also begun to assemble small wind bands of their own. For example, the bailiff's accounts of the city of Shrewsbury for 1457 lists the ensembles of three dukes.

> Quatuor ministrallis domini ducis de Bukyngham ... iiij ministsrallis d'ni ducis de Eboroco (York) iv minstsrellis d'ni ducis de Excestro.[84]

[82] Chambers, *The Mediaeval Stage*, 1:50.

[83] Stevens, *Early Tudor Court*, 307.

[84] Ibid., 300.

Kings of the House of York

Edward IV (1461–1470, 1471–1483)

With the reigns of Edward IV one begins to see the use of rather large numbers of wind instruments in the court. Twenty-five minstrels were issued livery for his coronation in 1461, nearly all of which were certainly winds.[85] In addition to winds there are also now some royal string players (called *strengemen*) and a large choral organization in the chapel. For the coronation of the queen, in 1465, the leader of the king's shawm ensemble[86] was given money to distribute to visiting minstrels, more than one hundred in all, who seem to have all belonged to the private wind bands of visiting nobles.[87]

From the household regulations of Edward there is an unusual extant document which gives the most complete picture we have of the life of the medieval court musician in England. This regulation discusses the basic duties of thirteen regular wind players, their yearly fees and livery, and cautions

[85] Henry Thomas Cart de LaFontaine, *The King's Musick* (London: Novello, 1909), 1.

[86] Called 'still minstrels.' This term was used through the reign of Henry VIII, but the players can be identified as shawm players.

[87] Cora L. Scofield, *The Life and Reign of Edward the Fourth* (London: Longmans Green, 1923), 1:376–377.

the players not to be too presumptuous in asking rewards from any of the lords of the land, citing an earlier prohibition of Emperor Henry II.

> Mynstrelles, xiii, whereof one is verger, that directeth them all in festivall dayes to theyre stations, to bloweings and pipynges, to suche offices as must be warned to prepare for the king and his houshold at metes and soupers, to be the more readie in all servyces; and all these sitting in the hall togyder; whereof sume use trumpettes, sume shalmuse and small pipes, and sume as strengemen, comyng to this courte at five festes of the yere, and then to take theyre wages of houshold after iiijd ob. a day, if they be present in courte, and then they to avoyde the next day after the festes be done. Besides eche of them anothyr reward yerely, taking of the king in the resceyte of the chekker, and clothing wynter and somer, or xxs. a piece, and lyverey in courte, at evyn amonges them all, iiij gallons ale; and for wynter season, iij candela wax, vj candells peris', iiij talwood, and sufficiaunt logging by the herberger, for them and theyre horses, nygh to the courte. Also havyng into courte ij servauntes honest, to beare theyre trumpettes, pipes, and other instrumentes, and a torche for wynter nyghts, whyles they blowe to souper, and other revelles, delyvered at the chaundrey; and allway ij of these persons to continue in courte in wages, beyng present to warne at the kinge's rydinges, when he goeth to horse-backe, as ofte as it shall require, and by theyre blowinges the houshold meny may follw in the countries. And if any of these two minstrelles be sicke in courte, he taketh ij loves, one messe of grete mete, one gallon ale. They have no part of any rewardes gevyn to the houshold. And if it please the kinge to have ij strenge Minstrelles to contynue in like wise. The Kinge wull not for his worshipp that his Minstrelles be too presumptuous, nor too familier to ask any rewardes of the lordes of his londe, remembring De Henrico secundo imperatore (1002–1024) qui omnes Ioculatores suos et Armaturos monuerit, ut nullus eorum in eius nomine vel dummodo steterint in sericio suo nihil ab aliquo in regno suo deberent petere donandum; sed quod ipsi domini donatores pro Regis amore citius pauperibus erogarent.[88]

[88] London, Public Records Office, Miscellaneous Books, Exchequer L.T.R., Nr. 206.

Another document discusses in detail the duties, pay and livery of the wind player who served wait duty for the court. He is better paid than the normal wind players, receiving housing and a servant, which reflects the importance of this basic duty.

> A wayte that nightelye from Mycelmas to Shreve Thorsdaye pipthe wathce within this courte fower tymes, in the somere nightes iij tymes, and makethe bon gayte at every chambere doare and offyce, as well for feare of pyckeres and pilleres; he eateth in the halle with mynstrielles

and taketh liverey at nights a loffe, a galone of alle, and for somere nightes ij candles pich, a bushel of coles; and for wintere nightes half a loaf of bread, a galon of ale, iiij candles piche, a bushel coles; daylye whilste he is presente in courte for his wages in cheque roale allowed iiijd. or else iijd. by the discresshon of the stewarde and tressore, and that aftere his coming and diservinge; also cloathinge with the household yeomen or mynstrelles like to the wages that he takethe; and he be syke he taketh twoe loves, ij mese of greatemeate, one gallon of, ale. Also he partethe with the hoseholde of general gyfts, and hath his beddinge carried by the comptrollers assyngment; and under this yeoman a groome watere. Yf he can excuse the yeoman in his absence then he taketh rewarde, clotheinge, meat and all other things lyke to other grooms of household. Also this yeoman-waighte at the making of Knightes of the Bathe, for his attendance upon them by nighte-tyme in watching in the chapelle, hath to his fee all the watchinge-clothing that the Knight shall wear uppon him.[89]

Of these court wind players, many were perhaps trumpeters; by 1468, in any case, there were nine trumpets organized under a 'Marshal of the Trumpets.' Perhaps he was trying to keep ahead of the powerful dukes, for it is known that the Duke of Clarence, for example, had six personal trumpets to announce his arrivals.[90] Another account tells of the Duke of York arriving in London, 'his trumpets and clarions giving loud notice of his arrival.'[91] In the same manner, the trumpets of Edward can be seen where ever he makes an appearance: for his arrival in London in 1471,[92] for his arrival in Paris in 1475,[93] and for the christening of Princess Elizabeth in 1466.[94]

In the regulation quoted above, one will see the emphasis on the minstrels appearing to play for the king's meals. When great banquets were given for visiting nobles, as in 1466, when Edward gave a fifty-course banquet for visiting Bohemian knights, all of the players must have participated, including the singers.[95]

It will be noticed in the same document that the wind players were given the special privilege of eating in the great hall with the nobles. As a further example of their unique access to the king, an old chronicle relates,

> as he (the king) was in the north country, in the month of September, as he lay in his bed, one named Alexander Carlile, that was sarjent of the minstsrels, came to him in great haste, and bade him arise, for he had enemies coming to take him, which were within six or seven miles.[96]

[89] *Liber Niger*, quoted in Crewdson, *Worshipful Company of Musicians*, 164–165.

[90] Rastall, 'Some English Consort-Groupings,' 189.

[91] Scofield, *Edward the Fourth*, 1:102–103.

[92] Kendall, *Richard the Third*, 62.

[93] Scofield, *Edward the Fourth*, 2:147.

[94] Ibid., 1:395.

[95] Kendall, *Richard the Third*, 64.

[96] Hayes, *King's Music*, 43.

Finally, there is a fifteenth-century miniature which pictures Edward's military band during the siege of Belle-Perche in 1468. One sees three clarions and a slide-trumpet on the left and three shawms on the right side of the picture.[97]

Richard III (1483–1485)

The twelve-year-old Edward V was king for only a brief time, and in name only as the real power was his uncle, Richard. Edward was trained in music, as one can see in a document of 1474.

> Item, we will that the sonnes of nobles, lords, and gentlemen beinge in householde with our sayde sonne ... be vertuously taught in grammer, musicke, and other cuninge and exercises of humanity.[98]

The evil Richard, with his 'ill-featured limbs, crooked back, hard-favored visage, and left shoulder much higher than his right,'[99] had a somewhat broader education, including riding, the sword, dagger, battle-axe, 'and completing the day's regimen by rehearsing the polite arts of harping, singing, piping, and dancing.'[100]

In one of the darkest chapters in English history, this Richard had young Edward and his brother Richard murdered in the Tower and then crowned himself Richard III. For his coronation a large number of minstrels were issued livery; some are identified as the king's trumpets and most were probably winds.[101] There were also a large number of visiting minstrels, including players from Austria and Bavaria.[102] One source says in all there were forty trumpets participating in the coronation ceremony.[103] During the ceremony these trumpets played with the organ and then led a procession over red cloth to Westminster Hall.[104]

Richard took his trumpeters with him into battle, for they were an important symbol of his person. Kendall gives us a picture of Richard in all of his glory at Bosworth Field.

> Richard was mounted on a white courser, a slight figure even in the casing of full armor. He bore a golden crown upon his helmet, that friend and foe alike might know that the King was going forth to battle. The banners of England and St. George floated above him. In his train blazed the heralds in their tabard coats of arms and trumpeters and drummers, their instruments flaunting the leopards and lilies and the white boar.[105]

---

[97] Berlin, State Library ('Chronik Jean Froissarts,' Depot Breslau I, Ms. Rehd. 2, fol. 23).

[98] Hayes, *King's Music*, 42.

[99] Holinshed, *Chronicle*, 3:712. Also Shakespeare, *Henry VI*, act 3, scene 3, line 2; and *Richard III*, act 1, scene 1.

[100] Kendall, *Richard the Third*, 52.

[101] LaFontaine, *The King's Musick*. Coronation liveries for William Herte the younger and Edmond Trumpet, mynstrals; John Hert, William Hert the elder, William Mayhue, James Hylle, Thomas Freman, William Wright, Edward Scarlet, Robert Trumpett, William Scarlet, John Bulson, John Browne, John Marshall, John Talbot, Henry Swan, Watkyn, Palvyn, William Davy, William Scarlet the younger, Rauf Hubert, William Wortley, Richard Dalamare, Henry Gyles, Janyn, taberetts and trumpetts ... John Crowland, marshal of the mynstrals; Richard Hylles, John Pryoure, John Paynell, Thomas Paynter, John Hatche, William Elyston, Nicholas Dennis, Peter de Casa noua, Saunder Marshall, Robert Grene, Thomas Mayhue, William Barley, Johannes William, mynstral, Lyefart Willerkyn, Walter, minstrel, and Gylkyn Couper.

[102] Chambers, *The Mediaeval Stage*, 1:53.

[103] Robert Davies, ed., *Extracts from the Municipal Records of the City of York* (London, 1843), 283ff.

[104] Kendall, *Richard the Third*, 274. Also, Sir Clements R. Markham, *Richard III: His Life & Character* (London: Smith, Elder, & Co., 1906), 127, where the original order of march is given. The 'Trumpets and Clarions' are third in the order, behind the 'Serjeants of Arms' and 'Heralds.'

[105] Kendall, *Richard the Third*, 428.

The House of Tudor

Henry VII (1485–1509)

The House of Tudor began with Henry VII, a strong and good king who achieved national unification and a centralized administration. It was his achievements which helped make possible the glories of Henry VIII. This Henry had a permanent indoor wind band of two, and sometimes three, shawms and two sackbuts.[106] Undoubtedly there were numerous trumpets for ceremonial occasions, for even the Earl of Northumberland maintained six trumpets at this time.[107] At his coronation, where Henry sat in golden satin and a purple robe, one heard all these instruments, as well as the visiting minstrels, who were called *Spielleute*.[108]

All court ceremonial occasions featured winds. When Prince Arthur married Katherine of Aragon in 1501, a great water-pageant featured the entire court traveling down the Thames river to Greenwich,

> with the moost goodly and plesaunt mirthe of trumpetts, clarions, shalmewes, tabers, recorders and other dyvyrs instruments, to whoes noyse upon the water hathe not been hard the like.[109]

Similarly, when his daughter, Margaret, left to marry James VI of Scotland, Henry sent along his wind players.

> Among the sayd Lords and the Qwene, was in Order Johannes and his companye, the Menstrelles of Musick, the Trompetts in displayed Banneres, in all the Departyngs of the Townes, and in the Intryng of the sam, playing on their Instruments to the Tym that she was past owt.[110]

The performers for the funeral of Queen Elizabeth, wife to Henry VII, included eighteen 'Gentilmen of the King's Chapell,' who were probably singers. In addition there were John Buntaunce, 'Mynstrell'; Steven Delalaund, Pety John, and Haskenet Delmers, 'Mynstrells to the prince'; and Gabriell and Kenner, 'Mynstrells to the Quene of Scottis.' Two wind ensembles are also listed:

[106] Rastall, 'Some English Consort-Groupings,' 196.

[107] Chambers, *The Mediaeval Stage*, 1:51.

[108] Jones, *Crowns and Coronations*, 147.

[109] Stevens, *Early Tudor Court*, 237.

[110] Ibid., 236.

SAKBUSSHES AND SHALMOYES
John de Peler   Hans Naille
William Burgh   Edward Peler
Adryan Wilmorth

THE KING'S TRUMPETTES
Peter de Cas a noua   Domonys
Thomas Freman   Adryan
John Gece   Fring
Jaket   John Decessid
William Freman[III]

For the funeral of Henry himself, in 1509, eleven children singers participated in addition to many performers of wind instruments.

MYNSTRELLS
Hakenett de Lewys   Stephyn de Lalaunde

MYNSTRELLS OF THE CHAMBRE
Gyles   Buntanes
Barbram

SEYKEBUDS AND SHALMEYS
Johannes   Edward John
Guyllam Borrow   Alexander Massu

THE KYNG'S TROMPYTTS
Jakett   Christopher
Peter   Adryan
Domynye   John Broune
John Beale   John Blank
Frank

TRUMPETS
John Hert   John Frere
Thomas Wrey   John Strutt
John Scarlet   Robert Wrey

THE MYNSTRELLS (SHAWMS)
John Chambre, marshall Thomas Mayre
John Furnes   John Abys
Thomas Spencer   Richard Waren
Thomas Grenyng   Thomas Peion

[III] LaFontaine, *The King's Musick*, 2.

TABRETTS WITH OTHERS
Marquesse Loreden   Janyn Marquesyn
Richard Anows[112]

[112] LaFontaine, *The King's Musick*, 2–3.

Notes on Court Wind Bands in Ireland and Scotland

The only reference I have found to medieval court wind bands in Ireland is a note regarding legal tracts of the early fourteenth century in which it is indicated that the king had flute players and also 'horn blowers.'[113]

[113] Wylie, *Henry the Fourth*, 2:153.

For this period in Scotland there are few available records, however its fourteenth-century literature offers a few clues. A ballad-historian, for example, recounting the Battle of Hallidon Hill (1333), when the Scots were defeated by Edward III, notes,

> This was do with merry sowne
> With pipes, trompes and tabers thereto
> And loud clarionnes thei blew also.[114]

[114] Farmer, *Military Music*, 15.

From the fourteenth century poem, *Orfeo and Heurodis*, one finds another reference to the army music of the Scots.

> Wele attourned ten hundred knightes
> Ich y-armed to his rightes;
> ...
> Tabours and trimpes yede hem bi,
> And al maner menstraci.[115]

[115] Quoted in Henry G. Farmer, 'Music in Mediaeval Scotland,' in *Proceedings of the Musical Association* 54 (1929–1930): 73.

Another portion of the same poem describes the same tradition we have seen in England of using the 'loud' instruments for banquets:

> In the castel the steward sat atte mete,
> And mani lording was by him sete.
> Ther were trompour and tabourers,
> Harpours fele and crouders,
> Miche melody thei maked alle,
> ...
> And Orfeo sat stille in the halle
> And herkneth.[116]

[116] Ibid.

During the fifteenth century, all four kings of Scotland, James I, II, III, and IV, were musicians. James I (1424–1437) composed and played several instruments. It was recorded that on the very eve of his assassination he spent his time

> yn redyng, yn syngyng and pypynge, yn harpynge, and yn other honest solaces of grete pleasance and disport.[117]

[117] Ibid., 76.

22 Court Wind Bands in France

BEFORE THE CRUSADES, references to court music in France mention only the trumpet and clarion for ceremonial use and a wide variety of instruments for entertainment. A typical example is the report of an eyewitness to the marriage of Louis I (814–840).

> Of the service there must be no question; All of the possible meats to be found were in abundance, and served between trumpets and clarions; and minstrels, lutes, psalterons and followers were many.[1]

[1] *Chronicle of St-Denis*. This quotation and others like it seems to separate 'minstrel' from lute, psalteron, etc., suppporting, I believe, the other, more direct, evidence that 'minstrel' usually implied a wind player.

According to Kastner, the French used the *carroccio* in the eleventh and twelfth centuries, but the tradition was short lived. As in the Italian version, multiple trumpeters performed on this vehicle, but the French model was richly decorated and drawn by cattle.[2]

[2] Kastner, *Manuel Général*, 80.

Louis IX, 'Saint Louis' (1226–1270)

It is possible to date the appearance of a wider variety of wind instruments in the French Court with the period following the Seventh Crusade, led by Louis IX. Louis was one of France's greatest kings, both as an administrator and as a man. Tall, handsome with finely cut features, rich blond hair and so outstanding in character that he has become known as 'Saint Louis.' His chronicler, Joinville, said, 'On no day of my life did I ever hear him speak evil of anyone.'[3] His government in every way was a model of organization and justice. William of Chartres said, 'men feared him because they knew he was just.'[4] A contemporary miniature pictures two heralds with the trumpets of Louis playing. From the trumpets hang the banners with the king's three lillies.[5]

The crusade itself (1249–1250) was not particularly successful but does provide us with some interesting details of the wind bands present. As Louis sailed into the Egyptian port of Damietta he heard 'noisy nacaires and cors sarrazinnois.'[6] Joinville describes Louis, by his standard, being heralded by 'a

[3] Jean de Joinville, *Chronicle of the Crusade of St. Louis* (Everyman's Library), 139.

[4] Dana Carleton Munro and George C. Sellery, *Medieval Civilization* (New York: Century, 1926), 520.

[5] Peter Panoff, *Militärmusik* (Berlin: Sigismund, 1944), 39.

[6] Joinville, *Chronicle of the Crusade of St. Louis*, also the following quotations.

great noise of trompes, nacaires and cors sarrazinnois.' This use of the term 'Saracen horn,' in French, by a French writer, clearly demonstrates that the influence on Western wind bands by the Eastern music heard in the earlier crusades had by this date become widely felt.[7]

Joinville goes into additional detail in describing the Saracen music. He discusses the use of this music with respect to the actual battles and describes concerts by the Sultan's band, which he calls *Haulequa* (from the Arabic, *Halqa*, 'circle'). This band, he says, consisted of 'cors sarrazinnois, tabours and nacaires,' although Farmer says other sources add reed-pipes and shawms.[8]

Philip III (1270–1285)

Philip III succeeded his father and tried to continue the crusade with the remnants of an army eager to quit. Shortly before he gave up and departed for France in 1270, he gave a royal welcome to his brother, Charles of Anjou, who came to visit him in Tunis. One who saw the procession recalled only the usual trumpet-types.

> If one commands to know what passed, the sound of trumpets, buisines and araines.[9]

Philip IV, 'The Handsome' (1285–1314)

Philip IV, who mounted the throne at age seventeen, was 'eaten up by the fever of avarice and cupidity,' according to a Flemish monk at Egmont.[10] A pay document for 1288 gives a complete list of his minstrels. In a few cases their instruments can be identified by their names, as in the case of 'Bill Trumpet.' Most interesting is the fact that a flute player is here called 'king of the flutes,' which is the earliest known use of the title 'king' for a wind player in France.[11]

[7] Reschke, 'Studie zur Geschichte der brandenburgisch-prussischen Heeresmusik' (PhD diss., Friedrich Wilhelms Universitat, Berlin, 1935), 5, points out that by the thirteenth century the French military bands consisted of brass, woodwind, and percussion instruments, a century before similar ensembles appear in Germany.

[8] Farmer, 'Crusading Martial Music,' 247.

[9] Bowles, 'Haut and Bas,' 149.

[10] M. Guizot, *France*, trans. Robert Black (New York: Co-Operative Publication Society, n.d.), 1:457.

[11] Ludwig, *Reliquioe manuscript omnis medii oevi*, 12:10, 25, 26.
  Ministeralli: Robertus de Berneville, Guillermus de Baudrecent, Rex Heraudum, Rex Flaioletus, Henricus de Lauduno, Tassinus, Guillermus Trompatorum, Guyotus de Bremireil, Guillermus le Ber ... Rex Ribaldorum.

Sons of Philip IV (1314–1328)

Philip had three sons who became king, although together they only served a total of fewer than fourteen years and none was distinguished. Louis X, 'The Quarreller,' had only a small musical company of four players: two trumpets, a drum and psalter.[12]

Philip V, 'The Long,' had a short reign, but a document from his first year announces that his minstrels had the right to share in the distribution of official clothes and the bread, wine and meat of the principal feasts.[13]

The Valois Kings

Philip VI (1328–1350)

As Philip V had no sons, a new line of kings begins with Philip VI, the king with whom one associates the beginning of the Hundred Years' War. Although he maintained an official household of at least one hundred and forty, only two of them seem to have been minstrels.[14] Given other evidence from this time, it is difficult to believe his court knew so little wind music. A poem, written in 1340 by Jean de le Motte, mentions a number of wind instruments, including 'cor, buisines et calimiaus menus (shawm), trompes, timbres, nacaires, tabours, estives (?), cor a doix, flagot et frestiaux.'[15]

This listing of instruments compares well with the wind players maintained by another noble during this period, Jean IV of Nantes. For festivities in 1341, his minstrels performed on tambours, nakers, shawms, and hunting horns.[16]

John II (1350–1364)

John, son to Philip IV, maintained a musical establishment with a very broad variety of instruments, as one can see in a document from near the beginning of his reign. It defines his 'menestreux' as those who play 'naquaires ou timbales, canon ou demi-flûte, du cornet, de la guiterne ou guitare Latine, de la flûte Behaigne ou bohemienne, de la trompette, de la guiterne Moresche ou guitare mauresque, et de la vielle.'[17]

[12] Ludwig, *Reliquioe manuscript*, 12:74. Johannes Trompator, Arnoldus Trompator, Micheletus de Nacriis, Guillotus de Psalterion.

[13] Bernhard, 'Recherches sur l'histoire de la corporation des ménétriers ou joueurs d' instruments de la ville de Paris,' in *Bibliothèque de l'école chantes* (Paris, 1842), 5.

[14] Grove, 12:350.

[15] *Parfait du paon*, quoted in André Pirro, *Histoire de la musique de la fin du XIVe siècle a la fin du XVIe* (Paris, 1940), 8.

[16] Grove, 13:21. A manuscript volume on the life of the fourteenth-century French noble, Gaston Phèbus, contains three miniatures which document the hunting horn. They show an instructor in the field teaching the use of the instrument, a hunter listening to the horns, and a group of four horn players playing for the chase of a wild pig. (Paris, National Library, Ms.fr. 616, fol. 54, 68, and 73—see images p. 210–212).

[17] Bernhard, 'Recherches,' 5. Documentation of this period of the French kings is made near impossible due to the destruction of the archives of the Chambre des Comptes in Paris in 1737.

Enseignement de la chasse: les veneurs apprennent à sonner de la trompe (Teaching hunting: the hunters learn to sound the horn), *Le livre de chasse* (The Book of Hunting), Gaston Phébus, folio 54

Chasse au cerf: laisser-courre du cerf (Deer hunting: unleash the deerhounds), *Le livre de chasse* (The Book of Hunting), Gaston Phébus, folio 68

212 THE WIND BAND AND WIND ENSEMBLE BEFORE 1500

Chasse à courre du sanglier (Hunting wild boar), *Le livre de chasse* (The Book of Hunting), Gaston Phébus, folio 73

During the second half of the fourteenth century, the descriptive poems begin to reflect not only this wider variety of instruments, but their clear division into 'loud' and 'soft' categories. The Romance, 'Floriant et Florete,' for example, identifies the 'loud,' or wind band as buisines, shawms, horns, and drums. These musicians, the poem says, tend to 'stir up too much gaiety.'[18] The anonymous, 'Eches amoureux,' ca. 1376, includes in the 'loud' band, 'trompez, tabours, tymbrez, naquaires, cymballes, cornemusez, chalemelles, and cornes.'[19] Eustache Deschamps, in 'Ballade pour Machaut,' includes shawms in the 'soft' ensemble, which is rare at this early date in other countries.[20]

[18] Bowles, 'Haut and Bas,' 120.

[19] Ibid.

[20] Ibid., 121.

Charles V (1364–1380) and Charles VI (1380–1422)

One can imagine such a diverse wind band performing when Charles V welcomed the Holy Roman Emperor to Paris. One reads of the silver trumpets poised with minstrels and the king in front, with knights and peers behind. As they played fanfares, the Emperor floated down the Seine in a boat designed like a house, hung with tapestries and filled with musicians.[21]

Whereas Charles V was one of the finest rulers in French history, the 'gamble of hereditary monarchy' now produced an idiot in Charles VI. He became king at age twelve; regents ruled until he was twenty, allowing Charles to devote himself to debauchery. He took control of the government in 1388, but was insane by 1392.

Several accounts exist which describe the use of the royal wind band playing for banquets at the time of Charles VI. The *Livre du duc des vrais amants*, by Christine de Pisan, speaks of a specific dinner which included wind instrument music after the meal.[22]

A royal banquet given at Hotel St. Pol by Charles, in 1393, seems to have included 'soft' background music during dinner, with trumpet fanfares announcing each course and special music by the court singers and wind band.

> For the company's pleasure they sounded hand instruments, such as flutes, tambours, shawms, harps, and vielle, and they had a great melodie of trumpets and clarions … at the head of the table there were singers of the royal chapel and the wind instrument minstrels.[23]

[21] Bowles, 'Musical Instruments in Civic Processions,' 150.

[22] André Pirro, *La Musique à Paris sous le règne de Charles VI* (Strasbourg: Heitz, 1930), 22.

[23] Ibid., 29.
Pour la compagnie esjoir, on y sonnoit maint instruments, comme flahutes, tambourins, chalemies, harpes, vielles et bedons, et se y avoit grand mellodie de trompettes et de clarons … Au lever de la table, estoient les chantres de musique de la chapelle royale et les haux menestreux.

A miniature from 1393 shows a wedding entertainment, a mask (of 'savages') with three shawms performing above in a balcony.[24] The wedding between Henry V, of England, and Catherine of France, which occurred in 1420, has been mentioned above. Here one heard large numbers of 'trompets, clarions, and minstrels.'

Charles VII (1422–1461)

Charles VII began the long overdue process of rebuilding villages, restoring the economy, and after regaining much of the lost land from England, signed a treaty to end the Hundred Years War.

During his five-hour long coronation ceremony in 1429, Joan of Arc stood beside the king, holding her banner. Finally the moment came when the archbishop poured the holy oil on his head and then placaed the crown upon him. At this moment the crowd cried, 'Noel!,' and the trumpets sounded so loud that it seemed as if the very vaults of the church would crack![25]

Aside from the inevitable horns and trumpets,[26] by this date Charles would have had shawms, which were in plentiful supply due to their use in civic wind bands. In 1457, King Ladislaus of Hungary sent envoys to Charles' court to seek his daughter's hand in marriage. Accompanying the envoys were musicians playing an instrument unknown to Paris, as an eyewitness describes.

> One had never before seen drums like big kettles, carried on horseback.[27]

The display of trumpet playing which welcomed the Duke of Bedford to Paris in 1424 has been discussed above. Another welcoming ceremony during the reign of Charles VII was one given the Duke of Orléans in his home city, on 24 January 1448. The celebration included allegories performed on twelve scaffolds and the wind band (*haults menestrals*) played under the direction of one called Oudin de St. Avry.[28]

[24] Jean Froissart, *Chroniques* (London, British Museum, Ms. Harley, 4380).

[25] Jules Quicherat, ed., *Procès de condamnation et de réhabilitation de Jeanne d'Arc* (Paris, 1841–1849), 5:128.

[26] A miniature from ca. 1460 pictures Charles VII and the Duke of Burgundy, traveling toward Paris, with the four royal trumpets of Charles. (Paris, National Library, *Grandes Chroniques de France*, Ms. fr. 6465, fol. 417.)

[27] Sachs, *The History of Musical Instruments*, 329.
On n'avoit ni mi oncques veu des tabourins comme de gros chaudrons qu'ils faisoient porter sur des chevaux.

[28] Bowles, 'Haut and Bas,' 130.

Louis XI (1461–1483)

One of France's best, but strangest, kings appears in the person of Louis XI. He lived very simply, dressed like an impoverished pilgrim in rough gray gown and shabby felt hat, and gave his entire energy and attention to the task of creating a unified nation. A contemporary said of him,

> If all the days of his life were computed in which joys and pleasures outweighed his pains and trouble, they would be found so few that there would be twenty mournful ones to one pleasant.[29]

[29] Philippe de Comines, *Memoirs* (London, 1900), 6:12.

The great Burgundian historian, Georges Chastellain, was an eyewitness to his coronation. He reports that at the moment Louis was crowned, there was such a noise of trumpets and bells that the whole world seemed to quiver and rock and all ears were deafened.[30] The procession following the coronation, from Reims to Paris, was led by no fewer than fifty-four trumpets.[31]

After the pomp of the coronation, the reign of Louis XI is rather characterized by an absence of the usual ceremonial flavor of French court life. He tended to enjoy the more simple, even rural, forms of music. The banquet following his marriage featured a peasant Morris dance with music by pipe and tabor, with bells.[32] As he lay dying, in 1483, Louis desired to hear music outside his window and sent out an order for performers of every kind. Some one hundred and twenty appeared, mostly shepherds playing pipe and flute.[33]

The rather spartan court life of Louis XI throws into even greater significance the rich musical establishment maintained by Rene I, Duke of Anjou (d. 1480). He loved music, sang, and played instruments himself. He supported a five-member wind band, in addition to minstrels who played, 'clarion, trompette, sarquebbute, tabourin, chalemie, fleute, herpe, leutz doulcine, musette et orgue.'[34]

A visitor to a dinner given by Rene II, of Anjou, in 1489, wrote that the various courses of the dinner were served with great ceremony and with the music of trumpets, shawms (*fifres*) and tambours and that during the entire duration of the meal there was music played by 'all sorts of instruments.'[35]

[30] Georges Chastellain, *Oeuvres* (Brussels, 1863–1866).

[31] Bowles, 'Musical Instruments in Civic Processions,' 154. A miniature from 1467 shows the army of Louis, with three long clarion-type trumpets. (Paris, National Library, Ms.fr,254, fol. 10)

[32] Dominic Bevan Wyndham Lewis, *King Spider* (New York: Coward-MacCann, 1929), 170.

[33] Ibid., 295.

[34] Jacques Levron, *La vie et les moeurs du bon roi René* (Paris: Amiot-Dumont, 1953), 187; G. Arnaud d'Agnel, *Les comptes du Roi René* (Paris: A. Picard, 1910), 3:75ff.

[35] Jean Jacquot, *La musique en Lorraine* (Paris, 1882), 8.

Charles VIII (1483–1498)

I close this account with one of the most colorful of all French rulers. He was a macrocephalic hunchback, eyes big, colorless and myopic, his underlip thick and drooping, speech hesitant, and hands which twitched spasmodically. Yet, Charles VIII was good natured and given to reading chivalric romances. One of these inspired him to make an ill-fated crusade to Italy and Jerusalem. He set out in 1494, but found Milan so enjoyable that he never proceeded further. His troops enjoyed the local citizens (Charles himself left a trail of natural children) and when they returned to France a year later, they carried with them both the *morbus gallicus* and the Renaissance. Charles, three years later, on his way to watch a tennis match struck his head against a door and died at age twenty-eight.

When Charles entered Rouen in April 1485 a great theatrical creation greeted him. With the town wind band providing music from behind the scaffold, built by the Church of Notre Dame, the eye saw a structure,

> large and very high, ingeniously constructed so as to revolve on a pivot "*by subtle means.*" There were three levels, or stages, on the highest of which was the figure of God the Father enthroned. In back of the chair were circles of gold and many colors. At the four corners of the stage were the four evangelists in the form of symbolic beasts, with pairs of angels and seraphims. On the middle tier, in front of the coat-of-arms of Rouen, was the Lamb of God, the symbol of the city, which moved out of its niche to greet the king as he passed by. On the lower level were seated 24 Old Men of the Apocalypse, sumptuously dressed, with elaborate headdresses and crowns. They held organs, harps, lutes, rebecs, shawms, crumhorns, and other instruments.[36]

[36] Bowles, 'Musical Instruments in Civic Processions,' 155.

23 Court Wind Bands in Spain

SPAIN DURING THE MIDDLE AGES was not yet a unified nation, consisting rather of the separate kingdoms of Aragon and Castile. With the unification under Ferdinand and Isabella,[1] Spain would transform itself from relative insignificance into one of the great powers of the Western world in fewer than twenty-five years.

ARAGON

The tradition of wind ensemble music in this region begins far before the records of the courts of its kings, as one can see in the ceramic depictions of ensembles of oboe and flute-types performing for ritual dances found near Valencia.[2]

Pedro III (1276–1285)

Among early kings, Pedro III seems to have been relatively enlightened, at least he accepted a decree of the Cortes of Catalonia in 1283 stating that thereafter no national legislation should be issued without the consent of the citizens.[3] He maintained an ensemble of three trumpets and a percussionist (*atabale*), as can be seen in extant court documents (*Ordenanzas*). In addition, he maintained a group of minstrels under the leadership of Cerveri de Girona.[4]

Jaime II (1291–1327)

During the fourteenth century, under Pedro's son, Jaime II, one can find a much more extensive and international gathering of minstrels. He hosted visiting musicians from England, Portugal, Castile, Navarre, France, Venice, Sicily, Majorca, as well as Muslim minstrels.[5] The historian, Anglès, gives Jaime's own ensemble as, 'trompes, trompets, tambor, viula, xebeba (flute), und meocanon der Araber.'[6]

Jaime's son, the 'Infant of Catalonia-Aragon,' once entered Toledo on a state visit accompanied by one hundred Moorish trumpeters.[7]

---

[1] Henry IV's only daughter, Joanna being regarded as the fruit of the queen's adultery, his sister, Isabella became heir. Her subsequent marriage with Ferdinand of Aragon joined the two most powerful of the Spanish kingdoms.

[2] Grove, 19:491.

[3] *Cambridges Medieval History*, 7:695–702.

[4] M. Balthasar Saldoni, *Diccionario biografico-bibliografico de Efemérides de musicos españoles* (Madrid, 1868), 1:334. Also, Jocelyn Nigel Hillgarth, *The Spanish Kingdoms* (Oxford: Clarendon, 1976), 1:54.

[5] Hillgarth, *The Spanish Kingdoms*, 1:54;

[6] Higino Anglès, 'Die Instrumentalmusik bis zum 16. Jahrhundert in Spanien,' in *Natalicia Musicologica* (Oslo: Hansen, 1962), 148.

[7] Hillgarth, *The Spanish Kingdoms*, 1:179.

Alfonso IV (1327–1336) and Pedro IV (1336–1387)

Alfonso IV employed Moorish players of trumpet, flute, psaltery, and rebec.[8] His successor, Pedro IV, continued to favor Moorish musicians, one of his favorite minstrels being the flutist, Cahat Mascum.[9] A surviving document orders his 'trompes, trompeta' and 'tabaler' to play music at the beginning and at the end of each royal meal.[10]

Juan I (1350–1396)

Juan I, son to Pedro IV, apparently placed great emphasis on music. Not only did he entertain minstrels from Portugal, Cyprus, and Bologna, but he turned to Western Europe to build his own wind band. A document of 1388 discusses five players of instruments of the shawm family: one, 'Jaquet of Paris,' was from France and two, 'Olin' and 'Stefan,' are said to have been from Germany.[11] Another shawm player, 'Venequi,' of Flanders, was mentioned in a document of the following year.[12] Juan also sent his own minstrels to Western Europe to study, as one can see in the example of two minstrels sent to Germany in 1391.[13]

This king also had international tastes as a gourmet, requiring cheese and dates from Majorca, trout from the Pyrenees, and Greek wine; it was said he could eat four partridges at a single sitting.

Don Ferdinand (1412–1416)

Don Ferdinand was patient and forbearing, tall, well formed, with 'very beautiful eyes, a little bloodshot.'[14] When he was crowned, an eyewitness said shawms, trumpets, and dancers filled the streets day and night.[15]

Alfonso V (1416–1458)

Finally, Alfonso V, 'the Magnanimous' represents the last of the great Aragon kings. According to Anglès, Alfonso maintained fifteen musicians who were divided between strings and 'instrumentos de viento.'[16] Alfonso traveled widely and apparently took musicians with him. Philip the Good, of Burgundy, made a gift to four minstrels of Alfonso, whom he heard in April 1423, in Paris.[17]

---

[8] Grove, 17:234.

[9] Ibid.

[10] Anglès, 'Die Instrumentalmusik,' 148–149.

[11] The entire document is quoted in Vander Straeten, *La Musique*, 7:81. See also, Anglès, 'Die Instrumentalmusik,' 148–149.

[12] Vander Straeten, *La Musique*, 72.

[13] Marix, *Histoire de la Musique*, 92.

[14] Juan Fontes, 'The Regency of Don Ferdinand of Antequera,' in *Spain in the Fifteenth Century*, ed. John Roger Loxdale Highfield (London: Macmillan, 1972), 123.

[15] Lauretius Valla (1405–1457), 'De Rebus a Ferdinando Aragoniae rege gestis,' in *Rerum Hispanicarum Scriptores* (Frankfurt, 1579), 2:1048.

[16] H. Anglès, 'La música en la corte del rey Don Alfonso V de Aragon,' in *Gesammelte Aufsätze zur Kulturgeschichte Spaniens* (Münster: Aschendorff, 1940), 355ff.

[17] Marix, *Histoire de la Musique*, 64.

Castille

Sancho IV (1284–1295)

Sancho IV maintained a court of some two hundred and fifty persons, including thirty archers, eighteen clerics, and 'thirty-six falconers, pages, cooks, minstrels, buffoons, Moorish drummers and trumpeters.'[18] We catch a glimpse of these minstrels in the writing of Ramon Lull (1232–1315), one of the most prolific writers of the Middle Ages. In his *Libre de contemplacio en Deu*, a million-word encyclopedia on theology (ca. 1272), he gives the social standing of various professions, beginning with the pope (God's representative on earth): kings, knights, pilgrims, judges, lawyers, doctors, merchants, seamen, minstrels, shepherds, painters, farm laborers, and artisans.[19] He grumbles that, while the poor shiver in rags outside the palace door, the minstrels are clothed in royal clothing, banquet with princes, and are loaded with gold and silver. Lull finds no king who rules as he should, few judges not corrupted by gold, and few minstrels who will not lie for money.

During the fifteenth century, one begins to find in Spain celebrations of the lesser nobles which include the participation of their private wind bands. For example, one of the Dukes of Medina Sidiona who controlled Seville until late in the century, took part in the annual Easter parade with shawm, cromorne, trumpet, and drum players.[20]

King Sancho IV of Castile and Leon (1284–1295), anonymous, thirteenth century

[18] Hillgarth, *The Spanish Kingdoms*, 1:54.

[19] Ibid., 46–47.

[20] *Memorial histórico español* (Madrid, 1855), 8:174.

Enrique IV (1425–1474)

Another ruler who was personally musical was Henry IV, King of Castile. As one might expect, his marriage in 1440 included almost continuous wind music. First the bride was honored at a great feast at the palace of the Count of Haro, during her journey to Valladolid for the actual ceremony. As she arrived at the palace, she was greeted by 'blaring trumpets, shrilling flutes, and pounding drums.'[21] The party entered the palace and the bride was immediately seated to a meal consisting of an endless succession of roasts, fowl, fish, pastries, and fruits, as the minstrels performed throughout.[22] The Count, determined that no visiter should accrue any debt during his visit, set up a fountain which gushed a stream of pure silver available to anyone.

[21] Townsend Miller, *Henry IV of Castile: 1425–1474* (New York, 1972), 20.

[22] Fernan Pérez de Guzmán, 'Coronica del Rey Don Juan II,' in *Biblioteca de Autores Espanoles* (Madrid: Ediciones Atlas, 1953), 565.

All entertainments paled in comparison to that held on the fourth day of the visit. The Count had a large field near the palace turned into a kind of fifteenth-century Disneyland. A forest was transplanted, together with puzzled deer, boars, and bears and nearby a man-made lake was stocked with fish. Behind the lake a huge creation of twenty levels was built, all carpeted with green sod. The guests took their places on the various levels and began a great banquet, while watching hunters kill the helpless game in the artificial forest and anglers pull fish out of the lake. After the meal, the party danced until breakfast, where each lady found a gold ring set with jewels by her plate. The Count also distributed two great sacks of coins among the exhausted minstrels.[23]

Finally, the wedding party continued its journey to Valladolid, where they were met by numerous trumpeters. Almost all ceremonial aspects of the wedding here were cancelled, due to a series of events which occurred during the following days. First, a great tournament got out of hand and turned into a bloodbath, then a kidnapping necessitated a public beheading, followed by a number of aristocratic (natural) deaths.

One of the important tasks of the royal trumpeters on this occasion was to play a fanfare the moment the royal bride ceased to be a virgin. They were placed by the door of the bridal chamber and three notaries were required by law to stand by the bed, ready to pass the word on to the trumpeters. The trumpets never played on this occasion, and history has named Henry, 'the impotent.'

The first great ceremonial event of Henry's reign was the investiture of Lucas as Constable of Castile, on 25 March 1458. During this ceremony which ennobled Lucas, 'whole choirs of silver trumpets' played.[24] An eyewitness described this event as also including shawms, dolcians, waits, timpani, and drums. These instruments, he wrote, played not only in the procession but also in the church ceremony.[25]

This constable's wedding procession in 1461 included trumpets (*trompetas bastardas e italianas*), shawms (*chirimias*), tabors, tamborinos, and other percussion instruments.[26] His contemporaries said that he never ventured out of his palace without his trumpeters and drummers.[27]

[23] Miller, *Henry IV of Castile*, 22.

[24] Ibid., 102.

[25] Anglès, 'Die Instrumentalmusik,' 152.

[26] *Memorial historico español*, 8:47.

[27] Bowles, 'Musical Instruments in Civic Processions,' 149.

An account of a welcome given Henry by Lucas in Jaén describes, in addition to 'platoons of silver trumpets,' also 'huge copper drums slung from Arabian horses and gleaming and pounding, cymbals.' At the dinner which followed, each course was announced by 'hautboys and tambors.'[28]

All during the reign of Henry IV, wind ensembles were used for every festive purpose. There were the 'flourish of instruments' at the investiture of Beltrán, Duke of Alburquerque (who had the habit of kicking down doors and blurting out obscenities); the midnight routs with shawms and castled pastries, 'a la borgoñesa,' held by Fonseca, Archbishop of Seville; and at the end, a strange mock trial in 1465, attended by 'the orchestra—shawms, drums and trumpets.'[29]

[28] Miller, *Henry IV of Castile*, 147.

[29] Ibid., III, 152, 172ff.

Fernando V (1474–1516) and Dona Isabel (1474–1504)

Ferdinand and Isabella, the patrons of Columbus, were fond of music and employed household wind players. A document dated 1498 lists all the officials at the House of Isabella, including three organists and the rest wind players. One finds here three players called 'wind players,' followed by a true wind band (*Menestriles Altos*), and five trumpeters.[30] An inventory of Isabella's instrument collection in the castle of Segovia in 1503 includes three shawms, three flutes, keyboards, and (now) eight string instruments.[31]

Ferdinand had six minstrels in service at his palace in Aragon in 1491; eight in 1500; seven trumpets, four drums and nine minstrels, one of which is identified as a player of '*sacabuche*' in 1505; ten musicians in 1510; and finally, in 1511, eleven players specifically identified as a wind band (*ministrils alta*).[32]

During the military campaigns which characterized the reign of Ferdinand and Isabella, and out of which the modern Spain emerged as a unified nation, one reads of the usual trumpets and drums, as for example in the Moorish ballad on 'The Loss of Alhama.'

[30] Vander Straeten, *La Musique*, 7:106. Vander Straeten says the three 'wind players' (Tañedores de las Cañas) were the same as *pijpers* (shawms) in Flanders.

[31] Anglès, 'Die Instrumentalmusik,' 153.

[32] Ibid., 155.

King Ferdinand II of Aragon (Fernando V), by Michel Sittow (ca. 1469–1525)

> When the Alhambra's walls he gained,
> On the moment he ordained
> That the trumpet straight should sound
> With the silver clarion round.
>   Woe is me, Alhama!
> When the hollow drums of war

> Beat the loud alarm afar,
> That the Moors of town and plain
> Might answer to the martial strain,
>   Woe is me, Alhama![33]

On occasion, larger varieties of instruments appear, such as those accompanying the troops of the Duke of Madina Sidonia in 1480–1481.

> Down the mountains rode the ducal forces in their customary battle array, trumpets, flutes, flageolets, and kettledrums raising the echoes and the banners of Andalusia flying.[34]

Finally, a great welcome was given Ferdinand upon his entrance to Naples in 1506, with 'Spanish kettledrums and pipes, Italian flutes, trumpets, horns, choirs of boys and chanters' filling the evening with music.[35]

Isabella I of Castile, from the *Rimado de la Conquista de Granada*, by Pedro Marcuello, 1482

[33] Quoted in Mary Purcell, *The Great Captain: Gonzalo Fernández de Córdoba* (New York: Doubleday, 1962), 57.

[34] Ibid., 67.

[35] Ibid., 201.

24 Court Wind Bands in Italy

After the fall of the Roman Empire, the most ancient reference to a large gathering of wind instruments seems to be a reception given the Greek exarch, Longinus, in Venice in the year 568. He was met with great rejoicing, to the sound of 'bells, flutes, and other instruments.'[1] One may assume the other instruments were primarily winds, for it was said the total effect was such that one could not have heard the thunder of heaven.

A similar welcome was given in Venice, on 7 April 1203, to Alexios of Constantinople, with 'a blast of trumpets.'[2] During the thirteenth century, one also finds the usual references to the use of trumpets with the Venetian army, such as an account from 1203 which speaks of the soldiers being awakened by the 'shrill braying' of these instruments.[3] During war time, the trumpets were often used as ambassadors of sorts, carrying messages between enemies, due to their close association with the aristocracy. One can see this relationship in a comment, made by an eyewitness, during the Italian wars against Charles of France in the late fifteenth century.

> The King straightway sent a herald who did not dare enter the camp without a Venetian trumpeter.[4]

It is possible that many such early references deal not with players under regular contract to a court, but with players paid for specific engagements. Such was the case in the court of Filippo di Savoia of Piedmont as we know from an extant document of 1295 which deals with the temporary employment of trumpet players.[5]

An early fourteenth-century treatise, *Lucidarium*, by Marchetto of Padua, mentions the use of horns (*cornui*) and trumpets (*tubae*) and other instruments in battle, as part of daily experience. In a section on instrumental music (*musica organica*), he lists 'tubae, cymbala, fistulae, organa, monocordum, and psalterium.'[6] It might be mentioned that a fourteenth-century

---

[1] William Carew Hazlitt, *The Venetian Republic: Its Rise, Its Growth, And Its Fall, AD 409–1797* (New York: AMS Press, 1915), 1:15.

[2] Ibid., 1:267.

[3] Ibid., 1:301.

[4] Alessandro Benedetti, *Diaria de Bello Carolino*, ed. Dorothy Schullian (New York: Ungar, 1967), 107. Additional references to fifteenth-century Venetian trumpets can be found in Hazlitt, *The Venetian Republic*, 2:944, 985.

[5] Vessella, *La Banda*, 49.

[6] Gerbert, *Scriptores*, 3:66, 68.

miniature from Padua (ca. 1390) shows an outdoor ceremony of the rings, during a wedding, and in a balcony are two timpani (one player), bagpipe, two shawms, and two clarions.[7]

One does not begin to find more numerous references to the broader use of court wind bands in Italy until the fifteenth century; they arrived with the Renaissance. Perhaps, if this enjoyment of the wind band came later than in most countries, it was due to the long hostile attitude of the Church and its influence. By the same token, perhaps it was the use of winds in the great ceremonies of the popes which was taken as a signal for acceptance of this aristocratic accouterment. One reads that during the coronation procession of Gregory IX, in 1227, 'the crowds were taken by the sound of the trumpets.'[8] An extraordinary variety of instruments is mentioned in an account of the coronation of Boniface VIII in 1295, including oboes, several trumpet-types, timpani, cymbals and corni.[9] The trombe and trombette were also used for the coronation of Gregory XI in 1377.[10]

During the fifteenth century a real papal wind band is found, called *i Musici Capitolini e i tamburini del Popolo Romano*. Now one finds 'trombe, nacchere, ciarsmelle,' and 'cornamuse' used for all sorts of festivals, ceremonies, battles, and proclamations of victory.[11] During the fifteenth century some of the other church princes also used wind ensembles for their entertainment. When the Cardinal of S. Sisto entertained Ercole d'Este in 1473 the meal was served to the music of 'tromba e pifferi in diversi modi' and the dancing was accompanied by shawms.[12]

One continues to read of winds in the coronation processions of the fifteenth-century popes, in particular those of Eugene IV, in 1436, and Nicholas V, in 1447.[13]

Nothing speaks more clearly of the change in the official attitude which occurred during fifteenth-century Italy than the miniature called *Le Jardin des delices*. Here one sees a 'musical bath,' complete with an aristocratic party, of both sexes, splashing around nude while three shawm players and a slide-trumpet, and an independent pipe and tabor player, perform.[14]

[7] Dublin, Chester Beatty Library (Hs. W 76A, fol. 113v).

[8] Vessella, *La Banda*, 35.

[9] Francesco Cancellieri, *Storia di solenni possessi de' Sommi Pontefici* (Rome, 1802), 33–34, quoting the original text,
> ... clanguntque tubarum aera, repercusso laterum per concava flatu at litui stridere vices, et cymbala strident, tympana congeminant sonitum, nec verbere tunsa discunt ferre gradum, tibi, sed connubia substant quae digitis commota canis. Ciet ergo juventam, corni pedumque animos extollit buccina clangens in stadium; clipeos, hastas, vexilla, togssque

[10] Vessella, *La Banda*, 36.

[11] Ibid., 46. The 'ciarsmelle' was a reed instrument.

[12] Corio, *L'historia di Milano*, 824ff.

[13] Archivio di Stato in Roma, Tesoreria segreta, 1447, N. 2037-Riportato in appendice. According to Vessella (*La Banda*, 52), there is an extant treatise by Cardinal Ascanio (1484) in the Biblioteca Trivulziana which deals with courtly entertainment, including the use of the trombetti. Vessella (p. 48) lists some of the many wind players and ensembles who visited the court of Nicholas V, including the four 'trombetti del Conte di Aversa,' the three 'trombetti di Monsignor Camerlengo,' 'Giorgio, trombetta dei Conservatori,' etc.

[14] Modena, Bibl. Estense (Mss. Nr. 209, fol. C 10r., from the Codice, 'De Sphaera').

Ferrara

The miniature mentioned above, which is known to be from Northern Italy, may well have been from the court of Ferrara, a city which, in the fifteenth century, ranked with Rome and Venice as one of the great cities of Italy. During the fifteenth century this court became one of the great patrons of art in Italy, in particular under the influence of its great ladies, Isabella and Beatrice d'Este. Throughout this century there are many accounts regarding the wind players of this court and the exchanges of these players with other courts (including an interesting reference to a lady musician, 'Barbara di Brandeburgo').[15]

The accounts of court music in this court begin with the Marquis of Ferrara, Niccolò III (1393–1441), an effective ruler who managed during his long reign to bring under the control of Ferrara the cities of Modena, Reggio, Rovigo, Parma, and for a time even Milan.[16] Niccolò employed a regular court band of three shawms (*pifferi*) and several trumpet players.[17] One first hears of these wind players when the Marquis sent 'six trumpets and three pair of minstrels, each playing his own instrument' to participate in the coronation of Pope John XXIII in 1410. The subsequent papal procession included 'thirty-six buisine or trumpets, ten pair of minstrels playing instruments of music.'[18] In 1426 Philip the Good, of Burgundy, ordered as a gift for the Marquis of Ferrara a set of new instruments for his wind band. The order to the maker, Loys Willay, in Bruges, was for '2 quatre grans instrumens de menestrelz, quatre douchaines et quatre fleutes,' all garnished with leather and in boxes.[19]

Long a papal state, under the House of Este Ferrara became an independent power and center of art. Borso d'Este (1450–1471), an able ruler who maintained peace and prosperity in Ferrara, was the first member of this family to carry the title, Duke of Ferrara. He himself did not care for the arts, but he supported them, as he loved court pageants and displays. His musical household included, in 1456, five trumpeters, one trombone, two shawms, five players of keyboard and strings, and one singer.[20]

[15] These accounts are given in part in Vessella, *La Banda*, 60ff.

[16] Will Durant, *The Renaissance* (New York: Simon and Schuster, 1953), 262. Durant adds that when one of the many wives of Niccolò committed adultery, he had her beheaded and ordered a similar fate for all Farrarese women convicted of the same crime. This was enforced until it became evident that Ferrara would become depopulated!

[17] Grove, 6:486.

[18] Marix, *Histoire de la Musique*, 56, fn. 7.

[19] Ibid., 105.

[20] Lewis Lockwood, 'Music at Ferrara in the Period of Ercole I,' in *Studi Musicali* anno 1, no. 1 (1972): 103.

We know that Borso's musical establishment was larger and included an independent shawm ensemble by 1465 from an extant letter written by his wife. She had earlier received a letter from Bianca Maria Sforza, mother to Maria Sforza who was to be married to Alfonso d'Aragón, asking if it would be possible to borrow Ercole's shawm band to help celebrate the forthcoming wedding. The letter in question explains why this request could not be met and, at the same time, reveals how important the shawm ensemble was to the court of Ferrara.

> Because the wedding will occur in April, which coincides with our own festival in honor of San Zorzo, the piffari are needed, indeed most needed to help honor our Saint. If the illustrious Bianca Maria Sforza would therefore accept our excuse we would be most content and if there are any other possibilities of repaying the declined favor we would be most happy.[21]

Borso had longed to gain the title of Duke of Ferrara and when he at last persuaded Pope Paul II to give him this title, and was summoned to Rome, he took his musicians to help dignify and add significance to the occasion. Thus he set out in 1471 with numerous officials, five hundred 'gentlemen,' with their valets wearing cloth of gold and their grooms attired in brocade of silver. His own trumpets and shawms (*piffari*) accompanied him, as well as huntsmen with Borso's dogs, falconers with falcons, and oriental keepers with tamed leopards, and members of his military.[22] Borso was met at the gates of Rome by seventeen cardinals. His trumpets played a 'blast of exultant music,' and Borso entered Rome, scattering coins on all sides while flowers showered down from windows and balconies.

In his brother and successor, Ercole I (1471–1505), one finds one of the great patrons of art of the fifteenth century in Italy. He was also a great builder of churches, palaces, and convents. He built an extension to the city, which was as large as the original city itself, and this 'new Ferrara' has been called 'the first really modern city in Europe.'[23]

For his court, Ercole enlarged the musical forces in order to create separate ensembles of singers, 'musici, trombeti, piffari,' and 'tromboni.'[24] The highest paid musician in 1476 was one of the woodwind specialists, Corado de Alemagna, at 26 Lire,

[21] E. Motta, *Musici alla Corte degli Sforza: ricerche e documenti milanesi* (Milano, 1887), 22ff.

> Ma considerando nui che l festa vostra nanti che la se cominci ha ad intrara parecchi dì in Aprile, et cussì simili feste, non vedemo che se mandassemo essi nostri piffari, potessereno esser tornati per modo alcuno a la festa nostra et a la solennità de San Sorzo, a l quale per nostro honore et de la terra, non solo sono necesari, ma necessarissimi. Et oltre de questo sapemo chel ni ha ad accadere cossa che ancora inanti loro ne bisognarono. Si che pregamo che la Ill.ma S.V. voglia acceptare questa nostra scuxa, como quella che e verissima et necessarissima, et reputare che se questo non fusse, molto piu voluntieri gli li haressimo mandati che lei non li haria acceptato, paratissimi ad ogni altro suo piacere più che per nuy proprio.

[22] Edmund G. Gardner, *Dukes & Poets in Ferrara* (New York: Haskell House, 1968), 109–110.

[23] Jacob Burckhardt, *The Civilization of the Renaissance in Italy* (London: G. Allen, 1914), 47.

[24] Werner L. Gundersheimer, *Ferrara: The Style of a Renaissance Despotism* (Princeton: Princeton University Press, 1973), 293–294.

while most of the musicians were paid from 13 to 19 Lire. By way of comparison, an engineer-builder received 26 Lire; a gardener, 9 Lire; physicians, ranging from 22 to 30 Lire.[25]

Of the many kinds of festivals and celebrations at the court of Ercole I which required music, the most lavish were the family weddings. When the bride, Maria Lucrezia of Montferrat, came in 1473 to Ferrara to marry Ercole's brother, Rinaldo, she rode in 'to the sound of trumpets, piffari, guns, and the ringing of bells.'[26]

The greatest of all celebrations was Ercole's own marriage in 1472 to Eleonora of Aragón. Although the purpose of this marriage was to cement the friendship with Naples, it must be pointed out out that among the results of this union were two of the most extraordinary women of the Middle Ages: Isabella and Bestrice d'Este. Ercole sent a large number of relatives, members of the court and horsemen to Naples to bring Eleonora to Ferrara for the wedding. They, together with those accompanying Eleonora, numbered fourteen hundred persons! First this enormous train stopped in Rome, the entry led by 'troops of trumpeters, piffari, and drummers.'[27] Here Eleonora celebrated a Mass with the Pope, and then was guest of honor at a sumptuous banquet. The theme of the banquet was classical mythology, each table containing a life-size mythological figure made of pastry. After the banquet there was a dance by sixteen 'great lovers of olden times'; fierce Centaurs rushed in to carry off the nymphs, only to be routed by Hercules, etc. Next, the vast traveling party was entertained in Florence, where a Florentine contemporary grumbled that the cost, some ten thousand Florin, was 'a bad and useless extravagance.'[28] Finally arriving in Ferrara, more than two months later, Eleonora rode dressed in cloth of gold, her hair flowing freely, down a long avenue of green trees planted for the occasion. She was met by musicians, bands of boys dressed as the Days of the Year, and troops of masqueraders representing the Seven Planets.

The tradition of the 'Ventura,' begun in 1472 by Ercole I, has been discussed above with regard to Italian civic wind music. This became an annual procession of nobles through the city, led by the duke, collecting donations of food for the needy. In 1473, on the day the Ventura was to be held a terrible snowstorm occurred. But, the 'trumpets, singers, and piffari'

[25] Ibid.

[26] Gardner, *Dukes & Poets in Ferrara*, 130.

[27] Ibid., 135.

[28] Isidoro Del Lungo, *Prose volgari ... di Angelo Ambrogini Poliziano* (Florence, 1867), 240–241.

were out there anyway, with the duke in the snow. It was the custom for the nobles to partake of this collection before giving it to the poor. In 1503, even considering the royal eating standards of the day, one has to assume the poor did rather well, for the duke and his party collected fifteen lambs, fifteen oxen, thirteen calves, five goats, five rabbits, two pigs, sixty-six ducks, one thousand five hundred and twenty-one capons, twenty-two turkeys, seventy-three partridges, eighteen peacocks, sixty quail, one hundred and ninety-one cheeses, two hundred and fifty boxes of candy, and one hundred and ninety large sausages![29]

Bologna

Most extant descriptions of fifteenth-century court wind music in Bologna are again found together with accounts of the great family weddings. The first of these, when Ginevra Sforza was married before the Bentivoglio palace in Bologna in May 1454, there were 'pifferi' and 'trombetti' playing from a garland-covered balcony.[30]

When Lucrezia, daughter to Duke Ercole of Ferrara, was married in March 1487, to Annibale Bentivoglio in Bologna, it was perhaps the greatest celebration of the ruling family and guests came from all of Italy. On the first evening a banquet was held which lasted seven hours, followed by a dance exhibition and a mask symbolizing the triumph of Matrimony over Chastity. At a following banquet each guest found before him a pastry creation of a personal nature: Lorenzo dei Medici had a peacock, the papal representative a model of the Castle of S. Angeleo, etc. There were tournaments and fireworks and more banquets; the three thousand guests consumed eight hundred casks of wine and thirty thousand pounds of meat before it was over. The procession to the Church of San Petronio, for the wedding itself, was led by one of the larger wind ensembles of the fifteenth century, '100 trombita e 70 pifari e trombuni e chorni e flauti e tamburini e zamamele.'[31]

Another great pageant occurred in Bologna on San Petronio's Day, 1490, as an aftermath of a discussion between Annibale Bentivoglio and Niccolo Rangoni as to whether Wisdom or Fortune wielded the greater influence over the affairs of men. To the sound of 'piffari' and drums the two appropriate

[29] John Fyvie, *The Story of the Borgias* (New York: Putnam, 1913), 250.

[30] Frati, *La Vita privata di Bologna*, 54.

[31] L. F. Tagliavini, 'La Scuola musicale bolognese,' in *Musiciati della scuola emiliana*, ed. Adelmo Damerini and Gino Roncaglia (Siena: Accademia Musicale Chigiana, 1956), 11.

goddesses pleaded their cause before a venerable man in the robes of a 'doctor of the university.' Unable to decide between them, he proposed a tournament, from which the eventual victor was 'Fortune.'[32]

Finally, a rather nice tale of chivalrous courtship is told of Annibale's father. Courting a lady living in Florence, he had the pavement before her house covered with flowers and fruit, stationed musicians by her window, and arranged to have rabbits and peacocks run and play in front of her house.[33]

Milan

The glory of Milan begins with Gian Galeazzo Visconti (1351–1402), who through expert intrigue, statesmanship, and success on the battle field brought all of Northern Italy under his control. He was also a builder: he began the cathedral of Milan, extended the Great Canal from Milan to Pavia, and promoted agriculture and commerce. He issued a code of laws which included the regulation of public health and the isolation of infectious disease.[34] Thus being a great duke in all but actual title, one can expect that he had at least a personal ensemble of trumpeters. Indeed, when the Emperor Wenceslas finally honored fact with form and gave him the title in 1395, a contemporary illustrator pictured the investiture as an outdoor ceremony with four trumpeters and a timpani player, all playing on horseback.[35]

One can see that Gian Galeazzo Visconti recognized the importance of music in his court celebrations from accounts of his great court entertainments. For the marriage of his daughter, Violanti, in 1368, the celebrations lasted eight days and included the usual tournaments, plays, dancing and singing. No fewer than four hundred instrumentalists participated and money and clothing were distributed to all.[36]

Another account describes the visit to Gian Galeazzo's court of the Prince d'Acaia. We are told the 'menestrelli e trombettieri' played constantly, from his arrival, throughtout the day, and throughout each meal. This dinner music consisted of five trumpets and five 'altri menestrelli del Duca.'[37]

Francesco Sforza, who established the Sforza dynasty in Milan, in 1450, was a restless and brilliant man. When still a general, his reputation was such that on occasion the enemy

[32] Cecilia Mary Ady, *The Bentivoglio of Bologna: A Study of Despotism* (London: Oxford University Press, 1937), 171.

[33] Ibid., 14.

[34] James Westfall Thompson, *Economic and Social History of Europe in the Later Middle Ages* (New York: Century, 1931), 236.

[35] Manuscript made for the duke, ca. 1395, by Fazio de Castoldis (Milan, Biblioteca della Basilica de S. Ambrogio, Mss 6, fol. 2).

[36] Corio, *L'Historie di Milano*, quoting a contemporary description:
Otto giorni la Corte si durare,
Torneri, giostre, bagordi facìa;
Ballar, cantar e sonar facean fare.
Quattrocento sonator, si dicìa,
Con buffoni alla Corte si trovoe:
Roba e danar donar loro si facia
Ciasun molto contento
si chiamoe.

[37] Vessella, *La Banda*, 50. Earlier (p. 49), Vessella gives the names of three pifferi players belonging to this Prince d'Acaia, who were sent by the Prince in 1378 to a minstrel school.

forces would lay down their arms at the sight of him. After his opportunity to become a duke arrived, he continued to live simply and work diligently on a broad range of government projects. He helped make Milan one of the great centers of the Renaissance. Even before he seized power, Francesco maintained in his personal service a number of wind players and trumpeters.[38] An illustration of his wedding to Bianca Maria Visconti, in Cremona, in 1441, shows no fewer than eight trumpets.[39] This court trumpet ensemble grew to nine by ca. 1450 and finally to eighteen by 1463. Among these players, those who traveled with the duke enjoyed special status and we are told that their expenses came to 400,120 lire per year.[40]

A miniature showing the wedding of another family member, ca. 1460, includes an ensemble of two clarions, a slide-trumpet, two shawms, and a bagpipe.[41]

Francesco's son, Galeazzo Maria Sforza, who ruled from 1466–1476, was a cruel man, given to pleasure, luxury, and the seduction of the wives of his friends. He was murdered as he worshiped in St. Stephen Church by a relative of one of the wronged ladies.

Scholars agree, however, that this was a great period for the cultivation of music in this court. Due to the high pay offered, Galeazzo Maria was able to attract the best wind players for his wind band (*piffari e tromboni e trombetti*), especially players from Germany and Flanders.[42] In addition, Galeazzo Maria frequently exchanged players with other courts as he attempted to improve his band. One notes that in 1474 he sent the Conte Giovanni Bononico in Ferrara a 'tromba de corno,' whom he described as having a 'good tone.'[43]

As was the case with the other Italian lords, Galeazzo Maria always traveled with his band. One reads of the 'i trombetti milanesi' accompanying him to Ferrara in 1454 and to Florence in 1474.[44] On at least one trip, perhaps a vacation, he took a very large band, no fewer than forty 'i trombetti e pifari.' We are told that the cost for these musicians, on his visit to the mountains of Appennini, in May 1471, cost him 200,000 ducati.[45] One wonders if these bandsmen appreciated these trips away from their families, for in 1471 as Galeazzo Maria was preparing to make a journey to Florence he perceived

[38] Grove, 17:210.

[39] Cremona, Bibl. S. Sigismondo (Codice di Donazione, 1464).

[40] Vessella, *La Banda*, 55.

[41] Milan, Castello Sforzesco, Musco d'Arte Antica (Wedding of Griselda and Gualtieri).

[42] Vander Straeten, *La Musique*, 5:26–27; Motta, *Musica alla Corte degli Sforza*; and Francesco Malaguzzi Valeri, *La Corte di Lodovico il Moro: La vita privata e l'arte a Milano nella seconda metà del quattrocento* (Milano: U. Hopeli, 1913).

[43] Vessella, *La Banda*, 54.

[44] Ibid., 55.

[45] Corio, *L'Historie di Milano*, ch. 6.

some misbehavior by his band and had them all thrown in jail! For his trip, he had to borrow a wind band from the Marquis of Mantua.[46]

Galeazzo left his throne to his seven-year-old son, Giangaleazzo Sforza, who was timid, frequently ill, and generally incapable. During most of his brief life the real power was held by his uncle, Ludovico Sforza. When Giangaleazzo married Isabella of Aragon, in 1488, in Milan, a wind ensemble of fifty woodwind instruments and trumpets participated. A painting from this reign, one of a series commemorating the festivities in honor of S. Giogio, shows the singers and trumpets of Giangaleazzo performing together.[47]

The marriage of another family member, Constanze Sforza, to Camilla of Aragon at this time (1475) is very interesting with respect to the music performed at the ceremony: a polychoral composition accompanied by a large wind band. An anonymous eyewitness wrote that the Mass was celebrated in the cathedral with the concurrence

> of numerous organs, shawms, trumpets, and drums, accompanying two separate groups of many singers, the one alternating with the other, and there were about sixteen singers in each.[48]

The most significant member of this family was Ludovico Sforza, the uncle to Giangaleazzo, who ruled Milan from 1481 to 1499. He was well educated and a wise and efficient ruler. During his reign extraordinary advances were made in the fields of agriculture and in every branch of Milanese industry (including that of musical instrument manufacture); he built hospitals and supported the Universities of Pavia and Milan. He might be considered one of the more civilized men in history, as one of Italy's greatest historians noted.

> If we consider the immense number of learned men who flocked to his court from all parts of Italy ... if we recall how many famous architects and painters he invited to Milan, and how many noble buildings he raised; how he built and endowed the magnificent University of Pavia ... we feel inclined to pronounce him the best prince that ever lived.[49]

[46] Reese, *Music in the Renaissance*, 174, says he took on his trip forty wind instruments. Salmen, *Der Fahrende Musiker*, 175, says it was German shawms, while another source, Motta, *Musici alla corte degli Sforza*, 4:32, maintains it was forty lutes.

[47] Vessella, *La Banda*, 53–54, takes their appearance here as a symbol of their importance in court life.

[48] Quoted in Grove, 14:568. See also, Otto Kinkeldey, *Orgel und Klavier in der Musik des 16. Jahrhunderts* (Leipzig: Breitkopf und Härtel, 1910), 165ff., quoting the original text, 'organi, piffieri, trombetti ed infiniti tamburini'; Reese, *Music in the Renaissance*; Haraszti, 'Les Musiciens de Mathias Carvin,' 59.

[49] Girollamo Tiraboschi, quoted in Julia Cartwright, *Beatrice d'Este* (London: Dent, 1928), 141.

Ludovico had the great fortune to marry one of the most exuberant young women of the fifteenth century, Beatrice d'Este, of Ferrara. She was vivacious, brilliantly intelligent, and loved life. She brought to the court a sense of joy and spirit, wrote one who knew her, by 'spending day and night in singing and dancing and in all manner of delights.'[50]

Although her time was brief (she died in childbirth at age twenty-two, in 1497), the combination of her influence and Ludovico's wealth made Milan the most splendid court in all of Europe. A contemporary was awed.

> Here was the learning of Greece, here Latin verse and prose flourished resplendently, here were the poetic Muses; hither the masters of the sculptor's art and those foremost in painting had gathered from distant countries, and here songs and sweet sounds of every kind and such dulcet harmonies were heard, that they seemed to have descended from Heaven itself upon this excelling court.[51]

For his wedding Ludovico appeared in a costume of gold, preceded by ninety-two trumpets, in pairs. All of his subjects, even the most humble, celebrated in the streets.[52] There is an extant letter written by Beatrice to her husband describing a banquet held in honor of her marriage in Venice.

> MOST EXCELLENT AND ILLUSTRIOUS LORD,
> MY DEAREST HUSBAND,
> ... A hundred lighted torches hung from the ceiling, and a representation was given on the stage, in which two big animals with large horns appeared, ridden by two figures, bearing golden balls and cups wreathed with verdue. These two were followed by a triumphal chariot, in which Justice sat enthroned, holding a drawn sword in her hand inscribed with the motto Concordia, and wreathed with palms and olive. In the same car was an ox with his feet resting on a figure of St. Mark and the adder. This, as your Highness will readily understand, was meant to signify the League ... Behind the chariot came two serpents, ridden by two other youths, dressed like the first riders. All these figures mounted the tribunal in the center of the hall, and danced round Justice, and after dancing for a while, their balls exploded, and out of the flames, appeared an ox, a lion, an adder, and a Moor's head suddenly appeared ... Then the banquet followed, and the different dishes and confetti were carried in to the sound of trumpets. First came (pastry) figures of the Pope, the Doge, and the Duke of Milan, with their armorial bearings and those of your Highness; then St. Mark, the adder, and the diamond, and many other objects, all colored and gilded sugar, as many as three hundred in all.[53]

Beatrice d'Este, by Bartolomeo Veneto (1470–1531), ca. 1510

[50] Quoted in Cartwright, *Beatrice d'Este* (New York: Dutton, 1899), 165.

[51] Corio, *L'Historia di Milano* (1554), quoted in Ella Noyes, *Story of Milan* (London: Dent, 1908), 165.

[52] Alessandro Luzio and Rodolfo Reinier, 'Delle relazioni di Isabella d'Este Conzaga con Ludovico e Beatrice Sforza,' in *Archivio storico italiano* (Milan, 1890), 85–86.

[53] Quoted in Cartwright, *Beatrice d'Este*, 200–201.

Perhaps the greatest celebration in fifteenth-century Milan occurred when a daughter to Galeazzo Maria Sforza, Bianca Maria (1472–1510) was married, in 1493, to Maximilian I, King of the Romans and the Emperor-Elect of the Holy Roman Empire. A letter from Beatrice d'Este to her sister, Isabella, described the wedding and the accompanying wind band music.

> Within the church, the aisles were hung with brocade as far as the choir, in front of which a triumphal arch had been erected on massive pillars. This was entirely painted, and bore in the center the effigy of Duke Francesco on horseback, in his ducal robes, with the ducal arms and those of the King of the Romans above … In the extreme corners of the choir were two raised stages, one for the singers, the other for the trumpeters, and in the space between were seated the doctors of law and medicine, with their birettas and capes lined with fur, each according to his rank … The street leading to the Duomo was beautifully decorated … On both sides of the street, the walls were hung with satin, excepting those houses which have lately been adorned with frescoes, and which are no less beautiful than tapestries. On the morning of the day, at about nine o'clock, the reverend and magnificent ambassadors of the King of the Romans rode to the church … At ten o'clock, her serene Highness the Queen ascended the triumphal car … which was drawn on this occasion by four snow-white horses. The queen wore a vest of crimson satin, embroidered in gold thread and covered with jewels. Her train was immensely long, and the sleeves were made to look like two wings, which had a very fine appearance … The chariot was followed by the ambassadors who have been sent by his Most Christian Majesty of France to honor these nuptials, and after them came the envoys of the different Italian powers, according to their rank … When we were all in our places, the Most Reverend Archbishop of Milan entered in full vestments, with the priests in ordinary, and began to celebrate mass with the greatest pomp and solemnity, to the sound of trumpets, piffari, and organ-music, together with the voices of the chapel choir, who adapted their singing to Monsignore's time … After mass had been celebrated with the greatest solemnity, the queen rose from her place between the ambassadors of his Most Christian Majesty, and, accompanied by the duke and my husband, Duchess Isabella and myself, and followed by all the princes of the blood, advanced to the alter. The ambassadors of King Maximilian advanced on their side, and we all stood before the alter, where Monsignore the Archbishop pronounced the marriage service, and the Bishop of Brixen first gave the ring to the queen, and then, assisted by the archbishop, placed on her head the crown, which act was accompanied with great blowing of trumpets, ringing of bells, and firing of guns and shells. And the said crown was of gold, enriched with rubies,

pearls, and diamonds, set in the form of arches meeting in the shape of a cross, and on top of all was a figure of the globe, crowned with a small imperial cross.[54]

[54] Cartwright, *Beatrice d'Este*, 212–215.

Another great celebration was held in 1499, when King Louis XII of France visited Milan.

The king himself made a gallant show in his long white mantle embroidered with golden lilies over a suit of royal purple ... Eight Milanese nobles carried an ermine-lined canopy over his head ... the procession paused, and the king walked up to the vaulted aisles to pay his dovotions at the Madonna's shrine. Then he rode on again, to the sound of trumpets and horns.[55]

[55] Ibid., 349.

Mantua

Court records for Mantua are very incomplete before the late fifteenth century, indeed the earliest reference to a court musician dates from a mention of 'Maestro Simone, piffaro del Gonzaga,' in 1434.[56] Two German wind players appear in the court by 1458, but it seems to be under the reign of Ludovico II Gonzaga (d. 1478) and his son and successor, Federico I Gonzaga, who ruled from 1478 to 1484, that a regular court wind band was founded. Ludovico Gonzaga, like the best of Renaissance princes, used his wealth to nourish literature, art and music. His *alta capella*, composed of 'pifferi' and 'tromboni,' can be documented from the 1460s.

[56] Iain Fenlon, *Music and Patronage in Sixteenth-Century Mantua* (New York: Cambridge University Press, 1981), 15, fn. 13. He also cites a forthcoming publication (in *Rivista italiana di musicologia*) by William Prizer which will provide extensive documentation of the Mantua court wind band between 1475–1525.

An early appearance of this wind band can be seen in the festivities given for the arrival of Margaret of Bavaria in 1463. An eyewitness, court chronicler, Schivenoglia, writes that her arrival was announced by 'Bufonij' and 'trombeti' and a subsequent procession included

107 trombi, pifari, tromboni, 26 tamburij, pive le quali erano venute con la spoxa et altri instrumenti ge nera senza fine; paria che tuto el mondo sonasse.[57]

[57] Quoted in Fenlon, *Music and Patronage*, 14.

Such an occasion obviously required the hiring of many extra musicians, for by 1468 the regular wind band consisted of only four wind players.

After the marriage of Isabella d'Este to Francesco II Gonzaga in 1490, the musical activities of the court took on much greater significance. Isabella was one of the extraordinary women of the fifteenth century; indeed, the poet Niccolo da Correggio called her, 'The first lady of the world.'[58] As a child she was an intellectual prodigy and one who knew her wrote, 'though I had heard much of her singular intelligence, I could never have imagined such a thing to be possible.'[59] These qualities, together with her ability to perform on several instruments, caused Ariosto to call her, 'liberale ed magnanime Isabella.'[60] As she became a woman, it was her vitality and high spirits which made her attractive. Her keen taste in art drew artists from all of Italy and helped create an atmosphere condusive to the support of all the arts. Fenlon speaks of the importance of the court wind band under the patronage of Isabella.

[58] Quoted in Julia Cartwright, *Isabella d'Este* (London: Murray, 1915), 1:83.

[59] Quoted in ibid., 4.

[60] Ludovico Ariosto, *Orlando furioso*, 13:59.

> From its origins as a simple band used on ceremonial occasions, this ensemble seems to have been transformed during the period of Isabella d'Este into a highly skilled and more versatile ensemble performing more sophisticated music. Throughout the sixteenth century frequent references to the *alta cappella* confirm that it remained an important feature of court life and a central institution of court music, performing at banquets, processions and triumphs, at public and private festivals, on major state and family occasions, on the battlefield, and sometimes in church, though presumably not in a liturgical context.[61]

[61] Fenlon, *Music and Patronage*, 14–15.

Naples

Naples was the only important city in the kingdom which occupied all of Italy to the southeast of the papal states. While this court was not one of the wealthy ones, there is evidence of court music from an early period. A court ordinance of 1344 sets the musical establishment at two horns, a trumpet, and timpani. These royal musicians were still called *juglars* in this ordinance and their duty was to perform before and after all public feasts, except during Lent.[62]

By the early fifteenth century, under the reign of Alfonso the Magnanimous (b. 1396) the wind band had grown with the addition of five piffari, trombones, and harps. Alfonso

[62] Alan Ryder, *The Kingdom of Naples Under Alfonso the Magnanimous* (Oxford: Clarendon, 1976), 74.

was particularly interested in classical literature and it is said he always carried some classic volume with him where ever he went.⁶³

During the second half of the fifteenth century, one finds a great period of development for art and music under the House of Aragon. An eyewitness who saw the procession after the coronation of King Alfons' II, in May 1494, reports seeing forty-six trumpet and ten shawm players, twelve small drums, four large field drums, and three pair of timpani, carried on mules.⁶⁴ A miniature exists of this very procession, but it shows only three trumpets and three woodwind instruments. One would expect the woodwind instruments to be shawms, but one player is also carrying a small drum and may thus be a pipe and tabor player.⁶⁵

Urbino

Urbino, although small in size, was certainly one of the most civilized courts in Italy. Federigo da Montefeltro (1444–1482), was both a great general (he never lost a battle), a wise ruler, and a very highly educated man. He built the greatest library in Italy, outside the Vatican, and loved to discuss his books with any who would listen. It was he who began to build the musical establishment at Urbino as well.⁶⁶ A Florentine bookseller, Vespasiano da Bisticci, wrote that Federigo employed excellent instrumentalists, including six 'trombetti,' two 'tamburini,' and two organists.⁶⁷

For great family marriages this court, as others, imported numerous extra players. For the marriage of Isabella of Urbino in 1475, to Roberto Malatesta, the visiting players included fifty trumpets, one hundred shawms, twenty-two drummers, and two cornett players, the latter from the service of the Bishop of Ferrara.⁶⁸

Florence

During 1438 the Patriarch of Constantinople visited Florence and a great welcome was planned. Unfortunately a fierce winter storm of torrential rain drove all the public off the streets. The trumpeters must have stood their ground, for the complaint was that the wind carried away their sounds.⁶⁹

---

⁶³ Durant, *The Renaissance*, 350.

⁶⁴ Ferraiolo, *Una cronaca napoletana figurata del quattrocento*, ed. Riccardo Filangieri (Naples, 1956), 93.
  Et ditta che fo laditta messa subito Sua Maiesta calva charedallo Piscopato che erano xviiii ore. Et in primis innante de tutta la giente andavano trombette schiate numaro xxxxvi, et ditte trombette portavano ippune (Dublette) vestute de divisa de inborchato et viliuto carmosino, et tamborrine numaro xii, et bifare numaro x, et liute badose et arpe et tremmune senza numaro de tutte guiste sune, et tamburre grusse a piede numaro iiii, et sey tamburre grusse sopra a tre mule, che le sonavano tre chiave nigre tutte vestute de seta verde et con divisa alle gamme.

⁶⁵ New York, Pierpont Morgan Library (Ms. M. 801, fol. 103).

⁶⁶ Earlier there seems to have been only choral music in the cathedral. See Grove, 19:463.

⁶⁷ Ibid.

⁶⁸ Nanie Bridgman, *La vie musicale au quattrocento* (Paris: Gallimard, 1964), 18, 46.

⁶⁹ Christopher Hibbert, *The House of Medici* (New York: Morrow, 1975), 66.

Once again the accounts of the great family marriages indicate the important participation of the wind players. One reads of a payment of 40 fiorini for pifferi and 80 fiorini for trombetti for the marriage of Nannina de' Medici to Bernardo Rucellai in 1466.[70] During 1469 there were numerous celebrations around the marriage of Clarice Orsini, which was an important political marriage allying the Medici with one of the powerful families in Rome. There was a great tournament with piffari and trumpets,[71] and later a banquet in the Medici palace, each course served with a flourish of trumpets.[72]

In Lorenzo, perhaps the best known of all these rulers today, one finds a man so liberal and so wealthy that his contemporaries called him, 'Il Magnifico.' His support of the arts is well-known and is what he had in mind when he said,

> When my mind is disturbed with the tumults of public business and my ears are stunned with the clamors of turbulent citizens, how could I support such contention unless I found relaxation in science?[73]

One tale of the great Lorenzo reveals the arduous demands on a court wind player. Lorenzo decided, after a party, at two o'clock in the morning, to throw snow balls at the palace of Marietta Strozzi. This was accomplished by light of flaming torches and the blowing of trumpets and shawms.[74]

Before leaving Florence, a note must be added regarding one of her citizens, Leonardo da Vinci. As everyone knows, his sketches cover virtually every facet of fifteenth-century thought. Among them,[75] one finds that he also gave some consideration to the chief problems of wind instrument construction of his day: the addition of diatonic notes on the trumpet and the problem of making tone holes in woodwind instruments where the human hand could reach them. By his sketches it is apparent that he was thinking in the direction of adding keyboards to these instruments!

[70] Vessella, *La Banda*, 42.

[71] A miniature of a joust in the Piazza S. Croce, in Florence, from this period shows three trumpet players on horseback. (Yale University Art Gallery, J. J. Jarves Collection)

[72] Hibbert, *The House of Medici*, 116–117. A miniature of a 'Triumph' given in Florence, ca. 1475, shows three shawm and a cornett player, with two trumpeters. (Musée Jacquemart-André, Paris)

[73] Quoted in William Roscoe, *Life of Lorenzo de' Medici* (London, 1877), 169.

[74] Ibid., 118–119.

[75] Leonardo da Vinci, *Arundel Codex*, 263.

25 Court Wind Bands in Burgundy

Philip the Bold

Due to its geographical location on the eastern side of France, consisting of the area around Dijon, together with the statesmanship of the dukes beginning with Philip the Bold, Burgundy was little damaged by the Hundred Years' War. When the Capetian line became extinct, the territory reverted to the French crown and King John II (then living in exile in London) who gave it to his son, Philip, as a reward for his valor at the Battle of Poitiers. Philip managed so well, adding more territory, including Flanders, that Burgundy began to function as an independent state, rather than as a province of France. It was the constant political aim of the next three dukes to achieve this recognition by having their title changed from duke to king by the Holy Roman Emperor. While in the end this was never achieved, Burgundy became for nearly a century the cultural center of Western Europe.

Soon after Philip's reign began (1363–1404), he traveled from London to his new estates and began buying horns for the watchmen of his castles for their protection.

> … for the purchase of a brass trumpet for the turret of the castle of Grignon, to (be) blown when the watchman sees men-at-arms.[1]
>
> 1 florin, 6 groschins for 6 field horns to be sounded, three for the Chateau of Cuisery and one for Sagy.[2]

In 1365 Philip made a payment to a visiting minstrel who played the cornamuse and, joining one of Philip's own players, Symon Guiteaul, 'accompanied him softly on his cornett.'[3] According to Bowles, by 1367 Philip already had twenty-eight musicians in his service.[4] One can see the variety of instrumentalists available to the dukes in the statement by the secretary to another duke, Johann IV of Burgundy, in 1365, that there were available the trumpet-types, percussion, shawms, bagpipes, and 'minstrels of all kinds.'[5]

[1] Michel Brenet, *Musique et Musiciens de la vieille France* (Paris: F. Alcan, 1911), 6.

[2] Bernard Prost, *Inventaires mobiliers et extraits des comptes des ducs de Bourgogne* (Paris: Leroux, 1902–1904), 1:24.

[3] Ibid., 1:82.

[4] Edmund A. Bowles, 'Instruments at the Court of Burgundy,' *The Galpin Society Journal* 6 (July 1953): 43.

[5] Quoted in Lionel de la Laurencie, 'La musique à la cour des ducs de Bretagne aux XIVe et XVe siecle,' *Revue de Musicologie* 14, no. 45 (Feb 1933): 1–5.

It has been said that at this time the court of Philip was more brilliant, with his musicians in greater number and chosen with greater care, than the court of the king of France.[6] We may be sure that the duke's own wind band was among the players who greeted him upon his return from the Battle of Tournai, in 1385, an occasion when a contemporary reported having heard a large ensemble performing, apparently together, in a very pleasing manner.[7]

The general impression one has from the pay records of Philip is that he was a very strong supporter of music and that his musicians were well treated. This interest is expressed, for example, in the instances when Philip paid the expenses for sending his wind players to the famous minstrel schools of Europe. In 1378 he sent a group of musicians to a minstrel school in Ghent[8] and in 1386 sent them twice (once to Germany) and instructed them to buy new instruments while on their trip.[9]

There are two eyewitness accounts of contemporaries who heard the wind band of Philip near the end of the fourteenth century. One describes the wind band playing for a dance, describing the ensemble as 'trumpets, tambors, shawms, and minstrels.'[10] Froissart describes a large number of winds, and singers as well, accompanying the duke on a voyage in 1390.

> Much great beauty and pleasure to hear from the resounding trumpets and clarions, sounding, and other minstrels performing on bagpipes, shawms, and timpani, as well as the sound of the voice, resounding and echoing from the sea.[11]

John the Fearless

Politically, the reign of John the Fearless (1404–1419) is not a happy chapter in the history of Burgundy. Joining Sigismund of Hungary in his war against the Turks, John the Fearless saw his army totally destroyed and was taken prisoner in the battle of Nicopolis, only to be set free after the payment of an immense ransom. Otherwise, he was unscrupulous, dishonest and violent. He personally paid for the murder of Louis, Duke

---

[6] Marix, *Histoire de la Musique*, 16–17.

[7] Kervyn de Lettenhove, 'Fragment inedit de Froissart,' in *Bulletin de l'Académie royale de Belgiques* 25 (1886), 57.
   ... les trompettes, clarons et ménestreuls de toutes manières d'instruments commencèrent à jouer et sonner tout à une fois que c'estoit chose plaisante et mélodieuse à ouyr.

[8] Vander Straeten, *La Musique*, 4:122:
   Aux ménestriers de Monseigneur, pour don fait à eulx par Monseigneur, ceste foix de grâce espécial, pour aler de Gand en Allemaine aux escoles, et retourner dever Monseigneur, et pour supporter les frez et missions que il feront oudit voiaige, par mandement de Monseigneur donné à Paris, vj de mars mccclxxvij c frans.

[9] Marix, *Histoire de la Musique*, 97, fn. 3, and Prost, *Inventaires mobiliers*, 2:1372, who provides the names of the minstrels making the trip: Nicolas d'Alfous, Jehan de Dynant, Loyset Mulier, Jossequin de Jardins, Villemote de Honcoigne, Claux le Taborin, and Nicolas la trompete. A few more players in Philip's musical establishment can be identified, including Henri Baudet, a timpanist hired in 1386, and the trumpet players Berthelemi Lyon (1372) and Nicholas de la Marche (1384).

[10] Kervyn de Lettenhove, ed., *Collection des chroniques belges* (1873), 5.

[11] Jean Alexandre C. Buchon, *Chroniques de Froissart* (1853), III, iv, 13:
   Moult grand beauté et plaisance fut d'ouïr ces trompettes et ces claronceaux retenir, bondir, et autres menestriers faisant leur mestier de pipes, de chalemelles et de naquaires, tant que du son et de la voix qui en issoient en retentissoit toute la mer.

of Orleans, and was himself killed by an assassin. One might say his reign made possible the sobriquet, 'the Good,' by which his son was known.

John's musical education began, in a sense, at age one, for a 'ménestrier de guiterne' was provided for his 'edification.' In 1383 he acquired a few woodwind players, who perhaps were among the musicians who performed for his marriage in 1385 to Margaret of Bavaria at Cambrai. The music of the Mass on this occasion was reported to have been performed by 'excellent singers and flute players.'[12]

Our earliest view of the wind band of John the Fearless is a document regarding the purchase of new scarlet robes for his four minstrels and two trumpeters in 1407. An account in 1410 of the duke at war mentions his six trumpets and four percussion.[13]

Aside from the trumpeters, it is clear that by at least 1413 John the Fearless had a true indoor wind band of six players. This is confirmed in a very important document of that year sent to the instrument maker Pierre de Prost, of Bruges. One sees here the purchase of a complete set of new instruments for the duke's wind band: two shawms, two bombards 'with key,' a 'contre' (surely a bass to the bombards), and a trumpet 'to be played with the other instruments', which must be taken as the slide-trumpet and not another trumpet of the kind used for military purposes.[14]

Perhaps it was this band, together with the ceremonial trumpets, which an eyewitness reported hearing when the duke met with Henry V, of England, in 1419,[15] for we know from a letter written by Philip the Good, on 10 October 1419, that this basic wind band was still maintained by the court up to the time of the death of John the Fearless.[16]

Philip the Good

The reign of Philip the Good (1419–1467) saw the complete separation politically from France and the annexation of large parts of what is now The Netherlands. It was truly a kingdom in wealth and power, but still not in name. To lend stature to his argument that he should be given a crown by the emperor, Philip sought to create the most regal possible court. The result, in music, art, and poetry, was a cultural life envied by

[12] Prost, *Inventaires mobiliers*, 1:1577, and 2:757, 767; and Marix, *Histoire de la Musique*, 18 (molt brafs contres et flusteurs musicals).

[13] L. Chauvelaye and P. de Coligny, 'Les armées des trois premiers ducs de Bourgogne,' in *Mémoires de l'académie des sciences, arts et belles-lettres de Dijon* (1854–1855), 5:117ff.

[14] Quoted in Vander Straeten, *La Musique*, 7:38–39:
A Pierre de Proos(t), demourant à Bruges, la somme de vingt quatre escus du pris de xl gr. monnoie de Flandres chascun escu, laquelle, du commandement et ordonnance de mondit seigneur, lui a esté paiée, baillée et délivrée comptant, pour les causes qui s'en suivent; c'est assavoir: pour V paires d'instruments, les deux appelez bombardes à clef, une contre et deux chalémies, que mondit sr a fait prendre et acheter dudit Pierre pour ses ménestrels, xiiii (livres); et pour une trompette servant avec lesdits instruments, que semblablement il a de lui fait prendre et acheter, x (livres); font ladite somme de xxiii (livres), si qu'il puet apparoir par mandement de descharge de mondit seigneur sur ce fait, donné à Paris, le viii jour de septembre MCCCCXIII, garni de quittance sur ce dudit Pierre, ensemble de certificacion de Henry Du Houx, ménestrel de mondit seigneur sur les pris, achat et reception desdits instruments, tout cy rendu pour ce XXIIII escus de XL gros.

[15] Quoted in Richard Vaughan, *John the Fearless: The Growth of Burgundian Power* (New York: Barnes and Noble, 1966), 270. (the trumpeters and musicians were playing on their instruments …).

[16] Marix, *Histoire de la Musique*, 109, fn. 1.

all of Europe; here the Renaissance began in music. In the following generation, even such powerful figures ss Maximilian of Austria and Henry VIII of England would imitate many aspects of Philip's chivalric court life.

What was this man like, who dominated the cultural scene in the fifteenth century? One of his official (thus biased in his favor, of course) court chroniclers, George Chastellain, described his person as follows:

> In stature he was a fairly tall man ... his legs and arms were thin ... he was lean of hand and foot, and bony rather than fleshy, with full-blooded veins that stood out. He had the rather long face of his father, brown and weather-beaten. The nose was long but not aquiline, his forehead was high and large, but not bald ... He had large bushy eyebrows which stood out like horns when he was angry ... His eyes varied considerably, sometimes looking fierce, at other times amiable. His face reflected his inner feelings ... He deserved a crown on the strength of his physical appearance alone ... He walked solemnly ... He sat but little, stood for long periods ... was always changing his clothes ... He was skillful on horseback, liked the bow and shot well, and was excellent at tennis ... He lingered over his meals. Though the best-served man alive, he was a modest eater.[17]

A more balanced assessment might point out that he was not above flares of wrath, as when he once pursued his son through the palace with a sword, or cruelty (he was responsible for destroying the town of Dinant and drowning six hundred of the citizens in the river). He had twenty-four mistresses and sixteen illegitimate children, to whom he was a good father.[18]

He had an unusual state of musical awareness, dating perhaps from some guitar instruction in his youth. He often personally auditioned his court musicians, sometimes more than once. Perhaps no prince of the fifteenth century was more generous in his gifts to visiting musicians. Such was his reputation in this regard that even the minstrels of the lands with whom he was at war would slip behind the lines to play for him and be rewarded! In this way he kept his eyes open for the better players. Thus, for example, when Charles VI died (1422), Philip immediately engaged two of his best musicians, Jehan Facien, known as 'king of the minstrels' in Paris, and Antoine le Blanc, a trumpeter. Perhaps because he was convinced of his

[17] Quoted in Richard Vaughan, *Philip the Good: The Apogee of Burgundy* (New York: Barnes and Noble, 1970), 127–128.

[18] He seems to have set the court standard, in this regard, for even the Bishop of Cambrai and the Bishop of Liege had thirty-six and twelve children respectively, born out of wedlock.

[19] Almost all of these players are listed in Marix, *Histoire de la Musique*, 264–274.

[20] Bowles, 'Instruments at the Court of Burgundy,' writes, without attribution, 'Trumpeters, vielle-players, lutenists, harpists, and wind-players ... all constituted a part of the ducal household. The actual number of minstrels at the court varied from time to time. During the early years of his reign, Philip ... had only players of "soft" instruments and one harpist.' I find this summary very misleading and impossible to substantiate. In fact, the records demonstrate the ensemble was consistent: it was primarily a wind band and not of strings; no where to my knowledge is there evidence that 'soft' instruments were at any time most prominent.

own authority in this regard, once he hired a musician for his permanent ensemble, usually the man stayed for many years, if not for life.

In addition to his fine group of singers, Philip retained from his father and maintained a small wind band, together with trumpets for ceremonial use, throughout his reign. While this permanent ensemble may seem small, one must remember that for any festive occasion Philip had access to numerous minstrels from cities and other courts.

From the very beginning of his reign Philip maintained five or six minstrels and five or six ceremonial trumpets (*trompette de guerre*) until the final ten years or so when they averaged four.[19] One sees a harpist retained in the first year only; the instrument does not reappear for nearly fifteen years. String players do not appear until the same year (1433).[20]

The nucleus of Philip's musical establishment was the group called minstrels, which seems beyond doubt a wind band.[21] For one thing the records of instrument purchases demonstrate this fact. In 1423, according to Marix, Philip placed an identical order to the one his father placed in 1413 with the instrument maker Pierre de Prost in Bruges.[22] This strongly implies that Philip maintained the six-member wind band of his father (two shawms, two bombards, a 'contre,' and a slide-trumpet). A similar order to the same maker in 1425 for three 'new' instruments;[23] the mention of the same wind band, with the same instrumentation in 1430 and 1435;[24] and the ordering of still additional instruments in 1439[25] all suggest these minstrels were in fact a continuing wind band.[26]

Philip's permanent instrumental ensemble was, then, a wind band of four, five, or six members, to which additional players would be added for public ceremonies. Because, as I have noted, these public ceremonies had political ramifications, these additional players were more a necessity than a luxury. By the calculated splendor of these public festivities, Philip hoped to instill in all observers a sense of awe toward the entire political state. It is a tactic not entirely unfamiliar to the twenty-first century as well!

The first of these great political festivities was Philip's marriage to Isabel of Portugal, which was celebrated early in 1430. While Philip's first two marriages had been politically tied

[21] This view is strongly held by Marix, *Histoire de la Musique*, 264–265, and Polk, 'Ensemble Instrumental Music,' 28.

[22] Marix, *Histoire de la Musique*, 102. I have not been able to establish the accuracy of this document.

[23] This document is quoted in Vander Streaten, *La Musique*, 7:39.

[24] Besseler, 'Alta,' and *Bourdon und Fauxbourdon* (Leipzig: Breitkopf und Härtel, 1974), 188.

[25] Archives du Nord (B 1966, fol. 242v).

[26] Bowles, 'Instruments at the Court of Burgundy,' 47, makes the statement that Philip preferred the trumpet above all instruments, a statement I again find misleading. All rulers preferred the trumpet for ceremonial usage, but one does not find with Philip accounts of the trumpets playing in private chambers, as for example was the case with Elizabeth I and Maximilian I. Contemporary art also frequently pictures the wind band, with the instruments I have described. One sees them playing for a banquet (Miniature by Loyset Liédet, *Histoire de Renaud de Montauban*, Paris, Bibl. l'Arsenal, Ms.fr. 5073, fol. 148); for a dance (Miniature, ibid., fol. 117v.); and for a court picnic (1608 copy of an original painting by Jan van Eyck, Versailles, Musée du Château, Inv.-Nr. MV 5423).

to France, now it was the desire to break with France which necessitated the special pomp surrounding this marriage with Isabel, who had dynastic ties with England.

Philip's ambassadors traveled to Lisbon in July 1429 to sign the marriage alliance and to escort Isabel back to Bruges, where Philip was waiting with his court. The reception of these ambassadors in Lisbon demonstrates the significance of the new alliance from the point of view of Portugal as well.

> They went to the encounter by horseback in large numbers of chevaliers, squires, well-mounted and clothed, and the bourgeois and notable merchants of the City of Lisbon, and with the Jews and the Sarrazyns of the area, separately, clothed in their habit, singing and dancing in their manner. And thus was the lady led through the city to the Palais de l'infant, with great joy and solemnity, and there was a great number of trumpets, minstrels, players of organs, harps, and other instruments.[27]

The problems of fifteenth-century travel being as they were, Philip had to wait impatiently for more than six months. Isabel's small fleet of ships had been scattered by a storm; some arrived, some landed in England, and Isabel was unaccounted for. When her ship finally arrived in port, on 7 January 1430, one can understand the resultant sense of celebration in Bruges. An eyewitness described the arrival:

> On the feast day of Saint Estienne, before midday, the lady descended from her ship and at her descent were many barges and other small vessels decorated with flags, and many important siegneurs, squires, and notable people from diverse lands to see, serve, and accompany her. There were also many trumpets, minstrels, and players of many musical instruments, and each tried to play the best he could, for the coming of the lady was much desired … Naturally there were heralds, trumpets, minstrels … more than 120 silver trumpets, plus other trumpets, minstrels, players of organ, harp and other instruments without number; the force of the music made the entire city vibrate.[28]

Another chronicler, Jean Lefèvre, the seigneur de Saint-Rémy, adds the very interesting observation that at least some of the playing by the massed trumpets was co-ordinated.

[27] Louis Prosper Gachard, *Collection de documents inédits concernant la Belgique* (Bruxelles, 1833–1835), 2:65ff.

> Aussy allerent à l'encontre à cheval grant nombre de chevaliers, escuiers, bien montez et habillez, et les bourgois et marchans notables de la ville de Lisbonne, et avec ce les Juifs et les Sarrazyns du lieu, separeement, habillez à leur usaige, chantans et dansans selon leur guise. Et ainsi fut la dame amenee par la ville au palais de l'infant, a grant joye et solemnité, et y avoit grant quantité de trompetes, menestrelz, joueurs d'orgues, de harpes et autres instrumen …

[28] Anonymous Mss., late fifteenth century (Archives générales du Belgique, Brussels), published by Gachard, ibid.

> … feste de saint Estienne, avant midy, descendy madite dame de sa nave, et à sa descendue ot mainte barge et autres petiz navieres parez de draps, et autres portans pluiseurs siegneurs, escuiers et gens notables de divers estas, pour veoir, acompaignier et servir icelle dame. Grant foison y ot aussi de trompetes, menestrelz et joueurs de pluiseurs instrumens de musique, et tous s'efforçoient d'en faire le mieulx qu'ilz savoient, pour la feste et joye de la venue de madite dame tant desirée … Aussi ne fait à demander s'il y avoit heraulx, trompettes et menestrelz, car tant en y avoit, que long temps avant n'en avoient tant esté ensemble, et y ot trompetes d'argent bien VIxx ou plus et d'autres trompettes, menestrelz, joueurs d'orgues, de harpes, et d'aultres instrumens sans nombre, que de force de jouer faisoient telle noise, que toute la ville en rosonoit.

101 silver trumpets, without the other instruments made a great racket in the city … By the door of the duke's palace they assembled 76 trumpets and all played at the same time.[29]

Still another eyewitness counted one hundred and sixty-four trumpets which sounded 'very melodiously.'[30]

For the festivities which followed, the Burgundian court had been making preparations for a long time. A four hundred man escort accompanied goods sent north from the court centers of Dijon and Lille, including fifteen cart-loads of tapestries, one hundred wagons of wine, and fifty loads of furnishings and jewels.

For the wedding banquet numerous temporary buildings were constructed, including a single hall one hundred and fifty feet long, faced with a wooden lion pouring wine from its paw. Each main dish was accompanied into the hall by an elaborate pageant, one, for example, had some of the duke's men dressed as savages, riding in on wild pigs. With one serving came a castle with a 'wild man' in the central tower holding Philip's banner, while in each corner a lady held the banner of one of his territories. The most remarkable pageant featured a large pie, containing a live sheep dyed in the ducal colors and an actor as a 'wild beast.'[31] Later the reader will see such a pie filled with musicians!

The musicians who played for this banquet, and the dancing which followed, were placed high in a special gallery.[32] These wedding celebrations continued with tournaments and, on 10 January, the announcement of a new chivalric order, the *Toison d'Or*, which I shall describe below.

In many ways, this wedding set the style for royal marriages which followed in Burgundy, providing the noble could afford to imitate Philip's concept of celebration. For example, Philip was an honored guest, in February 1434, for the wedding of the son of the Duke of Savoy, held in Cambrai. On the first evening, the meal was served to the music of 'trumpets and minstrels from various lands.' Among these were the wind players of Philip, for we know they made the trip with him and received a special monetary gift.[33] On the following evening occurred the official wedding banquet, with the main dishes paraded in with pageants in the style of Philip. A huge model ship, complete with mast, sail, crow's nest with

[29] Jean Lefèvre, *Chronique* (Paris, 1876), 2:165–166.
> … cent et 1 trompectes d'argent sans les aultres instrumens, qui faisoient moult grant esbaudissement par le ville … Et auprès de la porte y avoit, tout en une compaignie, lxxvj trompectes qui toutes blandissoient en une foiz.

[30] E. de Monstrelet, *La Chronique d'Enguerran de Monstrelet* (Paris, 1857–1862), 4:371.

[31] Banquet description taken from Lefèvre, quoted in Vaughan, *Philip the Good*, 56–57.

[32] Lefèvre, *Chronique* (Paris, 1852), 450.
> Dedens la dicte salle, y avoit fait ung moult bel hourdys et hault sur l'um de des costez, la ou les héraulx se tenoit pour regarder les estatz et pour cryer les festes. Et la jouoient les trompectes et menestreux pour danses.

[33] Archives du Nord (B 1951, fol. 111v).

a man in it, was brought into the banquet hall between rows of singing syrens and discharged the fish course. Then a horse disguised as an elephant entered; a man dressed in peacock feathers representing the god of love, riding in a castle on the 'elephant' shot roses among the guests with a bow. A following meal featured another immense pie, this time with a man inside dressed as an eagle who flapped his wings and released a flock of doves.[34]

In 1440, Philip attended the marriage of Charles d'Orléans and Marie de Clèves held in Bruges. An eyewitness wrote, 'the streets were filled with silver trumpets, clarions, minstrels, and other instruments of music.'[35] Marie was a daughter to Philip's aunt, and like Charles came from a musical family. In the case of Charles, let me only mention that his Mother, Valentine de Visconti, had a gown upon which the chanson, 'Madame je suis plus joyeulx,' was notated with five hundred and sixty-eight pearls![36]

An account of the marriage of Anthoine de Villers, principal squire of Philip's stable, outlines the participation of wind instruments in the five-day tournament ritual which followed the wedding.[37] When the adversaries display their flags and banners, the trumpets and clarions are heard. On the day the arms of the duke are displayed, when the horses are tried out, and again on the day of the tournament itself, these instruments played their role.

A rather unique description of this same tournament was left in verse, by a lady chronicler, Christine de Pisan.

> Procession to the field
> > Minstrels, trumpeters, timpanists,
> > There were more than three pairs,
> > Who blew so loudly
> > That hill and dale resounded.
>
> Dinner
> > Then the minstrels came forward
> > And began to blow ...
> > Then the dances began:
> > New, joyous, and gay.
>
> Going to the tournament, the next day
> > Painted lances and banners
> > All accompanied very beautifully,
> > The player of the shawm
> > Was there to hear.

[34] Lefèvre, *Chronique*, 2:287–297.

[35] Monstrelet, *La Chronique*, 5:447.

[36] Pierre Champion, *La vie de Charles d'Orléans* (Paris: Champion, 1911), 132.

[37] Antoine de La Sale, *Des anciens tournois et faictz d'armes* (1872), 203–214.

The Jousts begin
> Then joyously the minstrels
> Sounded forth, heralds cried …
> Lances broke, heads clanked,
> And these minstrels played loudly
> As if one heard the thunder of God.

After supper
> … Minstrels blew,
> And dancing diverted
> Companions of noble blood.[38]

Since the joust and tournament were fundamental to the princely life, nobles who participated in these events, or merely viewed them, in foreign cities would also take their musicians. There are several such references regarding Philip; I mention only one, when he traveled to Bruges for a joust in 1457. A pay record indicates Jehan Caresme, 'king' of Philip's minstrels, and his colleagues, received a present of six livres.[39]

As Philip was constantly on the road, even regularly changing the place of his residence, the wind band had its own wagon to carry their belongings.[40] When Philip traveled within his own territories he was, of course, treated to a welcome worthy a king, which he was in all but title. An eyewitness describes such a welcome given Philip in Bruges.

> And in the evening there were many solemnities and pompous demonstrations, bonfires were lit in various streets and quarters … and all through the night (one heard) many sounds of trumpets, clarions, and many instruments.[41]

On another occasion, Philip was welcomed in Ghent at the city gate by the trumpeters of the city, who, with the six he brought with him, 'amounted to at least 30 or more.'[42] Here he was also treated to a series of allegorical pageants, dealing with the 'Prodigal Son, Mars, Solomon and Sheba, the Prophets,' etc. One of these included an elephant (a real one this time) upon which sat two instrumentalists and four singers performing a new chanson.[43]

Apparently when the duke traveled he acquired additional trumpets, for on these occasions they numbered twelve, organized under a 'chief' trumpeter. On mornings of a trip, these trumpets would play at the duke's window to awaken him and

[38] Christine de Pisan, *Le livre du duc des vrais amans*, in *Oeuvres poétiques* (Paris, 1886–1896), 3:79–94.
> Menestrelz, trompes, naquaires
> Y avoit plus de troys paires
> Qui si haultement cournoyent
> Que mons et vaulx resonnoyent.
>
> On dîne
> Puis menestrelz s'avancierent
> Et a corner commencierent …
> Adonc commençay la dance,
> Nouvelle, joyeuse et gaye
>
> Le lendemain, on va aux joutes
> Lances peintes et baniere
> Et compagnie moult belle,
> Maint joueur de chalemelle
> Veissiez et peussiez ouir.
>
> Les joutes commencent
> Lors menestrelz liement
> Cournoient, hairaux crioient …
> Lances brisent, cops resonnent,
> Et ces menestrelz hault sonnent
> Si qu'on n'oïst Dieu tonnant.
>
> Après le souper, grand et notable,
> … Menestrelz cornerent,
> Et de dancer s'ordennerent
> Compagnons de noble sorte.

[39] Archives du Nord (B 3661, fol. 39v).

[40] Vaughan, *Philip the Good*, 142.

[41] Georges Chastellain, *Oeuvres* (Bruxelles, 1863–1866), 3:301–305.
> Et celuy soir furent faits maintes solempnités, maintes grandes chières et pompes monstrées, maint feu allumé en diverses rues et quarrefours … long de la nuyt, maintes sonneries de trompettes et de clairons et de tous instrumens …

[42] Clercq, *Mémoires*, 111.

[43] Jean Chartier, *Chroniques de Charles VII* (Paris, 1858), 81ff.

then split up into groups of four and go into the streets of the city to play. After returning for breakfast, they would play to have the horses made ready (an important safety measure, to accustom the horses to the noise of the instruments), play for the assembly, etc.[44] When the traveling party was ready, the trumpets would be joined for the trip by the 'haults instrumens,' the wind band of shawms and bombards.[45]

The trumpets on regular employment under Philip also had to participate in the many battles of his reign. I pass over these typical notices, except for one. During the siege of Bouvignes, in 1430, the citizens of Dinant, taking an inspiration from the Trojan Wars (and the famous horse), constructed an enormous wooden cat. With ten pair of wheels, it carried two hundred men under cover to the walls of Bouvignes. A chronicler tells us they forgot to oil the wheels of this great cat and the subsequent 'meeowing' would have been heard for many miles, had it not been for the noise of the shouting and the duke's trumpets.[46] I regret to add that incendiary missiles shot from the walls set the cat afire and many occupants were burnt before they could escape. Perhaps they should have read the Trojan account more carefully, for a similar fate befell the giant horse.

We have seen many instances where Philip the Good drew upon his wind band, together with other ceremonial appendiges, to contribute to the aura of importance in his public festivities. There remains one further example by which he is most widely known, his creation of a new chivalric order called the Order of the Golden Fleece (*Toison d'Or*). This was an honorary group of twenty-four knights, who were men of noble and legitimate birth, chosen from his various territories. This order, again, was in part to give the appearance of significance to his reign, but also to create the illusion of a unified people during a time of political unrest.

The order was announced in 1430 and periodically during the following thirty years the group met at great banquets held in the principal cities of his realm. At the first of these, held in the city of St. André, on 29 November 1431, one reads that at the lavish dinner the trumpets and minstrels 'played sweet (doulce) music which lingered in the ears.'[47]

In 1440 the order met in Bruges where there was a solemn procession through the streets to church for a Mass. The citizens decorated their homes and constructed pageants along the

44 Marche, *Mémoires*, 4:70–71. One can see the trumpets of Philip on his 'triumphal return to Artois,' in Jean Froissart, *Chron. de France et d'Angleterre*, ca. 1460 (copy in London, British Museum, Ms. Royal 18 E. I, fol. 12).

45 Marix, *Histoire de la Musique*, 61.

46 Kervyn de Lettenhove, 'Chroniques relatives à l'histoire de Belgique sous la domination des ducs de Bourgogne,' in *Livre des trahisons de France* (Brussels, 1873), 201.

Philip the Good, by Rogier van der Weyden (1400–1464), 1450. Philip is wearing a chain holding the Order of the Golden Fleece.

47 Lefèvre, *Chronique*, 2:201ff.

route. An eyewitness wrote, 'as to the silver trumpets, clarions, minstrels, and other instrumentalists, they were so numerous that the entire town vibrated with their music,' an expression frequently used.[48] In the church portion of the meeting held in Ghent, in 1445, a chronicler notes that the trumpets and minstrels performed as well, during the long service.[49]

There are somewhat more details for the meeting of the order in Mons, in 1451. One learns that there were ten minstrels and trumpets, 'wearing robes of silver gilt linen cloth.' After the Mass, the chevaliers returned to their lodging, where Philip had arranged for them to be serenaded by trumpets and minstrels.[50] Later, at the banquet, the various main dishes were brought out to the music of trumpets and minstrels, followed by such officials as army officers, the *maître d'hostel*, etc.[51]

By far the most elaborate of these meetings of the Order of the Golden Fleece was held in Lille on 17 February 1454. Known as the Feast of the Pheasant (*Banquet du Voeu*), this banquet was the most celebrated of the fifteenth century and is the most widely mentioned single event in the life of Philip the Good. Several first-hand accounts of this banquet exist, differing in small details, and from all of them I have drawn the following description.[52]

In 1453 Constantinople fell to the Turks, an event considered a great blow to all of Christendom. Philip used the opportunity to call for a gathering of the Order of the Golden Fleece to propose a new crusade to recapture the city. While this goal was never achieved, and perhaps never really intended by Philip, it did serve as an excellent opportunity to gather new taxes.

Three long tables were set up inside a banquet hall, which was guarded by uniformed nobles and crossbowmen. The duke's place was at the center table, beneath a canopy of velvet and gold. Here he sat 'with so many diamonds, rubies and fine pearls in his hat that there were no room for any more.' The tablecloths were of silk damask, touching the floor, with individual cushions embroidered with coats-of-arms on the benches. The service was of gold; the glassware of crystal with jewels encrusted.

The decorations included two statues, one the figure of a naked girl, leaning against one of the supporting columns of the hall with Hippocras spraying from her right breast and

[48] Monstrelet, *La Chronique*, 447.

[49] Marche, *Mémoires*, 2:87ff.

[50] Mathieu d'Escouchy, *Chronique* (Paris, 1863–1864), 1:350ff.

[51] Marche, *Espitre pour tenir et célébrer la noble feste du Thoison d'Or*, quoted in Marix, *Histoire de la Musique*, 37.

[52] National Library, Brussels (Anonymous Ms.fr. 5739); d'Escouchy, *Chronique*; Marche, *Mémoires*; and a letter of J. de Pleine (22 February 1454) quoted in Vaughan, *Philip the Good*, 145.

Above: *Le voeu du faisan* (The Feast of the Pheasant), anonymous, sixteenth century

guarded by a live lion. She symbolized the city of Constantinople being protected by the lion of Flanders. Similarily, the naked statue of a small boy sprayed rose-water in the most natural fashion.

The two major constructions in the hall also contained the musicians. One was a model church, complete with stained glass windows and a bell in the steeple. It contained four singers and an organ. Across the room was a great pastry pie which contained twenty-eight musicians.[53] One can not be entirely sure of the instrumentation of the musicians in the pie, but, taking all the sources together, there were mentioned bagpipes, cornetts, trumpets, lutes, dulcians, flutes, and drums; most likely Philip's wind band was there, with additional musicians.

There were further tableaux: a replica of a Flemish ship in port, with rigging, sailors, bales and casks and a replica of a Flemish town, by a desert scene of tigers and snakes fighting (Christendom and the infidel again). There was a 'monster' in white and green silk, its upper part man, its lower part griffin, riding astride a boar; and a dragon spouting fire as it flew across the room and then mysteriously disappeared.

When all the guests were seated, a bell rang in the model church, followed by a chanson sung by the musicians inside. This was apparently the first of the musical selections performed as the food was being made ready. The chanson was followed by a musician of the bagpipe, dressed as a shepherd. Then a performing horse entered the hall, walking backward,

[53] Since the duke's colors were half-black and half-gray, one can not help but wonder if this were the origin of the song, 'Sing a song of sixpence,' with its 'four and twenty black birds, baked in a pie.'

and on its back were two trumpeters, sitting back to back and dressed in gray and black robes and wearing masks and 'surprising' hats. The organ in the church played next, followed by a 'German cornett' from the pie, 'sounding very strange.'

Now the food was ready to be served but due to the congestion, there was no room for the usual procession by which food paraded in at these events. Here it had to be lowered from the ceiling by cranes! The duke, being an exception, was served by a 'two-headed horse' and later by 'a monster, consisting of a man riding on an elephant, with another man, whose feet were hidden, on his shoulders.' We may rest assured that the variety of food was adequate, as we are told each meat course alone consisted of more than forty different dishes!

As the banquet proceeded there was continual music. One heard the singers again in a motet and a three-part chanson, 'La saulvegarde de ma vie.' In through the doors of the hall came four trumpeters, in white robes and playing gold trumpets, followed by more vocal music now by a young boy (one account says a girl) seated on an artificial white stag with gilded antlers. The boy wore a short costume of crimson silk, a little black hat and shoes of pony skin and sang Dufay's chanson, 'Je ne vis oncques la pareille,' accompanied by the stag (another hidden musician).

Next a play, 'Mystery and Adventures of Jason,' was performed on a stage, followed by more singing and organ playing from the model church. One heard a fanfare by the gold trumpets, from behind the green stage curtain, and then a four-part recorder performance from inside the pie. The duke's two blind vielle-players performed with a young girl, followed by an instrumental work for the pipe and tabor players in the pie, and then yet another chanson.

Now a real elephant entered the hall; in the howdah was a lady dressed in white, representing the captive Church begging for delivery by a crusade. At this time Dufay's 'Lamentatio sanctae matris ecclesiae Constantinopolitanae,' was performed.

Finally the grand chivalric moment arrived, with the entrance of two knights of the Order of the Golden Fleece and a pheasant, which had a gold collar around its neck decorated with rubies and large pearls. The duke handed to the Golden Fleece King-of-Arms a vow to read. It announced his intention to make the crusade, even going so far as to say that if challenged, he would accept single combat with the Turk! Everyone was amazed at this and one by one the other knights took the vow.

A procession of torch-bearers and musicians now preceded the circulation of large bowls glittering with precious stones (after dinner favors?) and a dance by the twelve actors who had participated in the play now brought the banquet to a conclusion. One of the guests, de Pleine, reports he got tired and left just before four o'clock in the morning!

Charles the Bold

Shortly before he died, Philip the Good turned over the government to his impatient son, known today as Charles the Bold but during his lifetime as Charles the Rash (*Téméraire*). Even in an age long inured to violence, Charles was extraordinary. Dreams of even greater realms brought him into war with France and the Holy Roman Empire. When some of his own cities voted to join the French, Charles gave them over to pillage by his troops, burned buildings to the ground, and drowned captives by the hundreds. This mad reign lasted only some ten years, until 1477, when, defeated by the Swiss, the body of Charles was found in a pond, with his face frozen fast in the ice.

Charles continued the wind band of his father, although the instrumentation seems not to have been so consistent. An ordinance of 1469 lists five 'trompettes de guerre,' six 'trompettes de ménestrels' and three 'joueurs des instrumens bas,' organized under a 'escuier d'escuyrie.' Since de La Marche, a member of the court, says that Charles had six 'haulz menestrelz,' or players of wind instruments, we assume that they are the same as those listed as 'trompettes de menestrels.'[54] Thus his band consisted of six players of the loud winds and three players of the string or soft winds. The number of trumpets, who continued the tradition of playing a 'brazen fanfare' under his window on days Charles traveled, increased as his attention was forced more and more toward war.[55] Already in 1467, when he took the field against Liege, one reads of twelve trumpets playing a fanfare.[56]

[54] Marche, *Mémoires*, 4:71, fn. 2, and Richard Vaughan, *Charles the Bold* (London: Longman, 1973), 193. One can see Charles' wind band playing for a dance in a miniature by Louis de Bruges, in Jean de Wavrin, *Chronique d'Angleterre*, 1 (copy in Vienna, National Library, Ms. 2534, fol. 17).

[55] Lewis, *King Spider*, 135–136.

[56] Vaughan, *Philip the Good*, 16.

Although trained as a child in the art of music, the life Charles chose to lead left little time to imitate the great festivities of his father. Only his marriage to Princess Margaret of England, in 1468, follows in the tradition of splendor.

An English eyewitness describes the arrival of Margaret for the wedding in Bruges riding in a litter lined with gold cloth and ermine.

> Next before hir, kynges of armes, and herrauldes of dyvers realmes, great compaignye of lordis and knightes ... all the towers and cornears of the gatt (gate) enramplysshid with mellodieus mynstralsye and besene richly with tappestry.[57]

The official wedding procession is described by the Flemish chronicler, de La Marche, as having included trumpets, clarions and minstrels from many lands.[58]

The wind band of Charles provided the music of the wedding service itself and this included a 'long trumpet fanfare,' a motet performed by three shawms and a slide-trumpet, and a motet and chanson performed by an ensemble of trombones, shawms, and bombards, with 'excellent effect.'[59]

One who attended this celebration, Jehan de Haynin, writes that the banquet festivities were held in a large banquet hall which had been constructed two months before for a meeting of the Order of the Golden Fleece. Now two galleries were constructed in the hall, one for the 'trumpets, clarions, and minstrels,' and the other for lady guests for whom there was no further room at the tables. At the banquet the food was brought in on thirty superbly made wooden ships, painted and gilded, 'complete with cords, masts, anchors and sails of gray taffeta.' The meal lasted from ten o'clock in the evening until one o'clock the following morning, when the tables were cleared for dancing.[60]

The following days saw a joust and banquet daily for a week. A large model of a castle Charles was building at Gorinchem was set up, consisting of a wooden frame covered with painted cloth. It had four windows which opened to reveal in turn four wolves who sang a ballad about the festivities, four rabbits playing on flutes, four boars blowing trumpets, and four donkeys performing on shawms.[61]

[57] Quoted in T. Phillips, 'Accounts of the Ceremonial of the Marriage of the Princess Margaret,' in *Archaeologica* (1846), 331.

[58] Marche, *Mémoires*, 3:109ff. toutes manieres d'instrumens par ordre, qui estoient de diverses nacions; et après iceulx venoyent clarions, menestreulx et trompettes ...

[59] Wangermée, *Flemish Music*, 213; Eric N. Simons, *The Reign of Edward IV* (London: Muller, 1966), 155; Marche, *Mémoires*, iii, 152ff; Emilie Dahnk, 'Musikausubung an den Hofen von Burgund und Orleans wahrend des 15. Jahrhunderts,' in *Archiv für Kulturgeschichte* 25 (Leipzig: Teubner, 1934–1936), 210; and G. Thibault in 'Le Concert Instrumental au XVe Siècle,' 31, who suggests several chansons which he believes may have been performed on this occasion.

[60] Jehan de Haynin, quoted in Vaughan, *Philip the Good*, 49ff.

[61] Léon de Laborde, *Les ducs de Bourgogne* (Paris, 1849–1852), 2:326–327.

The tournaments which were held are known collectively as the *Pas de l'Arbre d'Or*. The allegorical theme centered on the 'Lady of the Ile Cellee' who begged the 'Bastard of Burgundy' to undertake an enterprise, on condition that he should decorate a golden tree with the arms of famous warriors. She was to place at the knight's disposal her dwarf, 'Arbre d'Or' and a giant from the 'Forêt douteuse.' The tournament site had two entrances, one with a painted golden tree and the other with two towers filled with trumpeters. The characters of this tale appeared at intervals during the week of tournaments. The dwarf, for example, stood on a special platform and, by way of a great sand-glass and a blast on his horn, controlled the length of the individual bouts.[62]

In 1473 Charles met with the Emperor Frederick in Trier. For this meeting he outfitted the entire court in new robes, an account of which is extant in a document by his treasurer, Nicolas de Gondeval. It lists, in order of importance, the robes to be worn from the highest nobles (Cloth of Gold) down to the porters and humble servants (Woollen cloths of different qualities). The musicians who made the trip are listed somewhat below mid-point in this hierarchy: Ferrette, 'le roy des menestriers,' Rousset the new trumpet and others, 'Short robes of damask and pourpoints of black satin,' and two trumpeters of the guard, 'Robes of camlet and pourpoints of black satin.'[63]

At one final ceremony, relative to a treaty of alliance between Burgundy, Savoy and Milan, in 1475, one reads,

> and at once the trumpets began to sound, eight of them; then the pipers (shawms?) of which there were many.[64]

Charles the Bold was the final chapter of the Burgundian hopes to become an independent state. As he left no son, the territories passed through his daughter, Mary, to her husband Maximilian I of Austria and the Hapsburg empire.

[62] Sydney Anglo, *The Great Tournament Roll of Westminster* (Oxford: Clarendon, 1968), 28ff.

[63] Vaughan, *Philip the Good*, 143ff.

[64] Johanne Petro Panigarola, Milanese Ambassador at the Burgundian Court, quoted in Vaughan, ibid., 170.

26 *Court Wind Bands in the German-Speaking Countries*

THE STORY OF THE GERMAN COURT WIND BANDS must begin with the greatest of all the medieval kings, Charlemagne (742–814). Although church bans on secular amusements were already appearing in increasing numbers, Charlemagne took a strong interest in the jongleur. Later minstrels looked back on him as their greatest early patron, who had given them the best land in Provence as payment for their services.[1] Chambers believes the birth of the later *chansons de gestes* can be found at the court of Charlemagne.[2]

According to one source, Charlemagne even had prepared a collection of his hunting signals, called 'Frohliche Jagd.'[3] While this music is not extant, iconographic clues would suggest his hunting music was performed by various animal horns, trumpet-types, a variety of pipes, drums, bells, etc.

For his numerous military adventures, perhaps no better description will be found than that suggested by the later Minnesinger, Wolfram von Eschenbach.

> There were sounds of busine
> and drums were thrown and beat
> a thousand drum sticks and no crumhorns(?)
> and the noise of 800 pusinen one heard.[4]

Several attractive anecdotes of Charlemagne have survived. One tells of a jongleur who guided Charlemagne over Mt. Cenis in 773 and was then given as a reward all the land over which his *tuba* (trumpet) could be heard when played from a hill.[5] Another is the story of Roland, nephew to Charlemagne, who lay wounded in the Pyrenées in 778. This poem, known as 'The Song of Roland,' is the oldest major work in French literature, dating from the middle of the twelfth century. We may take the description of one thousand trumpets sounding as exaggeration, of course, as the troops are awaiting the aid of Charlemagne. His nephew, Roland, carries a horn made of ivory, in the copy of an animal horn and known as an Oliphant, which he raises to sound a call to summon help from his uncle, Charlemagne. The subsequent description is

---

[1] Philippe Mouskes, *de Poetis Provincialibus*, quoted in Chambers, *The Mediaeval Stage*, 1:37.
> Quar quant li buens
> Rois Karlemaigne
> Ot toute mise à son demaine
> Provence, qui mult iert plentive
> De vins, de bois, d'aigue, de rive,
> As lecours, as menestreus,
> Qui sont auques luxurieus,
> Le donna toute et departi.

[2] Chambers, *The Mediaeval Stage,* 1:37.

[3] Veit, *Die Blasmusik*, 20.

[4] Ibid.
> dâ wart vil busîne erschalt
> und tambûren ungezalt
> ... dâ wart geworfen und geslagen ...
> tûsend rottumbes sleht, ir keinu krumbes
> und acht hundert pusînen snar
> man hôrte dâmit krache gar.

[5] Chambers, *The Mediaeval Stage*, 1:37, fn. 2.

again poetic exaggeration, however, anyone who has blown an animal horn made into a crude trumpet will have immediate sympathy with this account.

> Count Roland brought the horn up to his mouth:
> he sets it firmly, blows with all his might.
> The peaks are high, the horn's voice carries far;
> They hear it echo thirty leagues away.
> Charles hears it, too, and all his company:
> the king says then: "Our men are in a fight."
>
> Count Roland, racked with agony and pain
> and great chagrin, now sounds his ivory horn:
> bright blood leas in a torrent from his mouth:
> the temple has been ruptured in his brain.
> The horn he holds emits a piercing blast:
> Charles hears it as he crosses through the pass;
>
> Count Roland's mouth is filling up with blood;
> the temple has been ruptured in his brain.
> In grief and pain he sounds the Oliphant;
> Charles hears it, and his Frenchmen listen, too.
> The king says then, "That horn is long of wind."

These stories, but for the poetic exaggeration, must represent many early contests. All of the early German kings probably had their personal trumpets, following the example of the rest of Western Europe, and one can see an early example in an icon from the late twelfth century which pictures Henry VI, Emperor of the Holy Roman Empire from 1190 to 1197, entering Palermo preceded by his three busine players (see image below).[6]

[6] Pietro da Eboli, *Liber ad Honorem Augusti* (Berne, Burgerbibliothek, Mss. del Cod. di Berna 120).

Frederick II

The first German ruler for which there is more specific information regarding wind instrument performance is Frederick II (1194–1250), another Holy Roman Emperor and son of Henry VI. In Frederick we have one of the most interesting and most brilliant of all early kings. Both parents having died by the time he was five, he was made a ward of the pope and was therefore reared in Rome. This precocious youth took over the government at age twelve and married at fifteen years of age. Few men who have ever lived can point to such a lifetime of devotion to self-education. He spoke nine languages and wrote in seven. During the obligatory crusade, the Saracen commander, al-Kamil, was so astonished to find a European who understood Arabic and was familiar with Arabic literature, science and philosophy, he made a favorable peace. Frederick maintained a large zoological garden for study and wrote a definitive treatise on the art of falconry. He was interested in such diverse subjects as mathematics and anatomy and founded the University of Naples in 1224.

It was after his return from his crusade that he established the musical side of his court life. He returned with many Arabic servants, among whom were his corps of trumpets.

> He selected negro boys between sixteen and twenty to form a musical corps; they were magnificently clad and taught to blow large and small silver trumpets. We may assume that the duty of this imperial band was to play at meal times, since the courts of Anjou and Aragon, whom Frederick copied in every way, indulged this custom.[7]

In 1241 Frederick received an English visitor, Richard of Cornwall, and the details of this visit are preserved through the chronicle of a contemporary, Matthew Paris. Richard found great pleasure and enjoyment in being shown 'various kinds of musical instruments' by the emperor, most likely instruments he had brought back from the crusade.[8] Among the various entertainments offered Richard, he found particular praise for

> two Saracen girls of handsome form, mounted upon four round balls placed upon the floor, namely, one of the two on two balls, and the other on the other two. They walked backwards and forwards, clap-

[7] Ernst Kantorowicz, *Frederick the Second*, trans. E. O. Lorimer (New York: Ungar, 1957), 312.

[8] Paris, *English History*, 1:370.

> ping their hands, moving at pleasure on these revolving globes, gesticulating with their arms, singing various tunes, and twisting their bodies according to the tune, beating cymbals or castanets together with their hands.[9]

[9] Ibid.

When Richard left, after a four-month stay, the emperor arranged that upon his travel through Italy (where Frederick was then holding court) he would be greeted officially in each city.

> By the emperor's command, he was met on his route by the inhabitants of the cities, mounted on noble horses, richly equiped, dressed in silk and other costly garments, attended by vocal and instrumental musicians, with elegant devices; but I shall here, omitting all the others, make particular mention of the rejoicings at one place. On his approaching Cremona, the Cremonese came joyfully to meet him, with the emperor's elephant in advance of them, handsomely decorated, and bearing a wooden sort of tower, in which the masters of the animal sat, playing on trumpets.[10]

[10] Paris, *English History*, 1:385.

Frederick's third marriage was to an English princess, Isabella, who was fond of music and maintained her own minstrels. A fragment of a document, which survived until the last war, contained an entry relative to the purchase of a sackbut for her ensemble.[11] This is a particularly interesting reference, for it is much earlier than any other known appearance of this word.

[11] Georgina Masson, *Frederick II of Hohenstaufen: A Life* (New York: Octagon, 1973), 270.

I pause briefly to mention a particularly charismatic trumpet player, who appeared in 1233 during a period of religious fanaticism known as the 'Great Halleluja!' in Italy. The man wore a black beard, a high Armenian cap, and a sack-like robe with a red cross on front and back. He played a copper trumpet from which he produced 'now sweet, now terrifying sounds.' When he played people followed him and when he arrived at a market place or public square it was said,

> all anmities were suddenly forgotten, and a time of happiness and joy began; knights and people, citizens and peasants struck up hymns and songs in praise of God; people fell on each other's necks, and there was no wrath, no strife, no confusion: only Love and Peace.[12]

[12] Kantorowicz, *Frederick the Second*, 397. One would like to have a copy of that composition!

The political jurisdiction of the emperor over Italy had always been only a nominal one,[13] but since Frederick II had lived so much of his life in Italy he sought to make Rome the political as well as the religious capitol of the Western world. The result was a continuing series of battles between the emperor's forces and those of various cities who wished to maintain their status as city-states.

In a famous battle at Cortenuova, Frederick defeated the army of Milan and had the good fortune to capture the Milan *carroccio*, banners, flags, trumpets and all.[14] Frederick then began parading this vehicle through the cities of Italy, pulled by his elephant with its wooden tower filled with trumpet players, to the humiliation of the Milanese and as a great symbol of his intent to control the cities of Italy. To help fuel the enthusiasm of the Romans for his grand design, he sent the *carroccio* ahead to Rome as a gift. The Romans placed it in the Capitol, mounted on five marble columns, with the following inscription:

RECEIVE, O ROME, AS AN ETERNAL ORNAMENT OF THE CITY, THIS CARROCCIO, THE GIFT OF THE AUGUST EMPEROR, FREDERICK II! CAPTURED THROUGH THE DEFEAT OF MILAN, IT COMES AS A GLORIOUS SPOIL OF VICTORY TO PROCLAIM THE EMPEROR'S TRIUMPH.[15]

For most of the fourteenth century evidence points to only a continuation of the royal preference for the trumpet. For example, in an illustration of a tournament attended by Heinrich VII, ca. 1310–1313, one still sees only the older straight busines.[16]

The successor to Heinrich VII was Ludwig II, of Bavaria. Emperor of the Holy Roman Empire, he was excommunicated by the pope and then created his own anti-pope to perform his coronation as emperor. In 1338 he had an historic meeting with Edward III of England in Koblenz. Surely for such a meeting, in order to impress Edward, Ludwig would have taken his minstrels, although reports still refer only to the 'resounding blast of trumpets.'[17]

By the end of the fourteenth century a much broader range of instruments was known to Germany, indeed Reschke maintains that there were numerous brass, woodwind, and percus-

[13] As one would later observe, the Holy Roman Empire was neither Holy, nor Roman, nor an Empire!

[14] The reader is referred to the discussion of the *carroccio* above, under 'Civic Wind Bands in Italy.'

[15] Thomas Curtis van Cleve, *The Emperor Frederick II* (Oxford, 1972), 408ff.

[16] Koblenz Staatsarchiv, Codex Balduini Trevirensis, illustration 34A (Mss. IC NR. I).

[17] James MacKinnon, *The History of Edward the Third* (London: Longman Green, 1900), 120.

sion military bands by this time.[18] A report of the court of Duke Albert IV in Vienna, for 1398, lists, '3 fistulatores (flutes), 3 phiffer (shawms), 2 trompeter, 2 possuner (trombones), 3 paukker (timpani), 1 leyrer, 1 fidler, and 1 lautenslaher.'[19]

Surviving documents from the fifteenth century in Germany begin to provide a more complete picture of the court wind bands, beginning with Sigismund.[20]

Sigismund

Sigismund was a man not without attractive personal qualities. He had kingly presence, slender and graceful with curly hair and a long beard parted in the middle. He was an unusually fine public speaker and, one might add, in seven languages. When someone critized his Latin grammar, he responded that he was *supra grammaticam* (above grammar!); as an emperor, we can grant him that.

His relatively small number of personal wind players was a manifestation of the fact that his reign was beset by financial problems, a characteristic which seems to have accompanied the position. For cash flow the emperor of the Holy Roman Empire was dependent on grants from the electors, princes, and cities of the empire, all of whom appear to have been rather niggardly. The Emperor Maximilian, in 1495, observed that, 'the Empire is a heavy burden, with little gain therefrom.' Granvella, minister to Charles V, said at the Diet of Speyer, 'The Emperor has, for the support of his dignity, not a hazel-nut's worth of profit from the Empire.'[21] Of course, this is just a matter of perspective, but in the case of Sigismund the want seems to have been genuine. There are even reports that he would appear sometimes in patched shoes and clothes with tears 'that showed to the skin.'[22] Certainly his inability to support a wind band on the scale of even minor dukes must be taken as an indication of his being unable to afford many of the status symbols of his rank. This must have been a constant embarrassment for Sigismund, for any important appearance on his part would always attract the other nobility with their many wind players. For example, when he held an assembly in Ofen, in 1417, one reported the presence of eighty-six shawms and trombones.[23]

[18] Johannes Reschke, 'Studie zur Geschichte der brandenburgisch-prussischen Heeresmusik' (PhD diss., Friedrich Wilhelms Universitat, Berlin, 1935), 5.

[19] Hans Joachim Moser, *Die Musikergenossenschaften im deutschen Mittelalter* (Rostock: C. Hinstorffs Buchdruckerei, 1910), 19. See also, Kurt F. Reinhardt, *Germany: 2000 Years* (New York, 1950), 1:186.

[20] The minstrels of his predecessor, Rupert, King of the Romans, 1400–1410, traveled to London where they were given a gift by the court. They must have been wind players, but no specific information is given in the account of the payment. (London, Public Record Office, Queen's Remembrancer Wardrobe Account for 6 July 1402).

[21] James Bryce, *The Holy Roman Empire* (New York, 1968), 229, fn. d.

[22] Henderson, *A Short History of Germany*, 1:168,

[23] Chr. d'Elvert, *Geschichte der Musik in Mähren und Österreichisch-Schlesien* (Brünn, 1873), 165.

Never was his relative poverty more evident than at the Council of Constance, 1414–1418, the historic Church gathering with its numerous nobles and countless wind players which I have described above.[24] With the great pomp displayed on this occasion, one can imagine how embarrassed Sigismund was to have had to hire wind players for his appearances just to save face. A miniature published by one of the eyewitnesses to this council shows Sigismund arriving with four trumpets and three shawms, but the trumpets are in identical uniforms and the shawms not, indicating they were hired for the occasion (see image below).[25] Another of his entrances, in March 1415, found him with twenty trumpets and forty shawms, clearly an attempt to buy respect.[26]

[24] chapter 11, page 101

[25] Copies in Prag, Universitní knihova (Ms. XVI A 17, fol. 70) and in the New York Public Library (Spencer Collection, Ms. 32, fol. 86, see image below).

[26] Richental, *Ulrichs von Richental*, 63.

Emperor Sigismund with the golden rose, from Ulrich von Richental, *Chronik des Constanzer Concils*.

One must point out, however, that if Sigismund could afford only a few players, at least there is some evidence he was quite up-to-date in the instruments they played. A miniature showing his entrance into Basel in 1432 pictures two shawm players and what clearly seems to be the more modern sackbut, rather than the medieval slide-trumpet (one can see the instrument extending over the shoulder).²⁷ Also, an anonymous drawing, ca. 1420, of a tournament in Austria, possibly representing Sigismund, shows shawms of three different sizes.²⁸

Having been so often upstaged by more impressive musical forces, one can see the human side of Sigismund when, upon leaving Boulogne in April 1416, and six hundred horsemen with trumpets and minstrels came to escort him on his way, he sent them away with an angry message to be gone!²⁹

As Sigismund was also King of Hungary, with its active commercial interchange with the West, I shall note here a few of the examples of their wind bands which followed in the Western tradition. Royal trumpeters (*buccinatores*) are first mentioned in a document dated 1257 in Hungary and in 1272 the royal trumpets (*trumbatores domini regis*) were owners of the village of Gajdosbogdány (the name coming from *gajd*, for shawm, or perhaps horn).³⁰ A miniature pictures the marriage, in 1307, of Karl I and Elisabeth of Hungary and shows the clarion instrument.³¹

A very important Hungarian king comes in the late fifteenth century in the person of Matthias Corvinus. He actually conquered Austria, even Vienna herself, driving Frederick III into exile. An eyewitness in 1486 mentions hearing the shawms and trumpets of Corvinus.³² A very nice story documents a psychological victory by Corvinus over the Poles during his war with them in 1471–1478. In 1473, Corvinus found himself and his troops trapped in the city of Wratislavia, surrounded by the Polish troops. Normally, in a siege of this kind, the troops on the outside expected to soon starve the troops within the city into surrender. Corvinus, to give the impression that the city was sufficiently stocked to withstand a very lengthy siege, set up tables on the walls and had his officers appear there, dining richly to the music of his wind band and dancing girls. After watching a day or two of this, the Polish troops, living on field rations, became disheartened and submitted very favorable terms for a peace!³³

27 Benedikt Tschachtlan, *Heinrich Dittlingers Berner Chronik* (Zurich, Central Library, Ms. A. 120, fol. 55v).

28 Erlangen, University Library (Graphische Sammlung, Inv.-Nr. B. 16).

29 Wylie, *The Reign of Henry the Fifth*, 3:7.

30 Otto Gombosi, 'Music in Hungary,' in Gustave Reese, *Music in the Renaissance* (New York: Norton, 1959).

31 Budapest, Országos Szechényi Konyvtár (Mss. lat.m.a. 404, fol. 70).

32 L. Ovary, 'La recontre de Mathias et Vladislas à Iglau, d'après des documents des Archives de Mantoue et de Modène,' *Századok* (Budapest, 1889).

33 Kastner, *Manuel Général*, 103.

Frederick III

The last in a series of relatively weak emperors in the fifteenth century, Frederick III (reigning 1440–1493) allowed the impetus to move to the cities with their strong commerce-oriented governments. He was an alchemist and astrologer and so happy strolling around his garden in Graz that he permitted Bohemia, Austria, and Hungary to effectively remove themselves from the Empire.

For the first of his two coronations in 1452, he went to Italy with his brother, Duke Albert of Austria, his nephew, King Ladislaus of Hungary and Bohemia, and a train of some twelve hundred horsemen.[34] Following the coronation in Rome, Frederick was the guest of honor at a great cetebration in Ferrara, where one heard the 'mingling of martial trumpets with the softer strains of flutes (shawms?).'[35] For Frederick's coronation in Aachen the same year an eyewitness reported that his royal trumpets marched down both sides of the street during the processional.[36]

The best view of the use of wind instruments in the court of Frederick is found in the autobiographical book by his son, Maximilian I, called the *Weisskunig*. This book, which covers the life of Frederick as well, contains two hundred and fifty-one woodcuts, of which one hundred and eighteen are by Hans Burgkmair. Illustration Number 14 is called, 'Sea Journey of Queen Leonora,' and represents a visit of Frederick's wife to her home in Portugal. The scene pictures two ships, the one with Leonora containing three trumpet players playing a fanfare on short, folded instruments. There are in other illustrations the familiar facets of fifteenth-century court life, such as the trumpets playing for the joust and the pipe and drummer urging on the attack of the emperor's troops on the fortress of Monselice. The largest ensemble is found in illustration Number 136, which deals with Frederick's rescue of Maximilian when he was a prisoner in Bruges. Four ships fill the picture; the emperor's contains in addition to the standard-bearers, etc., four trumpeters, several woodwind players, and a drummer.

Finally, there are two extant eyewitness accounts of the performance of wind music during dinners hosted by Frederick III. During a dinner in 1473 in Trier, given for Charles of Burgundy, one heard a trumpet ensemble, an ensemble of

[34] Duke Albert had his own establishment of four trumpets, three minstrels, and a drummer, Jean le Noir, who received a special large gift when Philip the Good visited this court in 1454. See Marix, *Histoire de la Musique*, 70.

[35] Gardner, *Dukes & Poets in Ferrara*, 70ff.

[36] Bayerische Akademie, *Die Chroniken der deutschen Städte*, 364ff.

three (slide?) trumpets, two trombones and four shawms, and some performers on string instruments.[37] Another banquet given by the emperor in the same year offered only trumpets and timpani, but perhaps his budget was exhausted by the cost of the food, which consisted of forty-six courses![38]

I have been writing of German emperors and kings for the most part, but many dukes also maintained wind bands. An eyewitness records having heard the wind band of Duke Georg von Landshut, which in 1475 consisted of 'trumpetter, paugher und pfeyffer.' A similar account from 1496 mentions the band of Georg von Sachsen as consisting of 'tromether, pfeiffern, peugker, und trumslaher.'[39] In Dresden (for which there are virtually no surviving fourteenth-century accounts) one reads of six trumpets and five shawms being in residence in 1470–1471.[40]

An identical instrumentation performed for the marriage of Albrecht of Brandenburg (1440–1486) and Anna von Sachsen in 1472.[41] Lang finds in the records of this court the comment that the 'Musikanten erfüllten solche Tage mit ihren Harmonien' and the very interesting receipt for a gift of a shawm player with crumhorn (Pfeiffer mit der Krummpfeiffen).[42] The wind band of this duke traveled to Regensburg in 1454 to play for the visiting Philip the Good.[43]

These northern German dukes were the models for the courts of Denmark and the wind players frequently traveled from one country to the other. For example, one reads of the Danish winds visiting Augsburg in 1495 and Braunschweig in 1473,[44] while on the other hand, the coronation banquet of Christian IV included not only his corps of fifteen trumpets, but an additional seventeen from the German courts of Torgau and Dresden.[45] A very interesting reference of a Danish royal wedding in 1404 mentions music played by shawms and *bassooners*.[46] This was too early for the bassoon and the word must be taken as a Danish corruption of the old German word, *Pusuner*, or trombones.

[37] F. J. Mone, ed., *Quellensammlung der badischen Landesgeschichte* (Karlsruhe, 1848), 1:510.
  Item als man den letzsten gang nach dem essen ginge, da stunden 10 trumpter ime sale und trumpten, darnach 3 trumpter, 4 pfiffer, 2 pusuner, darnach 3 mit luten and darnach 3 mit gygen.

[38] Karl Schellhass, 'Eine Kaiserreise im Jahre 1473,' in *Archiv für Frankfurts Geschichte und Kunst* (1893), 4:195.
  ... und als oft man essen in den sal trueg, so was pawkn und trummetten, und standen da vor der tuer.

[39] G. Pietzsch, 'Die Beschreibungen deutscher Fürstenhochzeiten von der Mitte des 15. bis zum Beginn des 17. Jahrhunderts als musikgeschichtliche Quelle,' in *Anuario Musical* (Barcelona: 1960), 31–73.

[40] Grove, 5:616.

[41] Günther Schmidt, *Die Musik am Hofe des Markgrafen von Brandenburg-Ansbach vom ausgehenden Mittelalter bis 1806* (München: Ansbach, 1953), 4.

[42] Karl Heinrich Ritter v. Lang, *Neuere Geschichte des Fürstentums Beiruth* (Göttingen, 1798), I, 12.

[43] Marix, *Histoire de la Musique*, 71.

[44] Salmen, *Der Fahrende Musiker*, 168.

[45] Ehmann, *Tibilustrium*, 13.

[46] *Chronicle of Rythm. Majus*, in Eric Michael Fant, ed., *Scriptores Rerum medii Aevi* (Upsala, 1818), I, ii, 61.

Maximilian I

Maximilian I (1459–1519) was the last great figure of the Middle Ages and is often thus referred to as 'the last knight.' Son of Frederick III, Maximilian established his court in Innsbruck, which because of its location on the primary north–south trade routes made it a much more progressive town, culturally, than the more provencial Vienna.[47] Maximilian's introduction to the arts came at age eighteen when he went to Flanders to wed Mary of Burgundy. Here he saw the works of the Van Eycks and Memling, heard the music of Dufay and Binchois, and began his own lifetime of encouraging the arts. He assembled his own *Hofkapelle* between 1486 and 1496, combining Burgundian musicians with those of his father's court.

Maximilian's first title was 'King of the Romans' and at his ceremony of investiture, following a Mass and a sung Te Deum, one heard 'clarons, trompettes, tambours,' and a herald shouting loudly, 'Long live the King of the Romans.'[48]

We have an extradorinary document from which to see the wind ensembles found in the mature period of Maximilian's reign, the *Triumph of Maximilian I*. The *Triumph* is one of the world's richest and most unusual monuments of art, a sequence of one hundred and thirty-seven woodcuts by the foremost graphic artists of the fifteenth century. It portrays not only his autobiography (Maximilian dictated the entire plan to his secretary, Treitzsaurwein, whose written text also survives), but also the entire court, from the lowest page to the emperor himself.

After an initial two plates which announce the procession, one sees the first ensemble, consisting of four fifes and five drummers on horseback. Maximilian specified that this ensemble should appear in their traditional military jackets and blue caps, and each should carry a long sword and wear a laurel wreath. The fifes appear to be seven-hole flutes and it seems, judging by their finger positions, the three players are playing in two-parts. The drums are large field drums, with adjustable tension. One fife player is not playing, but is rather holding a large sign which was to have read,

> I, Anthony of Dornstätt, have played my fife
> For Maximilian, great in strife,
> In many lands on countless journeys,

[47] Even today, the trains follow these ancient routes.

[48] Louise Cuyler, *The Emperor Maximilian I and Music* (London: Oxford University Press, 1973), 35.

> In battles fierce and knightly tourneys,
> At grave times or in holiday,
> And so in this Triumph with honor I play.

> (Gladly and oft my fife I blew
> In proper style, with honor true,
> Serving the Imperial arms
> In knightly joust and war's alarms.
> Always prepared, the fifer blows
> Tunes gay and stern, as this Triumph shows.)[49]

It seems apparent that one has here the basic military wind and percussion ensemble. Another autobiographical work, *Weisskunig*, mentioned above, describes his father's court and also has several plates showing fife and drums. One of these carries the following text:

> The young *Weisskunig* (Maximilian) brought the manly and cheerful fife and drum. When he went to battle, the fife and drum not only gladdened the hearts of men, but filled the air with the sound that proclaimed that the young king conquered many lands, and always defeated his enemies.[50]

The texts also tell us that this ensemble apparently always traveled with Maximilian and also played for tourneys and for entertainment, as well as for purely military needs.

Next (Plates 19 and 20), one sees the basic indoor wind band, thus they appear riding in a wagon rather than on horseback. This band would perform for banquets, dances, and perhaps concerts. Shown are two shawms, two crumhorns, and the trombonist, Neyschl, who was the leader of this court wind band.[51] The text for this wind band reads,

> And Neyschl shall direct them, and his verse, borne by a boy, shall read: How to the Emperor's joy and by his command he combined such diverse instruments in the merriest way.

> (The trombone and the shawm adorn
> The joyous sound of curving horn,
> Each to the others well adjusted.
> Since musical command to me
> I have performed quite frequently.)[52]

---

[49] Quoted texts are those which Maximilian dictated to his secretary, but as these were incomplete, additional materials for the project, found after his death, are included in parentheses, taken from Stanley Appelbaum, *The Triumph of Maximilian I* (New York: Dover, 1964), 2.

[50] Plate 33, quoted in Christine Mather, 'Maximilian I and his Instruments,' *Early Music* 3, no. 1 (Jan 1975): 44.

[51] Louise Cuyler, 'Music in Biographies of Emperor Maximilian,' in *Aspects of Medieval and Renaissance Music*, ed. Jan LaRue (New York: Norton, 1966), 120.

[52] Appelbaum, *Triumph of Maximilian I*, 4.

Plates 25 and 26 are called, 'Choir,' and represent Maximilian's church musicians. Here one sees seven adult singers, six boy singers, a trombonist and a cornettist, whom are believed to be Stewdl and Augustin, respectively. Maximilian's original instructions were for multiple trombones and cornetts, but no doubt the artist simply could not find the room on the wagon for everyone. Maximilian requested further,

> Stewdl shall be leader of the trombonists, Augustin of the cornet players, and their verse, borne by a boy on the car, shall read thus: How by the Emperor's instructions they attuned the trombones and cornets in most joyous manner.
>
> (The cornets and trombones we placed
> So that the choral song they graced,
> For His Imperial Majesty
> Has often in such harmony
> Taken great pleasure, and rightly so,
> As we have had good cause to know.)[53]

53 Ibid., 5.

One plate requested by Maximilian was apparently not created. It was to have been called, 'The Emperor's Journey to His Burgundian Wedding,' and would have shown three drummers and fifteen trumpeters in Austrian uniforms. One does find the trumpeters later, under 'Imperial Trumpeters' (Plates 115–117). Maximilian desired,

> After them shall come on horseback a goodly number of trumpeters and drummers with the Imperial flags on their trumpets, and wearing laurel wreaths.[54]

54 Ibid., 15.

One finds a total of twenty-five trumpet players and five players of timpani, two per man, also on horse. This corresponds rather accurately with a survey made of musician's names which appear in Maximilian's household between 1490 and 1519.[55] Here one finds the names of twenty-seven trumpet and five timpani players.

One of the most interesting ensembles is that called the 'Burgundian Fifers' (Plates 77–79). Maximilian said,

55 Smithers, *The Music and History of the Baroque Trumpet*.

> After them shall come on horseback Burgundian fifers in the Burgundian colors with bombardons, shawms, and rauschpfeiffen. And they shall all be wearing laurel wreaths.[56]

56 Appelbaum, *Triumph of Maximilian I*, 9.

Triumph of Maximilian I, plate 20

Triumph of Maximilian I, plate 26, 'Choir'

Pictured is an ensemble of twenty-five wind players, consisting of ten trombones, and five each of the instruments requested by Maximilian. All of these players are pictured with their cases, which, in addition to being on horseback, implies they were members of the traveling music. Perhaps they were among those musicians mentioned by Cuyler.

Triumph of Maximilian I, plate 78

Triumph of Maximilian I, plate 79

> Evenings in camp and the long intervals when no engagement was actually joined could have been tedious indeed, except that the Emperor retained a group of musicians who would have been called *menestrels* in Burgundian days. The favourite was Artus, a lutenist, who was often present in Maximilian's personal entourage. Besides Artus and other lutenists, there were, from time to time, players of shawm, cromorne, sackbutt, and flutes (recorders) of various sizes.[57]

[57] Cuyler, *The Emperor Maximilian I and Music*, 81–82.

In addition to the woodcuts described above, other records indicate wind music was used for processions, at the table, and for all festive celebrations. Another woodcut, for example, called, 'Maximilian I Divertissement masque,' shows the players standing next to a large table filled with a great variety of instruments, ready to 'trade-off' to provide variety in instrumental color.[58]

[58] *Der Weisskunig*, fol. 147v, by Hans Burgkmair (copy in Vienna, National Library, Mss. Nr. 3032).

There is another account of a very special nature, a firsthand report by a visiting French journalist, describing Maximilian having dinner alone in 1492.

> His Majesty sits in a hall covered with tapestry, without another person except his court jesters. At every meal, mid-day or evening, there were 10 trumpeters and 10 other kinds. There were two large timpani of fine copper covered with ass skins and standing in two baskets. In the middle sat a man with a thick stick which he let loose in beats on (the timpani) so that the tone was in unison with the other instruments, as is used in Hungary or Turkey, it was amazing and humorous to hear.[59]

[59] Quoted in J. F. Huguenin, ed., *Les chroniques de la ville de Metz* (Metz, 1838), 586.

Aside from having a regular ensemble of twenty-one players for meals, there are some very interesting insights in this report. First, the journalist seems to have been hearing timpani for the first time and was impressed with a fact nearly forgotten today: the timpani were first used in ensembles, particularly trumpet ensembles, as a melodic and harmonic bass, not as a percussive element. Second, one wonders what the other ten instruments were which this journalist did not recognize. Surely they were not trombones, for example, but perhaps representatives of the new Renaissance instruments.

Finally, there was the Congress of Vienna, hosted by Maximilian in 1515, the opening for which he arranged to have a fanfare performed by forty-five trumpets, forty-five trombones, and six timpanists![60] The foreign journalists who covered this congress found great interest in the wind and percussion bands which accompanied the diplomats from the

[60] Ibid.

East.⁶¹ In their chronicles they speak of the great, wide and loud sounding trumpets of the Tartars and Turks. The impression one gets is that the Western journalists were hearing for the first time the ancient medieval instrument which was apparently still being used in the East.⁶² The journalists found the trumpets out-of-tune and described their tones as a 'buzz,' not unlike that of 'wasps and horseflies.'⁶³ They describe the tone of the horns as 'unclean,' the crumhorns as 'torrid,' and the shawms as 'coarse.' They further observed that the Hungarian trumpet and timpani players played in the German style (*auf teutsch*). In general they found the foreign ensembles did not play together as well as the Western ones, the trumpets in particular they heard as playing 'in confusion.'⁶⁴

I close this narrative with the court of 'the last knight,' for here one sees not only the epitome of the fifteenth-century court wind band and its usage, but the arrival of some of the new instruments and traditions of the following period, the Renaissance. Their story will require a separate volume.

⁶¹ I might add here that in the Middle Ages Russia generally followed the Aisian models, using shawms, many kinds of percussion (including giant wooden timpani, with copper timpani being reserved for the leader), and trumpets. An early reference to 'the blare of trumpets' is found in a description of the *Zadonscina*, the battle with the Tartars in 1380.

⁶² This impression is strengthened by an icon called, 'Charlemagne in battle with the Sarazen,' but which actually is a pictoral document dating from ca. 1460. Here, while the Western armies have the normal straight trumpets of the fifteenth century, the Eastern armies are pictured with a bizarre collection of exotic looking trumpets, all bent at strange angles. (Copy in the Royal Library, Brussels, Ms. 9068, fol. 212.)

⁶³ Salmen, *Der Fahrende Musiker*, 151.

⁶⁴ Huguenin, *Les Chroniques*.

PART VI
Notes on the Instruments

Notes on the Instruments

THE PURPOSE OF THIS SECTION is two-fold: it will, of course, present some of the important facts about the principal wind instruments of the Middle Ages for the reader who may not recall their nature, but a more important purpose is to present some interesting contemporary descriptions of these instruments as insights into traditions which, for the most part, are long lost.

The medieval shawm

The primary soprano woodwind instrument of the medieval wind band derives its name from the Latin *calamus*, meaning simply 'reed.' From the same cognate comes the word *chalumeau*, a term sometimes used in France for the shawm at this time. Late in the fifteenth century the term *hautbois* appears in France, meaning of course, 'high wood.' In England, the name 'wait,' or 'wait-pipe,' was sometimes given the shawm. A typical English reference might read thus, while meaning shawm, 'Wayte who nightely … pipethe watch.' Most confusing is the Italian *piffaro*, which many English writers, especially authors of general history, confuse with the Italian *fiffaro* and therefore translate as 'pipe,' which is etymologically correct for the latter. Unfortunately this gives the impression of a flute-type or bagpipe instrument, whereas in the later Middle Ages *piffaro* nearly always meant the shawm.

The larger, and lower, shawm in the fourteenth century began to be known under a new name, *bombard* (in German the corruption, *Pumhart*), from the Latin *bombus* or 'drone or buzz.' In 1376 Jean Lefevre de Ressons described a *Grosses bombardes* as being then new.[1]

The medieval shawm, as opposed to the renaissance instrument, remained closely related to its Saracen origin: a key-less, conical instrument with seven finger-holes and a thumb-hole. The reed was held in a metal staple; the lips pressed against the staple but did not touch the reed.[2] Consequently the sound was perhaps primitive and the strength of the tone accounts for

[1] Sachs, *The History of Musical Instruments*, 314.

[2] This instrument can still be heard as a peasant instrument today in cities of Eastern Europe; the author has even heard them in Venice. A more musical survivor may be heard in the coblas bands. See Anthony Baines, 'Shawms of the Sardana Coblas,' *The Galpin Society Journal* 5 (March 1952): 9ff.

its use as a watch instrument. Several early references equate the power of the instrument with the trumpet. The Burgundian chronicler, Jean Molinet, speaking of the shawm, said, 'enleverent melodie tant extreme et fort haulte.'[3]

The most complete technical description of the fifteenth-century shawm is found in Tinctoris, ca. 1489.

> The tibia has two main orifices, one extremely narrow, through which the breath is impacted against the sound-producing reed ... the other wide, whence the sound is emitted.
>
> Nowadays the tibia called *celimela* (shawm) has seven holes. Provided that its holes are correctly placed, any composition can be played on it and it is completely perfect.
>
> Note that when the seventh hole of any tibia is set to one side and has an eighth hole set opposite to it, each of these holes gives the same note. This arrangement was adapted to accomodate the little finger, which is normally not long enough to close the seventh hole if it is aligned with the other six. In consequence some players prefer to place the right hand uppermost and use the hole on the left side, while others prefer the opposite.
>
> A single tibia is like a voice in being able to deliver only one part in a composition, and hence, just as singers perform different parts according to the varying height and depth of their voices, so do tibia players use instruments varying in size. Some are high, suitable for treble parts, and others are low, for the middle and lowest parts. Therefore, tibias, like the parts themselves, are described as suprema, tenor (commonly called bombards) and contratenor.[4]

At least one source suggests that the fifteenth-century shawm had the tendancy to overblow a twelfth, as one can read in an English proverb dating from the end of the century.

> A Shawme makithe a sweete sounde for he tunithe Basse,
> It mountithe not to hy, but kepithe rule and space.
> Yet yf it be blowne with a too vehement wynde,
> It amkithe it to misgoverne out his kynde.[5]

---

[3] Albert van der Linden, 'La Musique dans les chroniques de Jean Molinet,' in *Mélanges Ernest Closson* (Brussels: Société Belge de Musicologie, 1948), 178–180.

[4] *De inventione et usu musicae*, quoted in Baines, 'Fifteenth-century Instruments in Tinctoris's *De Inventione et usu musicae*,' *The Galpin Society Journal* 3 (March 1950): 21.

[5] The 'Leckingfield Proverbs' are originally believed to have been inscribed on the walls of a building on the estate of Henry Percy, fifth Earl of Northumberland (1487–1527) in Yorkshire. The extant copy is found in London, British Museum, R.M.18.D.2. My quotation is taken from Christopher Welch, 'Literature Relating to the Recorder,' *Proceedings of the Musical Association* 24 (1897–1898): 152–153.

The doucaine

This instrument (no relation to the 'dulzian' or 'dolzian') is assumed to have been a double reed, but the lack of existing folk-types, or early iconographic examples, leaves the instrument somewhat ambiguous. Tinctoris distinguished it from the shawm by indicating that on the doucaine one could not play all the notes. Grove suggests it may have been a straight-capped shawm with a soft tone.[6]

[6] Grove, 5:531.

Bagpipe

An instrument of rustic origin and found throughout Europe, the bagpipe was a common court dance instrument during the Middle Ages. Its popularity, which may seem strange to those of us who know only the modern instrument, lay in the fact that it was the only wind instrument which could play a continuous melody for dancing. The medieval bagpipe, by the way, usually had *no* drone.

By the fourteenth century it had begun to become associated with the military, where it has remained ever since, as one can see in a description of a victory of Edward III over the Scots.

> Then the Englishe mynstsrelles beaten their tabers and blewen their trumpes, and pipers pipendene loude and made a great schowte upon the Skottes.[7]

[7] Quoted in Lilla Margaret Fox, *Instruments of Processional Music* (London: Lutterworth Press, 1967), 106.

Its impact on the battle field is testified to by the father of the astronomer, Galilei, who observed in 1581,

> To its sound this unconquered, fierce and warlike people (the Irish) march their armies and encourage each other to deeds of valour. With it they also accompany their dead to the grave, making such mournful sounds as to invite—nay, almost to force—the bystanders to weep.[8]

[8] Ibid.

The flute family

Because of the great variety of flute-type instruments (of both open mouth-hole and whistle mouthpiece sound production) and the even greater confusion of names given these instruments, it is difficult to sort out the nomenclature for the early Middle Ages.

A fourteenth-century French poet and musician, Guillaume de Machaut, speaks of the two basic kinds of flutes familiar to us, 'cross flutes and flutes that you play straight when you play.'[9]

The recorder can be traced only to the twelfth century, but soon became very popular. An early poem, 'Du metier profitable,' by Eustache Deschamps, says that playing the recorder well is the path to better profits, money, clothes, heritage, friends, and access to the Prince, who is always happy to hear the recorder well played.[10]

The fifteenth-century English proverbs, mentioned above, hint at the sophisticated system of full and partial fingerings needed to play this instrument well.

> The recorder of his kynde the meane dothe desyre,
> Manyfolde fyngerynge and stoppes bryngithe hy (him) from
> Who so lyst to handill an instrument so goode
> Must se in his many fingeryne yt he kepe tyme, stop and moode.

The transverse flute came west from Asia early during the Christian era. One type of transverse flute was very common during the Middle Ages, the military fife being common from the period of the crusades. The instrument is found first in the German-speaking countries, hence the colorful efforts at spelling in English. Under Henry VII one reads of 'drommers and viffleurs' and under Henry VIII, 'phiphes.' A sixteenth-century writer speaks of the character needed by these early military musicians as being,

> faithfulle, secret, yngenious, of able personage to use their instruments ... of sundrie language, for often tymes they are sent to partie with their enemies, to summon their forts and towns, to reddeme and conducte prisoners, and diverse other messages ... if such drummers or phiphers shall fortune to fall into the hands of their enemies, no gifte or force should cause them to disclose any secrete they know.[11]

---

[9] Sachs, *History of Musical Instruments*, 287 (flaustes traversaines et flaustes dont droit joues quand tu flaustes).

[10] Eustache Deschamps, *Oeuvres complètes* (Paris, 1878–1903), 6:128.
  Neantmoins, pour plus proufiter
  Avoir argent, robe, heritaige,
  Compains, apran à flajoler.
  Car princes oyent voluntiers
  Le flajol; qui en aprandra
  Advancez sera des premiers,
  Puis que bien jouer en sçara.

[11] Quoted in Fox, *Instruments of Processional Music*, 69.

One of the most frequently pictured 'dance bands' in medieval iconography is the one-man band, the 'pipe and tabor.' The flute-type he used began with the second harmonic, making it possible to play a complete scale with only three holes. The early medieval musician usually played with a drum suspended from the same hand which held the flute, the free hand playing the drum. He was the king of the dance until the appearance of two-part music in the fourteenth century.

The trumpet

Medieval trumpets are best thought of as being either long or short. The long instrument was usually known as *buisine* (from the Latin *buccina*), but in France sometimes as *cor sarrazinois* (Saracen horn, from the crusades). The word *trompe* appears only late in the Middle Ages.

Pictures of this early long trumpet in Western Europe can be found as early as Anglo-Saxon manuscripts.[12] All references before 1200 are probably the long instrument and most references are military in nature, although it was no doubt used for many court functions as well. Probably only the fundamental and the first four or five partials were used and medieval iconography almost always pictures the player with inflated cheeks, suggesting both the range limitations and the fact that the instrument was probably played at maximum volume. In the famous poem, 'Chanson de Roland,' it was said to be so loud as to pain the ears.[13] This instrument has survived, but only as a heralding, ceremonial trumpet.

During the thirteenth century the shorter trumpet, two or three feet in length, begins to appear. It is usually called *claro*, *clarion*, or *trompe petite*. Soon it begins to appear folded, often called the 'S-trumpet' by modern writers. In this form it became the primary signal giving instrument of the military, replacing the more unweildy buisine, as its narrower bore allowed it to sound the higher harmonics which were easier to hear in the heat of battle. One medieval poem says that it was played loud enough to wake the dead.[14] By the fifteenth century there were calls for a more refined style of playing.

> Immoderate wyndes in a Clariion causite for it to rage;
> Soft wynde and moderate makithe the sownde to assuage.

[12] Early examples: Seventh century: London, British Museum (Add. 30045) and Vienna, National Library (Cod.lat.1100); Ninth century: London, British Museum (Add. 10546) and Utrecht, University Library (Psalterium); Tenth century: London, British Museum (Add. 24199); Twelfth century: London, British Museum (Cott., Nero C. vi) and Turin, University Library (J.11.1. Cod. xciii); and Thirteenth century: Paris, National Library (Collection B. Delessert, Apokalpse), London, British Museum (Add. 21926), and Munich, University Library (Ms.24.40).

[13] Thomas Atkinson Jenkins, ed., *Le Chanson de Roland* (Boston: D.C. Heath, 1924), 243ff.
> Met a sa buche une clere buisine,
> Sonnent la cler que si paien l'odirent,
> Par tot lo champs ses compaignes ralient.

[14] Jean Guillaume Antoine Cuvelier, *Chronique de Bertrand du Gueslin*, ed. Ernest Charriere (London, 1910), 201ff.

> Therfore he whiche in that instrumente wolde have swete modulacion,
> Bustius wyndes must love and use moderacion.[15]

During the later Middle Ages the folded trumpet appeared in a version which we call the slide-trumpet, a form which made it ideally suited for the bass line of the court dance wind band. Unlike the trombone construction, the slide-trumpet player held the mouthpiece, which was attached to a length of straight tubing, and then with the other hand moved the entire instrument back and forth, toward and away from the face. One can appreciate how striking this must have appeared to those who saw it played for the first time through an anecdote told by Castiglione (*Courtier*, 1516) which tells of a small-town boy who went to Venice for the Feast of the Ascension celebration. Upon his return to his village, he told his friends of the things he had seen.

> And when one of his companions asked him which kind of music he liked best of what he had heard, he said: 'It was all good; but I noted especially a man playing on a strange trumpet which with every move he would shove down his throat more than two palm-lengths, and then suddenly he would draw it out, then shove it down again; you never saw a greater marvel!'[16]

The medieval cornett

Although the cornett belongs, musically, to the Renaissance, it does appear during the later Middle Ages. Perhaps the earliest reference is this fourteenth-century poem:

> Ther myghte men here (hear) menstralsye
> Trumpys, taboms, snd cornettys crye.[17]

The name comes from the Latin *cornu*, 'horn,' which reveals it origin. It is the transition from the animal horn to the wooden instrument that is identified by the new name. As with any instrument fashioned from an animal horn, the early cornett must have been difficult to play in terms of 'centering' the pitch. Players soon found that by placing the cup mouth-

---

[15] Quoted in Vivian Safowitz, 'Trumpet Music and Trumpet Style in the Early Renaissance' (PhD diss., The University of Illinois, 1965), 50.

[16] Quoted in ibid., 46; see also Grove, 17:381.

[17] Fox, *Instruments of Processional Music*, 111.

piece not in the center of the lips but on the side, where the lips are thin and sensitive to the smallest vibrations, performance was enhanced.

The sackbut

The prototype trombone takes its name either from the fourteenth-century Spanish *sacabuche* (draw-pipe) or the medieval French *saguer* (to pull) and *bouter* (to push). In any case, the construction is derived from the slide-trumpet and the other early names give evidence of this: *trombone* in French, Italian, and English, from *tromba*; and *Posaune* in German, from *buisine*. This similarity in construction fooled most early scribes and until late in the fifteenth century it is usually difficult to know if the slide-trumpet or sackbut is under discussion in the literature.

Unlike the trumpet, the trombone seems to have begun its long association with the human voice from its earliest period. One finds such an association early in the fifteenth century in an account describing the arrival of the English prelates at the Council of Constance (1414–1418).

> The trombonists played together in three parts as one is otherwise accustomed to sing.[18]

Mersenne, writing in 1636, cautions that the trombone be played,

> so that it may not imitate the sound of the trumpet but rather assimilate itself to the sweetness of the human voice, lest it should emit a warlike rather than a peaceful sound.[19]

[18] Gerald Hayes, 'Musical Instruments,' in *New Oxford History of Music* (London: Oxford University Press, 1960), 3:425–426. die pusauner pusaunoten über einnander mit dreyen stymmen, als man sunst gerwonlichen singet.

[19] Fox, *Instruments of Processional Music*, 82.

The small drums

Two basic types of small drum were common in the Middle Ages, the cylindrical tabor and timbrel (the larger of the two) and the naker, which had a large head on one side and a smaller head on the other, giving somewhat of a bowl shape. More significant than the shape was the distinction in playing technique, the naker being played with two sticks (two hands) and the tabor and timbrel with one. Although these instruments are seen frequently in iconographic specimens, actual music is extremely rare before the eighteenth century. One must therefore write his own percussion parts when performing early wind band literature. One clue to appropriate style may perhaps be found in the names themselves, an ingenious observation made by Jeremy Montagu.

> Before AD 1500, all drum names in European languages had a *tam-* or *tab-* root; only during the sixteenth century did the *trom-* and *drum-* (dear reader: please remember to roll your "r's") words come into use. So much of our drum terminology is onomatopoeic that I believe that the name of the instrument is also and that strokes such as flams, drags, and rolls should not be used in music earlier than the first half of the sixteenth century, but that plain strokes only should be used.[20]

The naker is one of the instruments introduced to the west during the crusades and it is from the Arabic *naggara* that we get *naker* in English and *nacaires* in French. Played with two sticks, the naker was capable of a great deal of noise, hence was valued for its military potential. Marco Polo describes how King Kaidu and the great Khan waited for the nakers to begin the battle.[21] They were also welcome at outdoor entertainments of all kinds.

The tambor, being the easier to play, is found in all facets of medieval life: the battle, the tournament, at meals, festivals and the dance. If needed they could produce great volume, and in one description their sound helped 'shake the earth.'[22] An interesting observation is made by Johannes de Grocheo regarding the larger variety of the cylindrical drum. In festivals and tournaments, he says, 'it is possible that such an instrument moves men's souls more due to its deep sonority.'[23]

Timpani

The timpani came West also, apparently from Hungary, during the fifteenth century. I have quoted several examples of the reaction of persons hearing these instruments for the first time. By the early part of the sixteenth century, they had rapidly taken their place with the trumpet as the representatives

[20] Jeremy Montagu, 'On the Reconstruction of Mediaeval Instruments of Percussion,' *The Galpin Society Journal* 23 (Aug 1970): 114.

[21] James Blades, *Percussion Instruments and their History* (London: Faber, 1970), 223.

[22] Friedrick Dick, 'Bezeichnungen für Saiten- und Schlaginstrumente in der altfranzösischen Literatur,' in *Giessener Beiträge zur Romanischen Philologie* (Giesseni: Romanisches Seminar, 1932), 138.
  Et si grant tumulte de tymbres, de tabors, et de trompes, ke toute li terre en tramploit.

[23] Théodore Gérold, *Histoire de la musique des origines à la fin du XIIIe siècle* (Paris: H. Laurens, 1936), 741.

of royalty. To some, however, a little percussion is enough and these great new instruments must have seemed ominous indeed. Virdung wrote, in 1511,

> These drums are to the taste of those who cause much disquiet to pious old people, to the sickly and the weakly, the devout in their cloisters and those who have to read, study, and pray. I verily believe that the devil must have had the devising and making of them, for there is no pleasure nor anything good about them.[24]

[24] Sebastian Virdung, *Musica getutscht* (1511)

Bibliography

Bibliography

Adams, Joseph Quincy. *Chief Pre-Shakespearean Dramas*. Boston: Houghton Mifflin, 1924.

Ady, Cecilia Mary. *The Bentivoglio of Bologna: A Study in Despotism*. Oxford: Oxford University Press, 1937.

Aelianus. *On the Characteristics of Animals*.

Aerde, Raymond Joseph van. *Musicalia: Notes pour servir à l'histoire de la musique, du theatre et de la danse à Malines*. Malines: Dierickx-Beke, 1925.

Aeschylus. *Eumenides*. Edited by Rudolf Helm. Berlin: Teubner, 1931.

Anglès, Higino. 'Die Instrumentalmusik bis zum 16. Jahrhundert in Spanien.' In *Natalicia Musicologica*. Oslo: Hansen, 1962.

———. 'El músic Jacomi al servei de Joan I i Marti I durant als anys 1372–1404.' In *Homenatge a Antoni Rubió i Lluch*. Barcelona, 1936.

———. 'La música en la corte del rey Don Alfonso V de Aragon.' In *Gesammelte Aufsätze zur Kulturgeschichte Spaniens*. Münster: Aschendorff, 1940.

Anglo, Sydney. *The Great Tournament Roll of Westminster*. Oxford: Clarendon, 1968.

Appelbaum, Stanley. *The Triumph of Maximilian I*. New York: Dover, 1964.

Apuleius. *Metamorphoses*.

Ariosto, Ludovico. *Orlando furioso*, 13:59.

Aristides, Quintilianus. *On Music*.

Aristotle. *Politica*.

———. *Problemata*.

Arrian. *The Campaigns of Alexander*. New York: Penguin, 1978.

Athenaeus. *The Deipnosophists*. Edited and translated by C.B. Gulick. 7 vols. Cambridge, Mass.: Harvard University Press, 1927–41.

Augustine. *Confessions*.

Baillie, Hugh. 'A London Gild of Musicians, 1460–1530.' *Proceedings of the Royal Musical Association* 83 (1956–1957): 15–28.

Baines, Anthony. 'Shawms of the Sardana Coblas.' *The Galpin Society Journal* 5 (March 1952): 9–16.

———. 'Fifteenth-century Instruments in Tinctoris's *De Inventione et usu musicae*.' *The Galpin Society Journal* 3 (March 1950): 19–26.

Barbure, L. de. 'La musique à Anvers aux XIVe, XVe, et XVIe siècles.' In *Annales de l'Académie Royale d'Archéologie de Belgique*. 1906.

Bayerische Akademie der Wissenschaften (München), Historische Kommission. *Die Chroniken der deutschen Städte*. Leipzig, 1864.

Benedetti, Alessandro. *Diaria de Bello Carolino*. Edited by Dorothy Schullian. New York: Ungar, 1967.

Bernhard, Marie-Bernard. 'Recherches sur l'histoire de la corporation des ménétriers ou joueurs d'instruments de la ville de Paris.' In *Bibliothèque de l'Ecole chantes* (April, 1842).

———. *Notice sur la Confrérie des Joueurs d'Instruments d'Alsace.* Paris, 1844.

Besseler, Heinrich. 'Alta.' In *Die Musik in Geschichte und Gegenwart.* Edited by Friedrich Blume. Kassel-Basel: Bärenreiter-Verlag, 1949.

———. *Bourdon und Fauxbourdon.* Leipzig: Breitkopf und Härtel, 1974.

Blades, James. *Percussion Instruments and their History.* London: Faber, 1970.

Bonaini, Francesco. *Statuti inediti della città di Pisa.* Firenze, 1870.

Bonanni, Filippo. *Gabinetto armonico pieno d'instrumenti sonori indicati.* Rome, 1722.

Bonfadini, Romualdo. 'Le origini del Comune di Milano.' In *Albori della Vita Italiana.* Milano, 1897.

Bourgeois, Alfred. *Les Métiers de Blois.* Blois, 1892.

Bowles, Edmund A. 'Haut and Bas: The Grouping of Musical Instruments in the Middle Ages.' *Musica Disciplina* 8 (1954): 115–140.

———. 'Instruments at the Court of Burgundy.' *The Galpin Society Journal* 6 (July 1953): 41–45.

———. *Musikleben im 15. Jahrhundert.* Leipzig: Deutscher Verlag für Musik, 1977.

———. 'Musical Instruments in Civic Processions during the Middle Ages.' *Acta Musicologica* 33, no. 2/4 (Apr–Dec 1961): 147–161.

———. 'Musical Instruments in the Medieval Corpus Christi Procession.' *Journal of the American Musicological Society* 17, no. 3 (Autumn 1964): 251–260.

———. 'The Role of Musical Instruments in Medieval Sacred Drama.' *The Musical Quarterly* 45, no. 1 (January 1959): 67–84.

———. 'Tower Musicians in the Middle Ages.' *Brass Quarterly* 5 (1962).

Brenet, Michel. *Musique et Musiciens de la vieille France.* Paris: F. Alcan, 1911.

Bridge, Joseph C. 'Town Waits and their Tunes.' *Proceedings of the Musical Association* 54 (1927–1928): 63–92.

Bridgman, Nanie. 'Fêtes italiennes de plein air au Quattrocento.' In *Hans Albrecht in Memoriam.* Kassel: Bärenreiter, 1962.

———. *La vie musicale au quattrocento.* Paris: Gallimard, 1964.

Brie, Friedrich Wilhelm Daniel. 'The Chronicles of England.' In *Geschichte und Quellen der Mittelenglischen Prosachronik.* Marburg, 1905.

———., ed., *The Brut* or *The Chronicles of England.* London: Kegan Paul, Trench, Trübner, 1906.

Brunner, Karl, ed. *Der mittelenglische Versroman über Richard Löwenherz.* Vienna and Leipzig: Braumüller, 1913.

Bryce, James. *The Holy Roman Empire.* New York, 1968.

Buchon, Jean Alexandre C., ed. *Chroniques de Froissart,* bk. 3.

Burckhardt, Jacob. *The Civilization of the Renaissance in Italy.* London: G. Allen, 1914.

Burgkmair, Hans. *Der Weisskunig.* Copy in Vienna, National Library, Mss. Nr. 3032.

Byrne, Maurice. 'Instruments for the Goldsmiths Company.' *The Galpin Society Journal* 24 (July 1971): 63–68.

Calmo, Andrea. *Lettere.* Edited by Vittorio Rossi. Turin, 1888.
Cancellieri, Francesco. *Storia di solenni possessi de' Sommi Pontefici.* Rome, 1802.
Carpenter, Nan Cooke. *Music in the Medieval Universities.* Norman: University of Oklahoma Press, 1958.
Cartwright, Julia. *Beatrice d'Este.* London: Dent, 1928.
———. *Beatrice d'Este.* New York: Dutton, 1899.
———. *Isabella d'Este.* London: Murray, 1915.
Casson, Leslie Frank, ed. *Sir Degrevant.* London: Oxford University Press, 1949.
Casteele, D. van de. 'Préludes historiques sur la Ghilde des ménéstrels de Bruges.' In *Annales de la Société d'Emulation* (3e série), 3:65ff.
———. *Annales de la Société d'Emulation pour l'Étude de l'Histoire et des Antiquitiés de la Flandre.* 1868.
Catullus. 'Poem 63.'
Cellesi, Luigi. 'Documenti per la storia musicale di Firenze.' *Rivista Musicale Italiana* 34 (1927).
Chambers, E. K., *The Mediaeval Stage.* Oxford: Clarendon, 1903.
Champion, Pierre. *La vie de Charles d'Orléans.* Paris, 1911.
Chartier, Jean. *Chroniques de Charles VII.* Paris, 1858.
Chastellain, Georges. *Oeuvres.* Brussels, 1863–1866.
Chaucer, Geoffrey. 'The Knyghtes Tale.' In *Complete Works.* Edited by Walter William Skeat. Oxford: Clarendon, 1924.
Chauvelaye, L. and P. de Coligny, 'Les armées des trois premiers ducs de Bourgogne.' In *Mémoires de l'académie des sciences, arts et belles-lettres de Dijon.* 1854–1855.
Clerq, Jacques du. *Mémoires.* Edited by John Alexandre C. Buchon. Paris, 1838.
Cleve, Thomas Curtis van. *The Emperor Frederick II.* Oxford: Clarendon, 1972.
Closson, Ernest. *La facture des instruments de musique en Belgique.* Brussels: Huy, Degrace, 1935.
Cohen, Gustave. *Le théatre à Paris et aux environs à la fin du XIV siècle* in *Romania.*
Comines, Philippe de. *Memoirs.* London, 1900.
Corio, Bernardino. *L'Historia di Milano volgarmente scritta.* Padova, 1646.
Coulton, George Gordon. *Chaucer and His England.* London: Methuen, 1921.
———. *Medieval Panorama.* New York: Macmillan, 1944.
Crewdson, Henry A. F. *The Worshipful Company of Musicians.* London: Knight, 1971.
Cuvelier, Jean Guillaume Antoine. *Chronique de Bertrand du Gueslin.* Edited by Ernest Charriere. London, 1910.
Cuyler, Louise. 'Music in Biographies of Emperor Maximilian.' In *Aspects of Medieval and Renaissance Music.* Edited by Jan LaRue. New York: Norton, 1966.
———. *The Emperor Maximilian I and Music.* London: Oxford University Press, 1973.
d'Agnel, G. Arnaud. *Les comptes du Roi René.* Paris: A. Picard, 1910.
Dahnk, Emilie. 'Musikausubung an den Höfen von Burgund und Orlèans währand des 15. Jahrhunderts.' In *Archiv für Kulturgeschichte 25.* Leipzig: Teubner, 1934–1936.
d'Arcq, Louis Claude Douët, ed. *Soc. Hist. France.* Paris, 1857.
Davies, Robert, ed. *Extracts from the Municipal Records of the City of York.* London, 1843.

da Vinci, Leonardo. *Arundel Codex*.

d'Elvert, Chr. *Geschichte der Musik in Mähren und Österreichisch-Schlesien*. Brünn, 1873.

Deschamps, Eustache. *Oeuvres complètes*. 11 vols. Paris, 1878–1903.

d'Escouchy, Mathieu. *Chronique*. Paris, 1863–1864.

Dick, Friedrick. 'Bezeichnungen für Saiten- und Schlaginstrumente in der altfranzösischen Literatur.' In *Giessener Beiträge zur Romanischen Philologie*. Giessen: Romanisches Seminar, 1932.

Diodorus. *The Library of History*.

Doorslaer, George van. 'La Chapelle musicale de Philippe le Beau.' In *Revue Belge d'archéologie et d'histoire de l'art*, 4:159.

Duncan, Edmonstoune. *The Story of Minstrelsy*. Detroit: Singing Tree, 1968.

Durant, Will. *Caesar and Christ*. New York: Simon and Schuster, 1944.

———. *The Renaissance*. New York: Simon and Schuster, 1953.

Eboli, Pietro da. *Liber ad Honorem Augusti* (Berne, Burgerbibliothek, Mss. del Cod. di Berna 120).

Ehmann, Wilhelm. *Tibilustrium*. Kassel: Bärenreiter-Verlag, 1950.

Elsner, E. *Untersuchungen der instrumentalen Besetzungspraxis der weltlichen Musik*. Leipzig, 1925.

Embden, A. Meerkamp van, ed. *Stadsrekeningen van Leiden*. Amsterdam: Müller, 1913–1914.

Engel, Carl. *The Music of The Most Ancient Nations*. London: Reeves, 1909.

Ernst, Fritz. 'Die Spielluete im Dienste der Stadt Basel im Ausgehenden Mittelalter.' In *Basler Zeitschrift für Geschichte und Altertumskunde*, vol. 44 (Basel, 1945).

Euripides. *The Phoenician Women*.

Fallersleben, August Heinrich Hoffman von, ed. *Altniederländische Schaubuhne*. Breslau, 1834.

Fant, Eric Michael, ed. *Scriptores Rerum medii Aevi*. Upsala, 1818.

Faral, Edmond. *Les Jongleurs en France au moyen âge*. Paris: Champion, 1910.

Farmer, Henry George. 'Crusading Martial Music,' in *Music & Letters* 30, no. 3 (July 1949): 243–249.

———. 'Music in Medieval Scotland.' *Proceedings of the Musical Association* 54 (1929–1930): 69–90.

———. 'The Music of Ancient Mesopotamia.' In *The New Oxford History of Music*. London: Oxford University Press, 1966.

———. *The Rise and Development of Military Music*. London: William Reeves, 1912.

Federhofer, Hellmut. 'Beitrage zur altern Musikgeschichte Karntens.' In *Carinthia* (145), 1955.

Féderov, Vladimir. 'Des Russes au Concile de Florenz.' In *Hans Albrecht in Memoriam*. Kassel, 1962.

Fellerer, Karl G. 'Mittelalterlichen Musikleben der Stadt Freiburg im Uechtland.' In *Freiburger Studien zur Musikwissenschaft*. Regensburg, 1935.

Fenlon, Iain. *Music and Patronage in Sixteenth-Century Mantua*. New York: Cambridge University Press, 1981.

Ferraiolo, *Una cronaca napoletana figurata del quattrocento*. Edited by Riccardo Filangieri. Naples: L'Arte tipographica, 1956.

Fester, Richard. 'Die Fortsetzung der Flores temporum von Reinbold Slecht.' In *Zeitschrift für die Geschichte des Oberrheins*. Stuttgart: Kohlhammer, 1894.
Fetherston, Christopher. *Dialogue agaynst light, lewde, and lascivious Dancing*. London, 1583.
Fons-Mélicocq, Alexandre de la. 'Les ménestrels de Lille.' In *Archives historiques et littéraires du nord*. 1885.
Fontes, Juan. 'The Regency of Don Ferdinand of Antequera.' In *Spain in the Fifteenth Century*. Edited by John Roger Loxdale Highfield. London: Macmillan, 1972.
Fox, Lilla Margaret. *Instruments of Processional Music*. London: Lutterworth Press, 1967.
Frati, Lodovico. *La vita privata di Bologna*. Bologna: Zanichelli, 1900.
Freeman, Edward Augustus. *History of the Norman Conquest of England*. Oxford, Clarendon, 1870.
Frizzi, Antonio. *Memorie per la storia de Ferrara*. Ferrara, 1847.
Froissart, Jean. *Les Chroniques*, in *Historiens et Chroniqueurs du Moyen Age*. Bruges, 1963.
———. *Chron. de France et d'Angleterre*. ca. 1460 (copy in London, British Museum, Ms. Royal 18 E. I, fol. 12).
———. *Oeuvres*. Edited by Kervyn de Lettenhove. Brussels, 1867.
Froning, Richard. *Das deutsche Drama des Mittelalters*. Stuttgart, 1891.
Funck-Brentano, Frantz. *The Middle Ages*. Translated by Elizabeth O'Neill. New York: Putnam, 1923.
Furnivall, Frederick James, ed. *The Tale of Beryn*. London: Kegan Paul, Trench, Trübner, 1909.
Fyvie, John. *The Story of the Borgias*. New York: Putnam, 1913.
Gachard, Louis Prosper. *Collection de documents inédits concernant la Belgique*. Bruxelles, 1833–1835.
Galpin, Francis William. *Old English Instruments of Music*. London: Methuen, 1910.
Gardner, Edmund G. *Dukes & Poets in Ferrara*. New York: Haskell House, 1968.
Gayley, Charles. *The Classic Myths*. Boston, 1893.
Gerbert, Martin. *Scriptores ecclesiastici de musica sacra potissimum*. Saint Blaise, 1784.
Gérold, Théodore. *Histoire de la musique des origines à la fin du XIIIe siècle*. Paris: H. Laurens, 1936.
Godefroy, Frédéric. *Dictionnaire de l'ancienne langue francaise*. Paris, 1881.
———. *Dictionnaire de l'ancienne langue francaise*. Paris: Vieweg, 1902.
Goldron, Romain. *Minstrels and Masters*. New York: H.S. Stuttman, 1968.
Gombosi, Otto. 'About Dance and Dance Music in the Late Middle Ages.' *Musical Ouarterly* 27, no. 3 (July 1941): 289–305.
———. 'Music in Hungary.' In Gustave Reese, *Music in the Renaissance*. New York: Norton, 1959.
Gower, John. *The English Works of John Gower*. Edited by George Campbell Macaulay. Oxford: Oxford University Press, 1901.
Gregoir, Édouard Georges Jacques. *Notice historique sur les sociétés et écoles de musique*. Antwerp, 1869.
Guasti, Cesare. *Le Feste di San Giovanni Battista in Firenze*. Florence, 1884.
Guizot, M. *France*. Translated by Robert Black. New York: Co-Operative Publication Society, n.d.

Gundersheimer, Werner L. *Ferrara: The Style of a Renaissance Despotism*. Princeton: Princeton University Press, 1973.

Guzmán, Fernan Pérez de. 'Coronica del Rey Don Juan II.' In *Biblioteca de Autores Espanoles*. Madrid: Ediciones Atlas, 1953.

Haraszti, Emile. 'Les Musiciens de Mathias Corvin et de Béatrice d'Aragón.' In Jean Jacquot, ed., *La musique instrumentale de la renaissance*. Paris: Editions du Centre National de la Recherche Scientifique, 1955.

Harrison, Frank L. 'Tradition and Innovation in Instrumental Usage 1100–1450.' In *Aspects of Medieval and Renaissance Music*. Edited by Jan LaRue. New York: Norton, 1966.

Hayes, Gerald. *King's Music*. Oxford: Oxford University Press, 1937.

———. 'Musical Instruments,' in *New Oxford History of Music*. London, 1960.

Hazlitt, William Carew. *The Venetian Republic: Its Rise, Its Growth, And Its Fall, AD 409–1797*. New York, 1915.

Hegel, Carl, ed. *Die Chroniken der deutschen Städte*. Leipzig, 1864.

Heinzel, Richard. *Beschreibung des geistlichen Schauspiels im deutschen Mittelalter*. Hamburg, 1898.

Henderson, Ernest F. *A Short History of Germany*. New York: Macmillan, 1916.

Herodotus. *The Histories*. New York: Penguin, 1977.

Hibbert, Christopher. *The House of Medici*. New York: Morrow, 1975.

Hillgarth, Jocelyn NIgel. *The Spanish Kingdoms*. Oxford: Clarendon, 1976.

Holinshed, Raphael. *Chronicle*. vol. 3.

Homer. *Iliad*.

Horace. *The Art of Poetry*.

Huguenin, J. F., ed. *Les chroniques de la ville de Metz*. Metz, 1838.

Huizinga, Johan H. *The Waning of the Middle Ages*. New York: Doubleday Anchor, 1954.

Jacquot, Jean. *La musique en Lorraine*. Paris, 1882.

Jenkins, Thomas Atkinson., ed. *Le Chanson de Roland*. Boston: D.C. Heath, 1924.

Joinville, Jean de. *Chronicle of the Crusade of St. Louis*. Everyman Library.

Jones, William. *Crowns and Coronations*. London: Chatto & Windus, 1902.

Jordanes. *Getica*.

Josephus. *Jewish Antiquities*.

———. *The Jewish Wars*.

Journal d'un bourgeois de Paris. Paris: le Monde en 1018.

Jubinal, Achille. *Mystères inédits du XV siècle*. Paris, 1920–1934.

Kade, R. 'Die Leipziger Stadtpfeifer.' In *Monatshefte für Musik-Geschichte*. Leipzig, 1889.

Kantorowicz, Ernst. *Frederick the Second*. Translated by E.O. Lorimer. New York: Ungar, 1957.

Kastner, Georges. *Les Danses des morts*. Paris, 1852.

———. *Manuel Général de Musique Militaire*. Paris, 1848.

Kendall, Paul Murray. *Richard the Third*. New York: Norton, 1955.

Kinkeldey, Otto. *Orgel und Klavier in der Musik des 16. Jahrhunderts*. Leipzig: Breitkopf und Härtel, 1910.

Kolbing, Eugen, ed. *Amis and Amiloun*. Heilbronn, 1884.

———., ed. *Arthour and Merlin*. Leipzig, 1890.
Laborde, Léon de. *Les ducs de Bourgogne*. Paris, 1849–1852.
LaFontaine, Henry Thomas Cart de. *The King's Musick*. London: Novello, 1909.
Lambin. *Messager des Sciences*. 1836.
Lang, Karl Heinrich Ritter v. *Neuere Geschichte des Fürstentums Beiruth*. Göttingen, 1798.
Langwill, Lyndesay G. *The Waits* or *Waits, wind band [and] horn*. London: Hinrichsen, 1952.
Laurencie, Lionel de la. 'La musique à la cour des ducs de Bretagne aux XIVe et XVe siecle' *Revue de Musicologie* 14, no. 45 (Feb 1933): 1–15.
Laurent, J. *Aachener Stadtrechnungen aus dem XIV Jahrhundert*. Aachen, 1866.
Lauterbeck, George. *Regentenbuch des Hochgelerten weitberumbten Herr Georgen Lauterbecken, Fürstlichen Brandenburgischen Rahts ...* Frankfurt am Main, 1579.
Lefebvre, Léon. *Histoire du théâtre de Lille*. Lille, 1907.
Lefèvre, Jean. *Chronique*. Paris, 1876.
Lesure, François. *Musique et Musiciens Français du XVI Siècle*. Geneve: Minkoff Reprint, 1976.
Lettenhove, Kervyn de. 'Chroniques relatives à l'histoire de Belgique sous la domination des ducs de Bourgogne.' In *Livre des trahisons de France*. Brussels, 1873.
———., ed., *Collection des chroniques belges*. 1873.
———. 'Fragment inédit de Froissart.' In *Bulletin de l'Académie royale de Belgiques* 25. 1886.
———., ed., *Le livre des trahisons de France envers la maison de Bourgogne*. Brussels, 1873.
Levron, Jacques. *La vie et les moeurs du bon roi René*. Paris: Amiot-Dumont, 1953.
Lewis, Dominic Bevan Wyndham. *King Spider*. New York: Coward-MacCann, 1929.
Linden, Albert van der. 'La Musique dans les chroniques de Jean Molinet.' In *Mélanges Ernest Closson*. Brussels: Société Belge de Muiscologie, 1948. pp. 166–180.
Livy. *History of Rome*.
Livy. *The War with Hannibal*. New York: Penguin, 1980.
Livy. *The Early History of Rome*. New York: Penguin, 1979.
Lockwood, Lewis. 'Music at Ferrara in the Period of Ercole I.' *Studi Musicali*, anno 1, no. 1 (1972): 101–131.
Longeron, O. 'La trompette d' argent.' In *Mémories de la Commission des antiquitiés de la Côte d'Or* (9, second series), 92.
Longman, William. *The History of the Life and Times of Edward the Third*. London, 1869.
Lungo, Isidoro Del. *Prose volgari ... di Angelo Ambrogini Poliziano*. Florence, 1867.
Luzio, Alessandro, and Rodolfo Reinier. 'Delle relazioni di Isabella d'Este Conzaga con Ludovico e Beatrice Sforza.' In *Archivio storico italiano*. Milan, 1890.
Lydgate, John. *Prilgrimage of the Life of Man*. Edited by Frederick James Furnivall. London, 1905.
———. *Reson and Sensuallyte*. Edited by Ernst Sieper. London: Kergan Paul, Trench, Trübner, 1901.
———. *Troy Book*. Edited by Henry Bergen. London, Kergan Paul, Trench, Trübner, 1906.
Machaut, Gillaume de. *Musikalische Werke*. Leipzig: Breitkopf und Härtel, 1928.

Machiavelli. *The Art of War*. Translated by Peter Whitehorne. London: Niclas Inglande, 1560; reprint New York: AMS Press, 1967.

MacKinnon, James. *The History of Edward the Third*. London: Longmans Green, 1900.

Manniche, Lise. *Music and Musicians in Ancient Egypt*. London: British Museum Press, 1991.

Manning, Percy. *Some Oxfordshire Seasonal Festivals*. London: Nutt, 1897.

Marche, Olivier de la. *Mémoires*. Edited by H. Beaune. Paris, 1885.

Marix, Jeanne. *Histoire de la Musique et des Musiciens de la Cour de Bourgogne sous le règne de Philippe le Bon*. Strasbourg: Heitz, 1939.

Markham, Sir Clements R. *Richard III: His Life & Character*. London: Smith, Elder, & Co., 1906.

Martial, Valerius. *Epigrams*.

Masini, Antonio di Paolo. *Bologna perlustrata*. Bologna, 1649.

Masson, Georgina. *Frederick II of Hohenstaufen: A Life*. New York: Octagon, 1973.

Mather, Christine. 'Maximilian I and his Instruments.' *Early Music* 3, no. 1 (Jan 1975): 42–46.

Matthews, Brander. *Development of the Drama*. New York: Scribner, 1921.

Mazzarosa, Antonio. *Atti e memorie della R. Accademia di Lucca*, 1861?

McKinney, Howard D., and W.R. Anderson. *Music in History: The Evolution of an Art*. Boston: American Book Company, 1940.

McKinnon, James W. 'Musical Instruments in Medieval Psalm Commentaries and Psalters.' *Journal of the American Musicological Society* 21, no. 1 (Spring 1968): 3–20.

Memorial historico español. Madrid, 1855.

'Mémoriaux de l'abbe de St-Aubert.' In *Archives historiques du Nord de la France*. 1844.

Meyer, Clemens. *Geschichte der Mecklenburg-Schweriner Hofkapelle*. Schwerin, 1913.

Meyer, Paul. *La Manière de langage qui enseigne à parler et à écrire le Francais*. Paris, 1873, but written in 1396.

Migne, Jacques Paul. *Patrologiae cursus completus, series latina*. 1844–45.

Miller, Townsend. *Henry IV of Castile: 1425–1474*. New York: Lippincott, 1972.

Mills, Maldwyn, ed. *Libeaus Desconus*. London: Oxford University Press, 1969.

Mizwa, Stephen P. *Nicholas Copernicus*. New York: Kosciuszko Foundation, 1943.

Mone, F.J., ed. *Quellensammlung der badischen Landesgeschichte*. Karlsruhe, 1848.

Monstrelet, E. de. *La Chronique d'Enguerran de Monstrelet*. Paris, 1857–1862.

Montagu, Jeremy. 'On the Reconstruction of Mediaeval Instruments of Percussion.' *Galpin Society Journal* 23 (Aug 1970): 104–114.

Moser, Hans Joachim. 'Zur Mittelalterlichen Musikgeschichte der Stadt Köln.' In *Archiv für Musikwissenschaft*. Rildesheim, 1964.

———. *Die Musikergenossenschaften im deutschen Mittelalter*. Rostock: C. Hinstorffs Buchdruckerei, 1910.

Motta, E. *Musici alla Corte degli Sforza: ricerche e documenti milanesi*. Milano, 1887.

Munro, Dana Carleton, and George C. Sellery. *Medieval Civilization*. New York: Century, 1926.

Nabonne, Bernard. *Gaston Phébus, seigneur de Bearn*. Paris: Corréa, 1936.

Nearchus. *Indica*.

Nedden, Otto Carl August zur. *Quellen und Studien zur oberrheinischen Musikgeschichte im 15. und 16 Jahrhundert*. Kassel: Bärenreiter-Verlag, 1931.

Nef, Karl. 'Die Stadtpfeiferei und die Instrumentalmusiker in Basel.' In *Sammelbande der Internationalen Musikgesellschaft* 10, no. 3 (Apr–Jun 1909): 395–398.

Nerici, Luigi. *Storia della musica in Lucca*. Lucca, 1880.

Neustadt, Heinrich von. *Apollonius von Tyrland*. Edited by S. Singer. Berlin, 1906.

Noyes, Ella. *Story of Milan*. London: Dent, 1908.

Ovary, L. 'La recontre de Mathias et Vladislas à Iglau, d'après des documents des Archives de Mantoue et de Modène.' *Századok*. Budapest, 1889.

Ovid. *Amores*.

Ovid. *Fasti*.

Ovid. *Metamorphosis*. Translated by George Sandys. Lincoln: University of Nebraska Press, 1970.

Panoff, Peter. *Militärmusik*. Berlin, 1944.

Paris, Matthew. *Matthew Paris's English History*. Translated by John Allen Giles. London, 1852.

Phillips, T. 'Accounts of the Ceremonial of the Marriage of the Princess Margaret.' *Archaeologica* (1846).

Philostratus. *The Life of Apollonius of Tyana*.

Pietzsch, G. 'Die Beschreibungen deutscher Fürstenhochzeiten von der Mitte des 15. bis zum Beginn des 17. Jahrhunderts als musikgeschichtliche Quelle.' In *Anuario Musical*. Barcelona, 1960.

Pin, Ellies du, ed. *Joannis Gersonii opera omnia 4*.

Pirro, André. *Histoire de la musique de la fin du XIVe siècle a la fin du XVIe*. Paris: H. Laurens, 1940.

———. *La musique à Paris sous le règne de Charles VI*. Strasbourg: Heitz, 1930.

Pisan, Christine de. 'Le livre du duc des vrais amants.' In *Oeuvres poétiques*. Edited by Maurice Roy. Paris, 1896.

Plato. *Laws*.

Pliny. *Natural History*.

Plutarch. *Lives*.

———. *Vitarum comparatarum*.

Polk, Keith. 'Civic Patronage and Instrumental Ensembles in Renaissance Florence.' Unpublished.

———. 'Ensemble Instrumental Music in Flanders, 1450–1550.' Unpublished.

———. 'Flemish Wind Bands in the Late Middle Ages.' PhD diss., University of California, Berkeley, 1968.

Polybius. *Histories*.

Polybius. *The Rise of the Roman Empire*. New York: Penguin, 1981.

Prost, Bernard. *Inventaires mobiliers et extraits des comptes des ducs de Bourgogne*. Paris: Leroux, 1902–1904.

Purcell, Mary. *The Great Captain: Gonzalo Fernández de Córdoba*. New York: Doubleday, 1962.

Quasten, J. *Musik und Gesang.* Münster: Aschendorff, 1930.

Quicherat, Jules, ed. *Procès de condamnation et de réhabilitation de Jeanne d'Arc.* Paris, 1841–1849.

Rastall, Richard. 'Some English Consort-Groupings of the late Middle Ages.' *Music & Letters* 55, no. 2 (April 1974): 179–202.

Reaney, Gilbert. 'The Performance of Medieval Music.' In *Aspects of Medieval and Renaissance Music.* Edited by Jan LaRue. New York: Norton, 1966.

Reese, Gustave. *Music in the Renaissance.* New York: Norton, 1959.

Reinaert. 'Willems.' In *Altniederländische Schaubuhne.* Edited by A.H. von Fallersleben. Breslau, 1834.

Reinhardt, Kurt F. *Germany: 2000 Years.* New York, 1950.

Repetti, Emanuele. *Compendio Storico della città di Firenze, sua comunità, diocesi e compartimento fino all'anno 1849.* Firenze, 1849.

Reschke, Johannes. 'Studie zur Geschichte der brandenburgisch-prussischen Heeresmusik.' (PhD diss., Friedrich Wilhelms Universitat, Berlin, 1935).

Richard of Devizes. *The Chronicle of Richard of Devizes.* Edited by John T. Appleby. London, 1963.

Richental, Ulrichs von. *Das Konzil zu Konstanz.* Edited by Otto Feger. Konstanz: Starnberg, 1964.

Richental, Ulrichs von. *Ulrichs von Richental Chronik des Constanzer Conzils.* Edited by Michael Richard Buck. Tüblingen, 1882.

Riegel, Joseph. *Die Teilnehmerlisten des Konstanzer Konzils.* Freiburg, 1916.

Rokseth, Yvonne. *La musique d'orgue au XVe siècle et au début du XVIe.* Paris, 1930.

Roscoe, William. *Life of Lorenzo de'Medici.* London, 1877.

Roye, Jean de. *Journal de Jean de Roye connu sous le nom de chronique scandaleuse.* Edited by Bernard de Mandrot. Paris, 1894.

Ryder, Alan. *The Kingdom of Naples Under Alfonso the Magnanimous.* Oxford: Clarendon, 1976.

Sachs, Curt. *The History of Musical Instruments.* New York: Norton, 1940.

———. *World History of the Dance.* New York: Norton, 1937.

Sadie, Stanley, ed. *The New Grove Dictionary of Music and Musicians.* 20 vols. London: Macmillan, 1980.

Safowitz, Vivian. 'Trumpet Music and Trumpet Style in the Early Renaissance.' PhD diss., University of Illinois, 1965.

Saldoni, M. Balthasar. *Diccionario biografico-bibliografico de Efemérides de musicos españoles.* Madrid, 1868.

Sale, Antoine de La. *Des anciens tournois et faictz d'armes.* 1872.

Salmen, Walter. *Der fahrende Musiker im Europäischen Mittelalter.* Kassel: Hinnenthal, 1960.

Sargans, Anton Henne von., ed. *Die Klingenberger Chronik.* Gotha, 1861.

Sarton, George. *Introduction to the History of Science.* Baltimore: Williams & Wilkins, 1930.

Schellhass, Karl. 'Eine Kaiserreise im Jahre 1473.' In *Archiv für Frankfurts Geschichte und Kunst.* 1893.

Schmidt, Günther. *Die Musik am Hofe des Markgrafen von Brandenburg-Ansbach vom ausgehenden Mittelalter bis 1806.* München: Ansbach, 1953.

Schroeder, Rudolf. *Studien zur Geschichte des Musiklebens der Stadt Dormund.* Emsdetten, 1934.

Schuler, M. 'Die Musik in Konstanz während des Konzils 1414–1418.' *Acta Musicologica* 38, no. 214 (April–December 1966): 150–168.

Scofield, Cora L. *The Life and Reign of Edward the Fourth.* London: Longmans Green, 1923.

Sendrey, Alfred. *Music in the Social and Religious Life of Antiquity.* Rutherford: Fairleigh Dickinson University Press, 1975.

Seneca. *Ad Lucilium Epistulae Morales.*

Shih-chi.

Simons, Eric N. *The Reign of Edward IV.* London: Muller, 1966.

Sittard, Josef. *Zur Geschichte der Musik und des Theaters am Württembergischen hofe.* Stuttgart, 1890.

Slootmans, Korneel. 'De Hoge Lieve Vrouwe van Bergen-op-Zoom.' In *Jaerboek van de Oudheidkundige Kring de Ghulden Roos.* (25), 212.

Smithers, Don L. *The Music and History of the Baroque Trumpet Before 1710.* London: Dent, 1973.

Smithers, G.V., ed. *King Alisaunder.* London: Oxford University Press, 1952.

Snoeck, C. 'Notes sur les instruments de musique en usage dans les Flandres au moyen âge.' In *Compte Rendu de la Fédération Archéologique et Historique de Belgique.* 1896.

Söhner, Leo. *Die Orgelbegleitung zum Gregorianishcen Gesang.* Regensburg: Pustet, 1936.

Sophocles. *Ajax.*

Southern, Eileen. 'Basse-Dance Music in Some German Manuscripts of the 15th Century.' In *Aspects of Medieval and Renaissance Music.* Edited by Jan LaRue. New York: Norton, 1966.

Stevens, John. *Music & Poetry in the Early Tudor Court.* London: Methuen, 1961.

Stowe, J. *Survey of London.* London, 1618.

Strabo. *Geographica.*

Stubbs, William. *Constitutional History of England.* Oxford: Clarendon, 1903.

Subirá, José. *Historia de la Música.* Barcelona, 1947.

Suetonius. *The Twelve Caesars.* New York: Penguin, 1989.

Tacitus. *Annals.*

Tagliavini, L.F. 'La Scuola musicale bolognese.' In *Musiciati della scuola emiliana.* Edited by Adelmo Damerini and Gino Roncaglia. Siena: Accademia Musicale Chigiana, 1956.

Thibault, G. 'Le Concert Instrumental au XVe Siecle.' In Jean Jacquot, ed., *La musique instrumentale de la renaissance.* Paris: Editions du Centre National de la Recherche Scientifique, 1955.

Thompson, James Westfall. *Economic and Social History of Europe in the Later Middle Ages.* New York: Century, 1931.

Tinctoris, Johannes. *De Inventione et Usu Musicae.* 1487.

Tolkien, J.R.R., and E.V. Gordon, eds. *Sir Gawain and the Green Knight.* Oxford: Clarendon, 1925.

Toulmon, Auguste Bottée de. *Dissertation sur les instruments de musique in Memoires de la Société des antiquaires de France*. Paris, 1844.

Tschachtlan, Benedikt. *Heinrich Dittlingers Berner Chronik*. (Zurich, Central Library, Ms. A. 120, fol. 55v).

Tuetey, Alexandre, ed. *Journal d'un bourgeois de Paris*. Paris, 1888.

Türlin, Heinrich von dem. *Diu Crône*. Edited by Gottlob Heinrich Friedrich Scholl. Stuttgart, 1852.

Turrentine, Edgar. 'Notes on the Ancient Olympic.' *Instrumentalist* (April, 1969).

Twici, Guyllaume. *L'art de vénerie*. Translated by Alice Dryden. Northhampton, Mass.: W. Mark, 1908.

Valentin, Caroline. *Geschichte der Musik in Frankfurt-am-Main*. Frankfurt: Völcker, 1906.

Valeri, Francesco Malaguzzi. *La Corte di Lodovico il Moro: La vita privata e l'arte a Milano nella seconda metà del quattrocento*. Milano: U. Hoepli, 1913.

Valeri Maximi. *Factorvm et Dictorvm Memorabilivm*.

Valla, Lauretius. 'De Rebus a Ferdinando Aragoniae rege gestis.' In *Rerum Hispanicarum Scriptores*. Frankfurt, 1579.

Vander Straeten, Edmond. *La Musique aux Pays Bas avant le XIXe Siècle* (1867–1888). Reprinted, New York: Dover, 1969.

Van Severen, Louis Gilliodts-. 'Les ménestrels de Bruges.' In *Essais d'Archéologie Brugeoise*. Bruges: Imprimerie de L. de Plancke, 1912.

Varro. *On the Latin Language*.

Vaughan, Richard. *Charles the Bold*. London: Longman, 1973.

———. *John the Fearless: The Growth of Burgundian Power*. New York: Barnes ands Noble, 1966.

———. *Philip the Good: The Apogee of Burgundy*. New York: Barnes and Noble, 1970.

Veit, Gottfried. *Die Blasmusik*. Innsbruck: Verband Südtiroler Musikkapellen, 1972.

Vergil. *Aeneis*. Translated by John Dryden. London, 1803.

———. *Georgics*. Translated by John Dryden. London, 1803.

Vessella, Alessandro. *La Banda*. Milan: Istituto Editoriale Nazionale, 1935.

Viard, Jules Marie Édouard, ed. *Les grandes chroniques de France*. Paris, 1837.

Vinsauf, Goeffrey de. *Chronicle of Richard the First's Crusade*. London, 1914; written in 1191.

Virdung, Sebastian. *Musica getutscht*. 1511.

Walsingham, Thomae. *Historia anglicana*. Edited by Henry Thomas Riley. London, 1863.

Wangermée, Robert. *Flemish Music and Society in the Fifteenth and Sixteenth Centuries*. Translated by Robert Erich Wolf. New York: Dover, 1968.

Warwick, Alan Ross. *A Noise of Music*. London: Queen Anne Press, 1968.

Welch, Christopher. 'Literature Relating to the Recorder.' *Proceedings of the Musical Association* 24 (1897–1898): 145–224.

Werner, Arno. *Städtische und fürstliche Musikpflege in Weissenfels*. Leipzig: Breitkopf und Härtel, 1911.

———. *Vier Jahrhunderte im Dienste der Kirchenmusik*. Leipzig: Carl Merseburger, 1932.

Wille, Günther. *Musica Romana: Die Bedeutung der Musik im Leben der Römer.* Amsterdam: Schippers, 1967.

Wilmanns, G., ed. Inscriptiones Africae latinae, *Corpus inscriptionum latinarum.* Berlin, 1881.

Woodfill, Walter. *Musicians in English Society: From Elizabeth to Charles I.* Princeton: Princeton University Press, 1953.

Wulstan, David. 'The Sounding of the Shofar.' *The Galpin Society Journal* 26 (May 1973): 29–46.

Wylie, James Hamilton. *History of England under Henry the Fourth.* London, 1884.

———. *The Reign of Henry the Fifth.* Cambridge: Cambridge University Press, 1914.

Xenophon. *Anabasis.*

———. *Hellenica.*

Zavarsky, Ernest. 'Beiträge zur Musikgeschichte der Stadt Kremnitz.' In *Musik des Ostens.* Kassel: Bärenreiter, 1963.

Zippel, Giuseppe. *I Suonatori della Signoria di Firenze.* Trento, 1892.

Index

Index of Names

A

Adelinda (female minstrel, 1086, England), 182
Aelianus, Claudius (2nd century AD historian), 51
Aeschylus (ancient Greek playwright), 49
Agesilaus, King of Sparta (444–361 BC), 33
Aglais of Megacles (ancient Greek trumpet player), 32
Alcibiades (5th century BC), 32
Alfonso the Magnanimous (b. 1396) of Naples, 239
Alfonso V (1416–1458), 220
Apuleius (2nd century AD historian), 17
Aribert, Archbishop of Milan (11th century), 121
Aristides Quintellianus (2nd – 3rd century AD), 45
Aristotle (4th century BC), 29, 30, 33, 34, 39, 45
Arsinoe, Queen of Egypt (3rd century BC), 17
Asopodorus of Palius (ancient Greek professional aulos player), 39
Athenaeus (2nd century BC historian), 16, 29, 39, 40 [cites lost aulos treatises], 49
Augustine of Augsburg (15th century trombonist), 125

B

Beatrice d'Este of Ferrara (15th century), 231, 236
Bellini, Gentile (15th century Italian painter), 127
Berdic (royal minstrel, 1086, England), 182
Blondel (famous Trouvère with Richard 'Coeur de Lion'), 184
Borso d'Este (1450–1471), 229ff

C

Canus of Rhodes, famous aulos player (3rd century AD), 11
Caphisias (aulos teacher, court of Alexander the Great), 41
Castiglione (16th century author of *Il Cortegiano*), 175
Catullus (1st century BC, Roman poet), 58, 59
Caveron, Robert (1st official leader of minstrels in France, 14th century), 146
Chao-hao, Emperor of China (2,598 BC), 9
Charlemagne, 261
Charles the Bold, Duke of Burgundy, 256ff
Charles V of France, 213
Charles VI (1380–1422), 213
Charles VII (1422–1461), 214
Charles VIII (1483–1498), 216
Charon of Lampsacus (ancient historian), 37

Chastellain, Georges (Burgundian historian, 15th century), 215, 246
Chaucer, Geoffrey, 80ff
Claudius Aelianus (2nd century AD historian), 12
Clement V (pope, 14th century), 187
Ctesibius (3rd century BC inventor), 17

D

Darius III, King of Persia, 11
Diodorus of Sicily (Etruscan), 49
Dufay (15th century composer), 177, 178, 255

E

Edward I (1272–1307), 187
Edward II (1307–1327), 187
Edward III (1327–1377), 79, 84, 189ff
Edward IV, 86, 197ff
Elagabalus (Roman Emperor, 3rd century, performer on aulos & cornu), 65
Enrique IV (1425–1474), 221ff
Eratosthenes (Etruscan historian), 51
Ercole I (1471–1505), 230, 232
Euripides (ancient Greek playwright), 49
Evraardus Venator (English trumpet & horn player, 1087–1100), 182

F

Fernando V (1474–1516) and Dona Isabel (1474–1504), 223ff
Francesco Sforza (Duke of Milan, 15th century), 205
Frederick II (1194–1250), 263ff
Frederick III, Emperor, Holy Roman Empire, 186, 269
Friedrich III, emperor (15th century), 151, 165
Froissart, Jean (French historian, 1333–1405), 122, 178, 189

G

Galeazzo Maria Sforza, 233
Gideon (military leader, Old Testament), 23
Gilles de Zamore (12th century theorist), 95
Grosseteste of Lincoln, Robert (1175–1253), 99, 107
Gudea of Sumeria, King of Sumeria (2,600 BC), 10

H

Hannibal (Carthaginian general, 247–183 BC), 38, 57
Henry I (1100–1135), 183
Henry III (1216–1272), 131, 186
Henry IV of England (1399–1413), 194 [list of players in fn. Nr. 63]
Henry V of England (1413–1422), 195ff
Henry VI (1422–1471), 196
Henry VII (1485–1509), 201ff [with list of players]
Heradorus of Megara (ancient Greek trumpet player), 32
Hermann, Monk of Salzburg, (1350–1410), 100
Herodotus (Roman historian, 5th century BC), 10, 17
Hippolochus (3rd century BC), 42
Hirtius (1st century BC Roman historian), 56
Homer (9th to 12th century BC?, poet), 29, 30

I

Isabella d'Este (15th century), 231, 239

J

Jaime II (1291–1327), 219
Jean Lefèvre (Burgundian historian, 15th century), 248
Joan of Arc, 214
John de Hertford (13th century Abbot of St. Albans), 99
John II of France (1350–1364), 209
John the Fearless, Duke of Burgundy, 244
Joinville (13th century historian), 72, 183, 207ff
Joos Zoetens of Ghent (1493 teacher), 138
Juan I (1350–1396), 79, 220 [with names of players]
Jubal (musician named in Genesis 4:21), 23

K

Kastner, Georges (French 19th century historian), 9, 115

L

Langland, William (English poet, 14th century), 191
Lieu-Pang (Emperor of China, 2nd century BC), 9
Livy (1st century BC Roman historian), 52, 57, 59, 60
Lorenzo 'Il Magnifico' of Florence, 241
Louis IX, 'St. Louis' (1226–1270), 207
Louis IX, 145
Louis XI (1461–1483), 215
Ludislaus, King of Hungary (15th century), 214
Ludolf von Sachsen (Dominican monk, 14th century), 166
Ludovico Sforza, 235ff
Lull, Ramon (1232–1315, Spanish philosopher), 221
Lygate, John (1370–1451, poet), 160

M

Machiavelli (Italian politician, 1469–1527), 34, 45 [fn Nr. 63]
Marchetto of Padua (14th century Italian theorist), 227
Marcipor (slave aulos player, 2nd – 3rd century BC), 64
Martial (1st century Roman poet), 61
Martin le Franc (15th century French poet), 178
Maximilian I, 237, 258, 266, 269, 271ff
Maximus, Valerius (1st century AD Roman historian), 62
Menander (Roman poet, 342–291 BC), 42
Mersenne (French Philosopher, 17th century), 287

N

Nebuchadnezzar, 19
Neckham, Alexander (13th century English Abbot), 116
Nero (Roman Emperor, 1st century, performer as singer and bagpipe player), 65
Niccolò III of Ferrara (1393–1441), 229

O

Ovid (1st century BC Roman poet), 59, 60, 61

P

Parmenio (400–330 BC, Macedonian general), 11
Pedro III (1276–1285), 219
Pericles (Athens general, 495–429 BC), 40
Persaeus (Greek historian, 3rd century AD), 43
Phébus, Gaston (14th century nobleman), 77, 167, 210–211 [icons]
Philip III (1270–1285), 208
Philip IV (1285–1314), 208
Philip of Burgundy (son to Maximilian I), 140
Philip the Bold, Duke of Burgundy, 103, 243
Philip the Good, 103, 151, 161, 220 229, 245ff
Philip VI (1328–1350), 209
Philostratus, Flavius (3rd century AD biographer), 11
Pietro di Boldrani (14th century Treviso trumpet player), 124
Pilgrim von Puchheim (1365–1396, Archbishop of Salzburg), 99
Plato (424–348 BC), 42
Plautus (Roman playwright, 254–184 BC), 64
Pliny (1st century AD historian), 60
Plutarch (1st – 2nd AD historian), 10, 31, 36, 39, 40, 36, 56, 64
Polybius (2nd century BC historian), 41, 42, 55, 57, 62
Poseidonius (Greek writer, 135–145 BC), 11
Pythagoras (6th century BC), 29
Pythochares (ancient Greek aulos player), 40

R

Rahere (English minstrel under Henry I, 1100–1135), 183
Richard I, 'Coeur de Lion' (1189–1199), 184
Richard II (1377–1399), 191ff
Richard III (1483–1485), 200
Roland (nephew to Charlemagne), 261
Rutebeuf (1245–1285, poet), 74

S

Sancho IV (1284–1295), 221
Seneca (Roman historian 1st century AD), 64
Sigismund (Emperor, Holy Roman Empire), 266ff
Socrates (469–399 BC), 35
Sophocles (ancient Greek playwright), 49
Sostratus, aulos player (280–261 BC), 11
St. Augustine, 91, 92
St. Francis of Assisi, 95 (fn. Nr. 4)
Strabo (1st century BC geographer), 33, 40
Suetonius (1st – 2nd century AD, Roman historian), 57

T

Tacitus (1st century AD Roman historian), 58
Taillefer (minstrel to William the Conqueror), 181
Theodore of Cyrus (Churchman, d. 460 AD), 92
Theon (4th century BC Greek painter), 37
Thomas Aquinas (1225–1275), 95
Thomas de Cabham (d. 1313), 96
Thucydides (5th century BC historian), 45
Tinctoris, Johannes (15th century theorist), 162, 173
Tushratta (1,400 BC), 10

U

Urban IV (pope, 13th century), 102

V

Varro (Roman scholar, 1st century BC), 60
Vergil (1st century BC, poet), 30, 37, 50, 65
Vessella (19th century Italian historian, *La Banda*), 125
Virdung (16th century Theorist), 289

W

Wace (12th century poet), 159
William 'the Red' (1087–1100), 182
William the Conqueror (11th century), 181
Wolfram von Eschenbach (1170–1220), 261
Wulstan (10th century English deacon), 95

X

Xenophon (4th – 5th century BC), 30, 35

About the Author

Dr. David Whitwell is a graduate ('with distinction') of the University of Michigan and the Catholic University of America, Washington DC (PhD, Musicology, Distinguished Alumni Award, 2000) and has studied conducting with Eugene Ormandy and at the Akademie fur Musik, Vienna. Prior to coming to Northridge, Dr. Whitwell participated in concerts throughout the United States and Asia as Associate First Horn in the USAF Band and Orchestra in Washington DC, and in recitals throughout South America in cooperation with the United States State Department.

At the California State University, Northridge, which is in Los Angeles, Dr. Whitwell developed the CSUN Wind Ensemble into an ensemble of international reputation, with international tours to Europe in 1981 and 1989 and to Japan in 1984. The CSUN Wind Ensemble has made professional studio recordings for BBC (London), the Koln Westdeutscher Rundfunk (Germany), NOS National Radio (The Netherlands), Zurich Radio (Switzerland), the Television Broadcasting System (Japan) as well as for the United States State Department for broadcast on its 'Voice of America' program. The CSUN Wind Ensemble's recording with the Mirecourt Trio in 1982 was named the 'Record of the Year' by The Village Voice. Composers who have guest conducted Whitwell's ensembles include Aaron Copland, Ernest Krenek, Alan Hovhaness, Morton Gould, Karel Husa, Frank Erickson and Vaclav Nelhybel.

Dr. Whitwell has been a guest professor in 100 different universities and conservatories throughout the United States and in 23 foreign countries (most recently in China, in an elite school housed in the Forbidden City). Guest conducting experiences have included the Philadelphia Orchestra, Seattle Symphony Orchestra, the Czech Radio Orchestras of Brno and Bratislava, The National Youth Orchestra of Israel, as well as resident wind ensembles in Russia, Israel, Austria, Switzerland, Germany, England, Wales, The Netherlands, Portugal, Peru, Korea, Japan, Taiwan, Canada and the United States.

He is a past president of the College Band Directors National Association, a member of the Prasidium of the International Society for the Promotion of Band Music, and was a member of the founding board of directors of the World Association for Symphonic Bands and Ensembles (WASBE). In 1964 he was made an honorary life member of Kappa Kappa Psi, a national professional music fraternity. In September, 2001, he was a delegate to the UNESCO Conference on Global Music in Tokyo. He has been knighted by sovereign organizations in France, Portugal and Scotland and has been awarded the gold medal of Kerkrade, The Netherlands, and the silver medal of Wangen, Germany, the highest honor given wind conductors in the United States, the medal of the Academy of Wind and Percussion Arts (National Band Association) and the highest honor given wind conductors in Austria, the gold medal of the Austrian Band Association. He is a member of the Hall of Fame of the California Music Educators Association.

Dr. Whitwell's publications include more than 127 articles on wind literature including publications in Music and Letters (London), the London Musical Times, the Mozart-Jahrbuch (Salzburg), and 39 books, among which is his 13-volume *History and Literature of the Wind Band and Wind Ensemble* and an 8-volume series on *Aesthetics in Music*. In addition to numerous modern editions of early wind band music his original compositions include 5 symphonies.

David Whitwell was named as one of six men who have determined the course of American bands during the second half of the 20th century, in the definitive history, *The Twentieth Century American Wind Band* (Meredith Music).

A doctoral dissertation by German Gonzales (2007, Arizona State University) is dedicated to the life and conducting career of David Whitwell through the year 1977. David Whitwell is one of nine men described by Paula A. Crider in *The Conductor's Legacy* (Chicago: GIA, 2010) as 'the legendary conductors' of the 20th century.

'I can't imagine the 2nd half of the 20th century—without David Whitwell and what he has given to all of the rest of us.' Frederick Fennell (1993)

www.ingramcontent.com/pod-product-compliance
Lightning Source LLC
Chambersburg PA
CBHW081347230426
43667CB00017B/2743